RUBY PROGRAMMING

JERRY LEE FORD, JR.

COURSE TECHNOLOGY
CENGAGE Learning

Australia • Brazil • Japan • Korea • Mexico • Singapore • Spain • United Kingdom • United States

COURSE TECHNOLOGY
CENGAGE Learning™

Ruby Programming
Jerry Lee Ford, Jr.

Executive Editor: Marie Lee

Acquisitions Editor: Brandi Shailer

Senior Product Manager: Alyssa Pratt

Development Editor: Kent Williams

Content Project Manager: Lisa Weidenfeld

Editorial Assistant: Jacqueline Lacaire

Associate Marketing Manager: Shanna Shelton

Cover image credit: ©istockphoto/ jennyking

Copyeditor: Suzanne Ciccone

Proofreader: Kim Kosmatka

Indexer: Sharon Hilgenberg

Art Director: Faith Brosnan

Text Designer: Shawn Gersberger

Cover Designer: Cabbage Design Company

Compositor: Integra

For product information and technology assistance, contact us at
Cengage Learning Customer & Sales Support, 1-800-354-9706

For permission to use material from this text or product, submit all requests online at **www.cengage.com/permissions**
Further permissions questions can be emailed to
permissionrequest@cengage.com

Library of Congress Control Number: 2010935900

ISBN-13: 978-1-111-22237-6
ISBN-10: 1-111-22237-1

Course Technology
20 Channel Center Street
Boston, MA 02210
USA

Cengage Learning is a leading provider of customized learning solutions with office locations around the globe, including Singapore, the United Kingdom, Australia, Mexico, Brazil, and Japan. Locate your local office at **www.cengage.com/global**

Cengage Learning products are represented in Canada by Nelson Education, Ltd.

To learn more about Course Technology, visit
www.cengage.com/coursetechnology

Purchase any of our products at your local bookstore or at our preferred online store **www.cengagebrain.com**

Some of the product names and company names used in this book have been used for identification purposes only and may be trademarks or registered trademarks of their respective manufacturers and sellers.

Any fictional data related to persons or companies or URLs used throughout this book is intended for instructional purposes only. At the time this book was printed, any such data was fictional and not belonging to any real persons or companies.

Course Technology, a part of Cengage Learning, reserves the right to revise this publication and make changes from time to time in its content without notice.

The programs in this book are for instructional purposes only. They have been tested with care, but are not guaranteed for any particular intent beyond educational purposes. The author and the publisher do not offer any warranties or representations, nor do they accept any liabilities with respect to the programs.

Printed in the United States of America
2 3 4 5 6   24 23 22 21 20

Brief Contents

Contents

CHAPTER 2   Interacting with Ruby **41**

CHAPTER 3   Working with Strings, Objects, and Variables **77**

v

x

CHAPTER 10   Debugging **331**

CHAPTER 11   Ruby on Rails Web Development **368**

xi

Preface

Ruby is an object-oriented, interpreted programming language. It is object-oriented in that it views (and interacts with) everything as an object. Ruby is interpreted in that its programs are compiled and executed by an interpreter at runtime. This allows you to make changes to your Ruby programs and then immediately run the programs to see how they work, without having to go through the extensive compilation that is required by many other programming languages.

Ruby is a cross-platform programming language, which means that its programs can run on Windows, Mac OS X, UNIX, Linux, and many other operating systems. This allows you to leverage your Ruby programming skills, maximizing the investment you've made in learning Ruby. You can even apply your Ruby programming skills to the development of web applications, using a specialized Ruby framework known as Ruby on Rails.

Ruby is easy to learn, yet quite powerful. This makes it an excellent choice for first-time programmers. It is a great programming language for tackling all kinds of small tasks. At the same time, Ruby is powerful enough to support the development of the most complicated programming tasks, making it a great language for experienced programmers looking for an advanced object-oriented programming language.

Best of all, Ruby is free. If your computer is running on a UNIX or Linux operating system, Ruby may already be installed. If not, you can download and install it directly from the Internet. Free installation packages are available for Microsoft Windows users as well. This book is dedicated to teaching you what you need to know to begin programming with Ruby. By the time you have finished this book, you will have developed a good understanding of the fundamentals of Ruby programming and will have a solid foundation to build upon in becoming an effective Ruby programmer.

The Approach

This book uses various instructional techniques to teach you how to develop Ruby programs. Each chapter guides you through the creation of a Ruby program using concepts learned in the chapter.

And each chapter ends with both a Summing Up section and a set of Reinforcement Exercises designed to give you hands-on experience with the programming techniques and concepts covered in that chapter.

In addition, each chapter includes a series of Discovery Projects designed to further your understanding of important topics and concepts. And each chapter contains two short quizzes as well as a Comprehension Check designed to measure your understanding of the concepts and your mastery of the material.

Overview of This Book

This book consists of eleven chapters, each of which focuses on a specific aspect of Ruby programming. Here is an outline of the book's contents:

Chapter 1, **"Ruby Basics."** An overview of Ruby programming, including information about its history, major features, and capabilities.

Chapter 2, **"Interacting with Ruby."** How to interact with Ruby from the command line. How to use the interactive Ruby shell known as IRB. Here, you begin to learn about Ruby's syntax and its built-in support for object-oriented programming.

Chapter 3, **"Working with Strings, Objects, and Variables."** How to work with and manipulate string and numeric data. How to define variables and objects and use them to store and retrieve data.

Chapter 4, **"Implementing Conditional Logic."** How to use conditional logic as a tool for analyzing data and controlling the logical execution of script statements.

Chapter 5, **"Working with Loops."** How to formulate and control the execution of loops. How to create Ruby programs that are capable of processing enormous amounts of data or performing repetitive tasks.

Chapter 6, **"Working with Collections of Data."** How to store and process related collections of data more efficiently. How to store data in indexed lists that can then be processed efficiently using loops. How to define data in hashes, which provide an efficient means of storing large collections of data using key-value pairs.

Chapter 7, **"Working with Regular Expressions."** How to use regular expressions to evaluate and manipulate strings. This lays the foundation for dissecting user input and file contents.

Chapter 8, **"Object-Oriented Programming."** Here, you will learn more about Ruby's support for object-oriented programming, including the concepts of encapsulation, polymorphism, and inheritance.

Chapter 9, **"File and Folder Administration."** How to access and manage file-system resources. How to read from and write to files.

Chapter 10, **"Debugging."** How to fix program errors. How to develop exception handlers that trap and deal with errors. How to work with Ruby's integrated debugger to exercise detailed control over the execution of your Ruby scripts.

Chapter 11, **"Ruby on Rails Web Development."** An overview of Ruby on Rails and the technologies required to work with it. How to set up your own personal web server and database and how to use Ruby on Rails to develop web applications.

Features

To facilitate learning, *Ruby Programming* includes the following features:

CHAPTER OBJECTIVES Each chapter begins with a list of the important concepts to be learned. This is both a quick reference to the chapter's contents and a useful study guide.

ILLUSTRATIONS AND TABLES Illustrations help you visualize common components and relationships. Tables present conceptual items and examples in a readable format.

 POINTERS These provide you with practical advice and proven strategies related to the concept being discussed.

 FACTS These provide additional helpful information on specific techniques and concepts.

 CAREFUL These point out troublesome issues you need to watch out for when writing Ruby programs.

SHORT QUIZZES At the end of each major topic, these quick comprehension checks assess your understanding of the section's material.

SUMMING UP These brief overviews of a chapter's contents provide a helpful way to recap and revisit the ideas covered in each chapter.

COMPREHENSION CHECKS These sets of 20 review questions reinforce the main ideas introduced in each chapter and help you determine how well you understand the concepts covered in the chapter.

REINFORCEMENT EXERCISES Although it is important to understand the concepts behind Ruby programming, no amount of theory can improve on applied knowledge. Toward this end, each chapter provides a set of exercises for each major topic.

DISCOVERY PROJECTS These give you further opportunities to apply what you have learned or expand upon your understanding of Ruby programming.

Instructor Resources

The following supplemental materials are available when this book is used in a classroom setting. All the resources available with this book are provided to the instructor on a CD.

ELECTRONIC INSTRUCTOR'S MANUAL The Instructor's Manual that accompanies this textbook provides additional instructional material to assist in class preparation, including Syllabi, Chapter Outlines, and Teaching Tips.

EXAMVIEW® This textbook is accompanied by ExamView, a powerful testing software package that allows instructors to create and administer printed, computer (LAN-based), and Internet exams. ExamView includes hundreds of questions that correspond to the topics covered in this text, enabling students to generate detailed study guides that include page references for further review. The computer-based and Internet testing components allow students to take exams at their computers, and save the instructor time by grading each exam automatically.

POWERPOINT PRESENTATIONS Microsoft PowerPoint slides are provided for each chapter. These are meant as a teaching aid for classroom presentation and can be made available to students or printed for classroom distribution. Instructors can add their own slides for additional topics they present to the class.

DATA FILES Files that contain all the data necessary for completing the book's Reinforcement Exercises and Discovery Projects are provided through the Course Technology website at *www.cengage.com/coursetechnology*. They are also available on the Instructor's Resource CD and for student download at cengagebrain.com.

SOLUTION FILES Solutions to the end-of-chapter Comprehension Checks, the Reinforcement Exercises, and the Discovery Projects are provided on the Instructor Resources CD and through the Course Technology website at *www.cengage.com/coursetechnology*. The solutions are password protected.

DISTANCE LEARNING Course Technology is proud to present online test banks in WebCT and Blackboard, to provide the most complete and dynamic learning experience possible. Instructors are encouraged to make the most of the course, both online and offline. For more information on how to access your online test bank, contact your local Course Technology sales representative.

Acknowledgements

Ruby Programming represents the time, effort, and hard work of numerous individuals to whom I would be remiss if I did not offer thanks. First and foremost, I need to thank this book's Development Editor, Kent Williams, for his expert guidance and advice and for greatly improving the quality and presentation of this text. Special thanks also needs to be given to Ann Shaffer, Consulting Development Editor, Alyssa Pratt, Senior Product Manager, Amy Jollymore, Acquisitions Editor, and Lisa Weidenfeld, Content Project Manager, for all their help in making this book a reality.

Recognition must also be made to the reviewers who provided their time, talent, and advice throughout the development of this book: Diane DelMonte, Briarcliffe College, Sue Fitzgerald, Metropolitan State University, and Jim Innis, North Central Texas College.

Last but by no means least, I must thank my wonderful children, Alexander, William, and Molly, and my beautiful wife, Mary, for their patience and support during the duration of my work on this book.

Requirements for Completing this Book

To reproduce the examples presented in this book and to complete end-of-chapter program development projects, you will need a computer running Microsoft Windows, Mac OS X, or one of the many versions of Linux or UNIX. You can use a computer in your school lab or your own computer. To use your own computer, you will need the following development resources, which you can obtain for free:

- **Ruby**, which can be downloaded and installed for free at *http://www.ruby-lang.org*.

- **A program or text editor**. On Windows, you can use the Notepad application. On Mac OS X, you can use TextEdit, provided you configure it to save out as plain text. On UNIX and Linux, you can use vi or any other text editor that may be installed. A word-processing program will not work, as it inserts formatting information into the document that will cause your scripts to fail.

- **RubyGems**. A Ruby package that facilitates the installation of Ruby on Rails and related components. RubyGems is automatically installed with Ruby on Microsoft Windows. Users of other operating systems can obtain RubyGems at *http://rubygems.org/pages/download*.

- **Ruby on Rails**. An installation program for Ruby on Rails can be downloaded using RubyGems.

- **A web browser**, such as Microsoft Internet Explorer or later or Mozilla Firefox to support Ruby on Rails testing and execution.

- **A web server** to host Ruby on Rails applications and facilitate application execution and testing. Ruby on Rails can work with any web server. The WEBrick web server is automatically installed as a part of Ruby on Rails standard installation and is the web server used in this book.

- **A database** to store application data for Ruby on Rails applications. Ruby on Rails can work with many different types of database systems. By default, Ruby on Rails applications are automatically configured to work with an SQLite database. You download SQLite for free using RubyGems.

To the Instructor

To complete some of the exercises in this book, your students must work with a set of data files. You can obtain the data files through the Course Technology website at *www.cengage.com/coursetechnology*.

Course Technology Data Files

You are granted a license to copy the data files to any computer or computer network used by people who have purchased this book.

Visit Our Web Site

Additional materials designed especially for this book might be available for your course. Periodically search *www.cengage.com/coursetechnology* for more information.

## CHAPTER 1

Ruby Basics

In this chapter, you:

- ◎ Get a brief history of computer programming
- ◎ Get an introduction to Ruby
- ◎ Get ready to work with Ruby
- ◎ Use Ruby interactively
- ◎ Develop Ruby programs
- ◎ Create the Ruby Joke game

2

Ruby is a programming language developed in 1993 to run on UNIX. However, it has since been adapted to run on many other popular operating systems, including Microsoft Windows, Mac OS X, and Linux. Ruby is distributed under an open-source license, allowing anyone to install and use it for free. In this chapter, you learn background information required to begin creating and executing Ruby programs. You also learn how to use Ruby to create the first of a number of computer games presented in this book.

Project Preview: The Ruby Joke Game

In this chapter and in each chapter that follows, you learn how to create a new computer game. By following along and creating your own copies of these games, you gain practical, hands-on experience programming with Ruby, and you develop a foundation upon which you can develop larger and more complex Ruby projects, such as system and network administration programs or website applications.

In this chapter's game project, the Ruby Joke game, you learn the basic steps involved in writing a Ruby program. When the game begins, the screen shown in Figure 1-1 displays, prompting the player for permission to begin telling jokes.

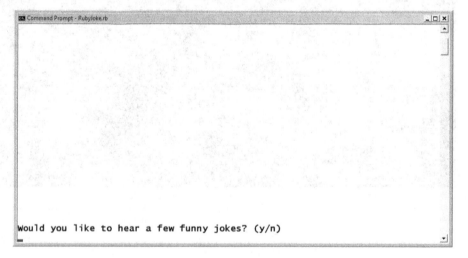

Figure 1-1 The player may elect to play the game or quit

If the player enters a value of n, the game responds by displaying a message that invites the player to return to play another time. However, if the player enters a value of y, the game responds by displaying the first of a series of jokes, as demonstrated in Figure 1-2.

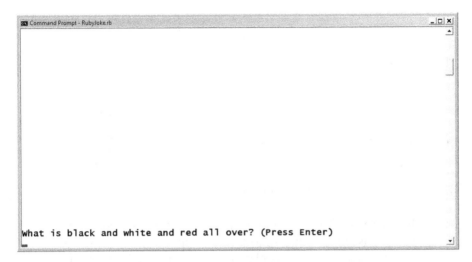

Figure 1-2 The player must press Enter to advance from screen to screen during game play

In order to view the first joke's punch line, the player must press Enter, after which the screen shown in Figure 1-3 displays.

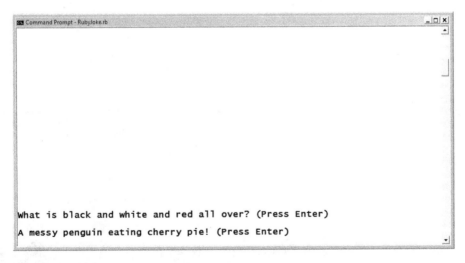

Figure 1-3 The punch line for the game's first joke

To view successive jokes, the player must continue to press Enter. Once the game's final joke has been told, the screen shown in Figure 1-4 displays, thanking the player for playing the game.

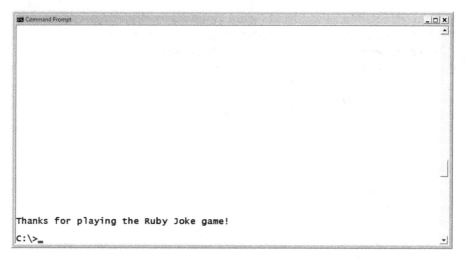

Figure 1-4   The game ends by thanking the player

In Figure 1-1 through Figure 1-4, you saw what the Ruby Joke game looks like when executed on a computer running Microsoft Windows. Ruby is a cross-platform programming language. This means Ruby programs can be created and executed on different operating systems, like Mac OS X or Linux. Figure 1-5 shows an example of how the screen would look if the game were run on Mac OS X.

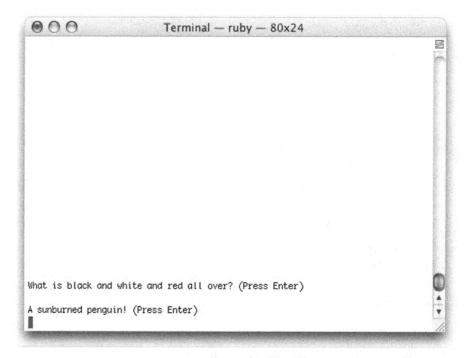

Figure 1-5   The Ruby Joke game runs exactly the same regardless of which operating system is used

By the time you have completed the development of the Ruby Joke game, you will have a good understanding of the basic mechanics involved in creating Ruby programs, and you will be ready to tackle more challenging projects.

A Brief History of Computers and Computer Programming

Computer systems have gone through a series of distinct changes over the last 70 years. These changes can be classified into different generations. Each generation marks a major jump in technology over the previous generation. **Computer programming**, often referred to simply as **programming**, is the process of developing, testing, debugging, and updating the code statements that make up computer programs. Computer programs tell the computer what to do. Like computer systems, computer programming has evolved significantly over the years.

The Mechanized Era

The art and science of programming goes even further back than the creation of the first computer. The earliest programming languages were made up of simple codes. Joseph Marie Jacquard developed the Jacquard loom in 1801. The loom was used to weave cloth. Its operation was managed by instructions provided on punch cards. Once programmed, the loom applied the programmed pattern into the resulting cloth. Although the loom did not perform any computations on the data it was provided, it is regarded as a precursor to today's computers.

Charles Babbage was an English mathematician and inventor. Many historians credit him with originating the first conceptual computer. In 1822, he began work on a machine that he called the Difference Engine, which was designed to process polynomial functions. He never finished building the Difference Engine. He later began work on a second machine, which he called the Difference Engine No. 2. He never completed building this device either. A complete version of the second machine was eventually built by the London Science Museum in 1991, based on Babbage's original specifications. It was programmed through the manipulation of mechanical gears and was capable of performing calculations resulting in as many as 31 digits of precision.

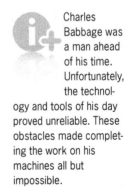

Charles Babbage was a man ahead of his time. Unfortunately, the technology and tools of his day proved unreliable. These obstacles made completing the work on his machines all but impossible.

Babbage later used punch cards as the basis for programming a third machine, which he called the Analytical Engine. This device introduced a number of new programming features that would prove to be essential elements in modern programming, including sequential processing, loops, and branching logic. Many historians regard the Analytical Engine as the direct precursor to the modern computer.

A mathematician named Ada Lovelace learned of Babbage's Analytical Engine. Although the device was never finished, her fascination led her to write extensively about it and theorize on its capabilities and possible use. She went on to write programs for the Analytical Engine, including one capable of generating Bernoulli numbers. Because of this work, Lovelace is regarded as the world's first programmer.

The First Generation

The period from 1937 to 1953 is generally regarded as the first generation of electronic computer systems. Among the earliest computers was Colossus, created by the British military during World War II to decrypt Germany's military code, and the Electronic Numerical Integrator and Computer (ENIAC) built at the University of Pennsylvania as part of a US Army project. ENIAC was originally intended to be used in computing ballistics during WWII. Later, it was used to perform calculations for the development of the hydrogen bomb.

The first computer programs that ran on these early computers were all written in **machine language** (sometimes referred to as **machine code**). At the most basic level, all computers see and process data as collections of numbers, made up of 0s and 1s. Machine language is a system of instructions used to write programs that can be executed by a computer's **central processing unit** (**CPU**). Machine language is regarded as the first generation of computer programming languages. Programming in machine language requires an intimate understanding of the computer's architecture and internal operation.

The Second Generation

The second generation of computer systems lasted from 1954 to 1962. During this time, major changes occurred in the design of computer circuits. Computer programming languages continued to evolve during this period as well. Beginning in the early 1950s, assembly languages were developed. **Assembly languages** replaced 0s and 1s with sets of symbols or mnemonics. They were therefore easier to work with.

Programmers translated their assembly programs into executable programs using a piece of software known as an **assembler**. Despite being significantly easier to program than machine languages, assembly languages were extremely complex and required considerable expertise to work with.

In the mid-to-late 1950s, a new set of higher-level programming languages began to supplant assembly language application development, although assembly languages were still commonly used in developing low-level system programs that managed hardware and component operations. These new languages included:

- Fortran (1956)—developed by IBM for science-based programming

- ALGOL (1958)—developed by a committee of American and European scientists and used primarily by computer science researchers

- COBOL (1959)—developed under the supervision of Rear Admiral Grace Hopper with sponsorship of the US Department of Defense, widely used for business and financial applications

Programs developed using these languages were **procedure oriented**. This means that program code was organized into collections of **procedures** (sometimes called functions or subroutines), each of which was designed to accept and process predefined types of data (**input**) and then return a result (**output**). To execute, programs written in these languages had to be compiled into executable programs using a program know as a **compiler**.

The Third Generation

The third generation of computer systems ran from 1963 to 1972. Innovations during this time included an enormous increase in computer processing power and speed and the development of the computer operating system. Two major programming languages were also developed during this period: Pascal and C.

Named after a French philosopher and mathematician, Pascal combined, simplified, and enhanced many of the language features found in Fortran, ALGOL, and COBOL. It was created as a way of teaching students structured programming, in which programs were designed in a modular fashion. A structured program would be broken down into separate modules, each module tested and integrated back into the structured program.

C is a general-purpose programming language. It was developed in 1972 at Bell Telephone Laboratories. Though originally created for the UNIX operating system, C has been **ported** so that it works on every major computing platform, and it has become the world's most popular programming language. With C, an application program written on one operating system can usually be ported to another operating system and then compiled for execution after making any changes specific to that operating system. This makes **cross-platform** program development a lot easier since programmers do not have to start over from scratch if they switch from one type of operating system to another (e.g., from UNIX to Windows).

The Fourth Generation

The fourth generation of computer systems lasted from 1973 to 1983 and was marked by a high level of component integration. Computers were no longer the size of buildings or rooms. They could now sit on your desk, which ushered in the age of the personal computer. Although C was still the most popular programming language, a new way of programming known as **object-oriented programming** (**OOP**) began to gain popularity in the late-1970s and early-1980s.

Instead of using procedures that accept and process input and then generate output, OOP focuses on the definition of objects. In OOP, an **object** interacts with other objects using its own internal methods (procedures), attributes (properties), and data. Objects represent files, folders, disk drives, customers, accounts, game characters, etc.

In OOP, objects are constructed based on predefined templates referred to as classes, which outline the objects' various components. A **class** controls object behavior (methods) and sets object properties (which describe the object). Through a process known as **instantiation**, objects are created based on classes. Objects interact with one another by executing their methods or changing their properties.

Adding the benefits of OOP, Bell Labs developed a new programming language in 1979 named C with Classes, later changing the name to C++. C++ gained rapid acceptance and went on to become one of the most popular programming languages ever developed. It has been used in the development of programs and applications that span the full range of computer programming, including:

- System software
- Device drivers
- Desktop applications
- Server software
- Computer games

The Fifth Generation

The fifth generation of computer systems, which lasted from 1984 to 1990, featured major advances in both **local area networking** (**LAN**) and **wide area networking** (**WAN**). Processor costs dropped, as did the cost of RAM, leading to the widespread deployment of desktop computers and network servers. A number of programming languages were developed during this period, including Perl, which was created in 1987. Perl supports both procedural and object-oriented program development. Although originally developed for UNIX, it (like most scripting languages that have followed) has been ported to most major computing platforms.

Perl is a general-purpose, interpreted scripting language. Interpreted programs are not compiled into executable programs at development time. They are interpreted (converted into executable code) at run-time, which means they must be reinterpreted every time they are executed. Interpreted programs are converted into executable code using an **interpreter** program.

With Perl, programmers develop programs referred to as scripts. **Scripts** are plain text files that contain program code, which can then be interpreted and executed. An advantage of scripting languages like Perl is that they are easy to write and execute. Once a scripting language has been installed, all you need to begin developing scripts is a basic text editor.

1990 and Beyond

Since 1990, we have witnessed the explosive growth of the public's use of the Internet. Network bandwidth, especially broadband technologies, has allowed the Internet to evolve into a major media for communication, commerce, education, and entertainment. Equally explosive has been the emergence of a new generation of programming languages, designed to enhance these new technologies.

A major advance is the movement towards **rapid application development** (**RAD**), which enables programmers to quickly develop high-quality applications. Programming languages like Visual Basic, C#, and Java are all examples of RAD languages. These are all object-oriented languages. To use them, programmers have to learn how to work with **Integrated Development Environments** (**IDEs**). Sophisticated and complex, IDEs provide a suite of development tools used to write, test, and debug computer programs.

Ruby is both an object-oriented programming language and an interpreted scripting language. Therefore, you will see it referred to as both a programming language and a scripting language, and you will see Ruby programs also referred to as scripts.

Programmers who have previous experience with Perl and Smalltalk (and to a somewhat lesser extent, Python, C++, Lisp, and ADA) should find many similarities between Ruby and these languages, making for a shorter learning curve.

Another major advance is the rise of **scripting languages**, such as Python, Java, and Ruby. These have gained great prominence on the web, where they are used to support the development of Internet applications. They have also found a place in other programming venues, including system administration and network programming.

Introducing Ruby

Ruby is an object-oriented programming language created by a Japanese computer scientist named Yukihiro Matsumoto, better known within the Ruby community as Matz. Matz created Ruby to address the shortcomings he found in other programming languages, which he viewed as overly complex and difficult to work with. He wanted to make programming less difficult and more fun.

Matz named his new programming language Ruby after joking with a friend that the Perl language's name sounded like "pearl." (Perl is an acronym for Practical Extraction and Report Language.) Unlike Perl, Ruby is the actual name of the programming language, not just a clever acronym. As a relatively new programming language, Ruby represents lessons learned from many other programming languages. For example, rather than adding support for object-oriented programming long after the language was created, as is now being done with Perl, Ruby was created from the ground up with object-oriented programming in mind.

As he worked on his new programming language, Matz was heavily influenced by Smalltalk, a pure object-oriented programming language created in the 1970s. Smalltalk programs tended to be cryptic, however, lacking Ruby's naturalistic programming style and syntax. Matz also drew heavily on another programming language, Perl. Unlike Ruby, Perl was not originally designed to support object-oriented programming. In slowly adapting to include object-oriented programming and other modern programming features, Perl's syntax has become cryptic and inconsistent. Other programming languages to which Matz attributed inspiration include Python, C++, Lisp, and ADA.

Matz began working on Ruby in February of 1993 and released his first version in December of 1995. It quickly gained notice and popularity in Japan. Elsewhere, few people gave it attention, however. Ruby 1.0 was released a year later, in December 1996. A big reason for the slow recognition of Ruby in its first few years was the lack of non-Japanese documentation. It was not until the end of 1998, when the ruby-talk mailing list was created, that Ruby began to be promoted in English. In 1999, *www.ruby-lang.org*, the home page which is shown in Figure 1-6, was set up as the official English-language website for Ruby.

Figure 1-6 The official English home page for Ruby is *www.ruby-lang.org*

Despite its obvious power and capabilities, Ruby still lacked the popularity of other programming languages like Perl and Python. What Ruby needed was a killer application that would demonstrate its capabilities and get everybody's attention. Then, with the introduction of Ruby on Rails, which allowed programmers to build website applications using Ruby, everything changed. Suddenly, programmers all over the world began to take notice of Ruby's capabilities, both as a general-purpose programming language and as a web-development language.

As of the writing of this book, the stable version of Ruby is version 1.9.1. This is currently considered by the Ruby community to be the general release version of the language.

Ruby on Rails, sometimes referred to as just **Rails**, is a web-based application-development framework that facilitates the development of database-driven applications. It was first released in 2004, and like Ruby, it is free.

Ruby Is Simple Yet Powerful

As an interpreted programming language, Ruby is simple to use. Just open a text or code editor, type in some Ruby code, save your program file, and your Ruby program is ready to execute. If all goes well, your program will do what it is supposed to do. Ruby can be used to develop complete applications that involve network and database access. Tight integration with the operating systems also provides Ruby with access to a wealth of system resources. Its devotion to object-oriented programming and its extensive set of classes and libraries give it capabilities that rival or surpass many other programming languages, especially those that fall into the scripting language category. In this sense, Ruby is quite easy to learn but, at the same time, difficult to master.

Ruby Is Interpreted

Because Ruby is an interpreted programming language, its programs, sometimes referred to as scripts, are not converted into executable code until you run them using a Ruby interpreter. An interpreter is an application that converts source code into a format that the operating system can execute. This makes Ruby a lot easier to work with than compiled programming languages, which require you to go through a formal compile process after creating or making a change to a program before it can be executed. Thus, if an error occurs in your Ruby program, you can open the program using your editor, find and fix the error, then save the program and run it again, at which time it will get interpreted and executed again.

Using Ruby, it is especially easy to create small programs and quickly get them executing, perhaps in just a fraction of the time required to create a similar program using a compiled programming language like C++. However, in exchange for this simplicity and ease of use, your Ruby programs will run slower than their compiled counterparts, because each time you run a Ruby program it must be reinterpreted before it can execute, whereas a compiled program can begin executing immediately.

Ruby Supports a Natural, English-Like Programming Style

Another feature of Ruby is its straightforward syntax, which makes learning how to work with it easier than is the case with many other programming languages. Ruby is generally regarded as a natural, English-like programming language. Unlike with other programming languages, such as Perl and Python, you can often tell exactly what a Ruby statement is doing just by reading it, even if you are unfamiliar with the specific commands that make up the statement. For example, consider the following statement:

```
3.times do print "What's up, Doc?" end
```

Without knowing anything about Ruby programming, you can probably figure out, in general terms, what this statement does when executed. It prints (i.e., displays on the screen) the question `What's up, Doc?` three times in a row.

Ruby Has Light Syntax Requirements

Yet another feature of Ruby that sets it apart from many other programming languages is its light syntax. Ruby does not force programmers to load up programming statements with brackets and parentheses, nor does it require that every statement end with a semicolon. Statements tend to be less wordy than with other programming languages. As a result, there is less opportunity for you to make mistakes when writing program code. As an example of Ruby's simple syntax, consider variable declaration. A **variable** is a pointer to a location in memory where a piece of data is stored. Ruby does not require you to formally declare a variable prior to its use. This greatly facilitates the development of small one- and two-line programs.

Despite its simplicities, Ruby is every bit as powerful and complex as any other modern programming language. Many programmers use Ruby to develop programs that tie together other applications, providing the programmatic glue needed to take disparate applications and get them to work together to be more efficient.

Ruby Is Object Oriented

Unlike many other modern programming languages, Ruby is as close to 100 percent object oriented as a programming language gets. In Ruby, everything is viewed as an object, even a file, a folder, or a printer. Things that describe or characterize an object are referred to as object **properties**. For example, a file has a name property and a length property. Properties are stored as variables. By accessing the contents of these variables, you can learn about object characteristics. You can even make changes to an object by modifying the values assigned to object properties. You might, for example, rename a file or folder.

Actions that affect the object, or that the object can be directed to perform, are stored as part of the object in **methods**. By creating objects and assigning program code to the objects' methods, you can create Ruby programs whose objects are able to perform any number of actions. For example, an object representing a character in a computer game might have methods that give it the ability to move, jump, and shoot.

Unlike many similar languages, Ruby is object-oriented programming to the nth degree. It treats everything as an object, even numbers. Since numbers are seen as a type of object, they are automatically associated with specific types of properties and methods.

Ruby Is Extremely Flexible

Using Ruby, you can create programs that automate any number of tasks. The programs can automate complex tasks, thus eliminating the possibility of human error. Alternatively, they can automate repetitive tasks, freeing you up to perform other tasks. In fact, you can use Ruby to perform just about any task you can think of, including the following:

- Writing to and reading from text files

- Retrieving network data and configuring network resources like network drives and printers

- Developing test programs (prototyping) before devoting the time to a particular programming problem using a more complicated language like C++

- Automating complex tasks and repetitive system-administration tasks, such as user-account management or disk cleanup

- Developing web applications by using Ruby in conjunction with the Ruby on Rails web-development framework

Ruby Exists in Many Different Environments

Ruby can run directly on Microsoft Windows, Mac OS X, and multiple versions of UNIX and Linux, as well as many other types of operating systems. Using the Ruby on Rails framework, Ruby also facilitates the development and execution of web applications. Finally, it runs within various virtual machines. A **virtual machine** is a program that looks and operates as if it were its own computer. It's like a "machine within the machine." A program can run within a virtual machine even if it is not compatible with the computer it is running on.

The .NET Framework is a collection of program-development tools provided by Microsoft that supports the creation of desktop, network, and Internet-based applications and programs.

One such virtual machine is **JRuby**, which is a Java-based Ruby environment developed by Sun Microsystems. Using JRuby, programmers can develop Ruby programs that run on any Java-supported platform. Since most modern web browsers, including Internet Explorer and Firefox, support Java, they are capable of supporting JRuby as well. Another virtual machine being developed for Ruby is Microsoft's **IronRuby**. IronRuby will support the development and execution of Ruby programs that can interact with the Microsoft .NET Framework. Although not available as of the writing of this book, IronRuby promises to make available to Ruby programmers all of the resources currently available to other .NET-compatible programming languages.

Getting Ready to Work with Ruby

You will not find Ruby already installed on a new computer running any version of Microsoft Windows. However, if you are running Mac OS X, version 10.3 or higher, Ruby should already be installed. And if you are running one of the many versions of the UNIX or Linux operating systems that are available today, there is a pretty good chance that Ruby is already installed on your computer.

If Ruby is not installed on your computer, you will need to download and install it, as explained in the sections that follow. If you are running a version of Ruby older than Ruby 1.8.2, you will need to upgrade to a new version, which you can do by simply installing a new version of the language.

As of the writing of this book, the current version of Ruby is 1.9.1. All the Ruby programs in this book were developed and tested using this version of Ruby. However, they should all work fine on any later version.

Determining Whether Ruby Is Already Installed

Depending on your operating system, there are a number of ways to check whether Ruby is installed on your computer. The following sections outline a number of these.

Looking for Ruby on Microsoft Windows

If you are running Microsoft Windows, the easiest way to see if Ruby is installed is to look for the Ruby program group. You do this by clicking Start > All Programs, then looking for a program group named Ruby-XXX-XX, where XXX-XX specifies the version of Ruby that is installed on your computer. If it is there, click the group to open it and look for an executable file named fxri–Interactive Ruby Help & Console. If it is there, Ruby is installed on your computer and should be ready for use.

Another way to determine if Ruby is installed on your computer (and to ascertain its version number, if it is installed) is to click Start > All Programs > Accessories > Command Prompt. This displays a Windows console window and provides you with access to the Windows command prompt. Type the following command at the Windows command prompt and press Enter:

```
ruby -v
```

If Ruby is installed, you should see output similar to that shown in Figure 1-7.

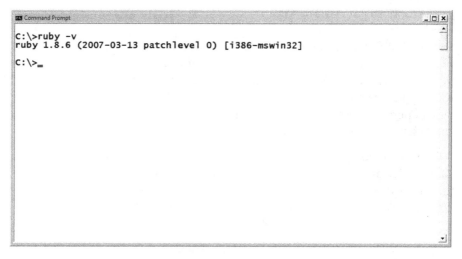

Figure 1-7 Information about the version of Ruby installed on the computer

Next, type the following command and press Enter:

`irb`

This command starts a new Interactive Ruby session. The following command prompt should be displayed:

```
irb
irb(main):001:0>
```

If you see this command prompt, Ruby is installed and ready for use on your computer. Type `exit` to end the IRB session.

Looking for Ruby on Mac OS X

Ruby comes installed on any computer running Mac OS X 10.3 or later. To determine if Ruby is installed on a Mac computer, open the Applications folder, scroll to the bottom of the list, and click Utilities. Inside this folder you will find the Terminal application.

To start the Terminal application, double-click its icon. Once started, it displays a UNIX-shell command prompt (Mac OS X is a UNIX-based operating system). To find out if Ruby is installed, type the following command at the command prompt and press Enter:

`ruby -v`

If Ruby is installed, a message similar to the following will display, indicating the version number:

`ruby 1.8.7 (2008-08-11 patchlevel 72) [universal-darwin10.0]`

Next, type the following command and press Enter:

`irb`

Ruby programmers who develop programs for Mac OS X will need to work with the Terminal application a lot. You may want to drag and drop the Terminal application icon onto the dock to have it nearby.

IRB stands for Interactive Ruby. It is a program supplied with Ruby that allows you to submit Ruby statements for processing and is commonly used to test language features to see how they work. You will learn more about IRB later in this chapter.

This command starts a new Ruby session. As a result, you should see the command prompt shown here:

```
irb
irb(main):001:0>
```

Depending on how things are configured, the exact format of IRB's command prompt may vary. For example, instead of the previous prompt, you might see something like the following:

```
irb
>>
```

Although different in appearance, this IRB prompt behaves no differently than the `irb(main):001:0>` prompt.

If everything worked as described, Ruby is installed and ready for use on your computer. Type **exit** to end the IRB session.

Looking for Ruby on UNIX and Linux

Ruby comes installed as part of many UNIX and Linux operating systems. To determine if it is installed on a particular UNIX or Linux computer, you need to start a new command shell session using whatever terminal shell program has been supplied with your operating system. Once at the command prompt, type the following command and press Enter:

```
irb
```

This command starts a new Interactive Ruby session. As a result, you should see the command prompt shown here:

```
irb
irb(main):001:0>
```

If everything worked as described, Ruby is installed and ready for use on your computer. Type **exit** to end the IRB session.

Installing or Upgrading Ruby

When you install Ruby, the Ruby interpreter is installed, too. You also get a collection of Ruby libraries that support the execution of Ruby on the particular platform on which it has been installed.

Depending on which operating system you are using, there are a number of different options for installing Ruby. The easiest option, when available, is to install an already packaged copy of Ruby. In the absence of a prebuilt installation package, you can download the appropriate Ruby source code and perform a manual installation.

Installing Ruby on Microsoft Windows

Microsoft Windows does not come with Ruby installed. So, unless someone else has already installed it on your computer, you will need to install it yourself. The easiest way to do this is to download to your desktop the one-click installer package made available at *www.ruby-lang.org/en/downloads*. Go to the Ruby on Windows section of the web page, as shown in Figure 1-8, click the Ruby One-Click Installer link, and save the file to your desktop when prompted.

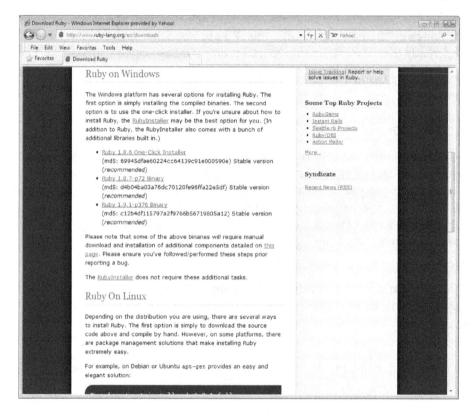

Figure 1-8 Searching for Ruby source code and installation packages

Once the download is complete, you can install Ruby on your computer by executing the steps outlined in the following procedure:

1. Double-click the installer program.

2. If Microsoft Windows displays a pop-up window with a security message, click the Run button to allow the installation process to continue.

3. When prompted by the install program, click Next to begin the installation process.

4. Continue to click Next, when prompted, to perform a standard installation of Ruby.

5. Once installation is complete, you will be prompted to click Next one last time, and then the Finish button. At this point, Ruby's installation is complete.

You can also use the Ruby-installation procedure to install a newer version of Ruby on your Windows computer.

Now that Ruby is installed, click Start > All Programs. You should see a new program group named Ruby-XXX-XX, where XXX-XX identifies the specific version of Ruby that has been installed. Within this group you will find a number of items, including:

- fxri-Interactive Ruby Help & Console—an interactive graphical application that provides access to Ruby help files and Ruby's interactive environment

- SciTE—a general code editor that can be used to create Ruby programs

- Uninstall Ruby-XXX-XX—a program for removing Ruby from your computer

- Ruby Documentation—links to online web pages and to Ruby's help files

- RubyGems—a package manager that provides a standard format for distributing Ruby programs

Finding a Ruby Installation for Mac OS X

Ruby comes preinstalled on all versions of Mac OS X starting with version 10.3. So, unless it has been removed from your computer or you want to install a more current version, you can simply begin working with it. If you do need to install Ruby on Mac OS X, go to *www.ruby-lang.org/en/downloads*. Here you will find several links in the "Ruby on OS X" section. Each of these links offers a different option for installing Ruby on Mac OS X. The names of these links and their respective URLs are listed here:

- Locomotive—*http://sourceforge.net/projects/locomotive/*

- MacPorts—*http://www.macports.org/*

- Fink—*http://www.finkproject.org/*

You will find instructions for working with each of these installation options on their respective websites.

Installing Ruby on UNIX and Linux

Many UNIX and Linux systems come with Ruby already installed. If yours doesn't, you can see whether it includes an option for installing Ruby. Many UNIX and Linux systems contain a program called a package-management utility that allows you to install Ruby by selecting it from a list of available applications.

You can also install Ruby manually. To do so, go to *www.ruby-lang.org/ en/downloads* and click the Ruby X.X.X link located in the Ruby Source Code section of the web page. Make sure the version of Ruby you click is listed as a stable version. Click Save when prompted to download the installation files to your computer. This downloads a compressed tar.gz file containing Ruby's installation files. This file is named ruby-X.X.X.tar. gz,where X.X.X represents the current stable version of Ruby. As of the writing of this book, the current version of Ruby is 1.9.1-376; therefore, the tar file would be named ruby-1.9.1-p376.tar.gz.

With the tar.gz file, you can install Ruby on your UNIX or Linux system if you are logged on with root access, which is a special security privilege that allows you to access and execute all the system's commands and files. Once you are logged on with root access, follow these steps:

1. Start a new shell session, and navigate to the folder where you saved the tar.gz file.

2. Uncompress the file by typing `tar xzvf ruby-x-x-x.tar.gz` and pressing Enter.

3. From the command line, open the folder created during the decompress process.

4. Type `./configure` and press Enter. This will generate a makefile file and config.h file for Ruby.

5. Compile Ruby by typing `run` and pressing Enter.

6. Type `make install` and press Enter.

Short Quiz

1. Which programming languages had an effect on the design of Ruby?

2. What is Ruby on Rails?

3. Is Ruby an interpreted language or a compiled language? What is the difference?

4. What is a variable?

5. What types of operating systems support the execution of Ruby?

Working with Ruby

There are many different ways of working with Ruby. One way is to access it from the operating system's command prompt, starting a temporary Ruby session to which you can submit individual Ruby statements for processing. You can also start IRB to set up a Ruby session. IRB is a Ruby shell, an interface that allows you to interact with Ruby and execute as many statements as you want.

Working at the Command Prompt

This option allows you to enter single-line Ruby statements and execute them immediately.

Working with Ruby from the command prompt is relatively straight-forward. To start, simply type the command **ruby** and press Enter. This starts up a new working session, and you can now enter any valid statement you would like Ruby to execute. Once you have finished typing in your statement, you need to inform Ruby that you are done. Press Control+D, and then press Enter. Ruby executes the statement you entered.

To see how all this works, consider the following:

Microsoft Windows

```
C:> ruby
puts "Hello World!"
^d
Hello World!
C:>
```

UNIX/Linux/Mac OS X

```
$ ruby
puts "Hello World!"
Hello World!
$
```

The UNIX/ Linux/ Mac OS X example shown here depicts the command prompt as a $ character. However, the command prompt may vary.

In the example on the left, a Ruby session is started at the Microsoft Windows command prompt, then the statement puts "Hello World!" is typed, after which the end-of-file character (Control+D) is typed. In response, Ruby displays the text string Hello World! on the console window. At this point, the Ruby session is closed, and the Windows command prompt is redisplayed. The example on the right shows the same process on a computer running UNIX or Linux. As you can see, the only difference between these two examples is the presentation of the command prompt.

IRB—Interactive Ruby

To start IRB, type irb at the operating system command prompt and press Enter. When you start IRB, an IRB shell is opened that provides a number of helpful features. For example, the shell maintains a history of all the commands that are entered during the current working session. This allows you to use the up and down arrow keys to move backwards and forwards in this history, retrieving and re-executing previous commands without having to type them again.

Using IRB, you can type snippets of code, press the Enter key, and get immediate feedback on the results. When started, the following command prompt is displayed:

```
irb(main):001:0>
```

As you can see, the command prompt consists of several parts, each of which is separated from the next by a colon. The parts are outlined here:

- (main)—The word listed inside the parentheses identifies the current class/object, in this case the main object.

- 001—This three-digit number represents a history, indicating the number of commands that have been entered during the current working session. A value of 001 indicates that the IRB is waiting for the first command to be entered.

- 0—This number represents the current queue depth when working with a class. (You'll learn what this means in Chapter 2, "Interacting with Ruby.")

- >—This identifies the end of the command prompt.

Here is an example of how to start and interact with IRB:

```
C:\>irb
irb(main):001:0> 5 + 4
=> 9
irb(main):002:0>
```

You can stop the current IRB session at any time and return to the operating system's command prompt by typing the word exit at the command prompt and pressing the Enter key.

Here, a new IRB session is started by typing irb at the command prompt and then pressing Enter. Next, a simple mathematical expression is typed. Then the Enter key is pressed. In response, Ruby evaluates the expression and displays the result. Notice that the result is preceded by the => characters. An **expression** is a piece of program code that, when evaluated, returns a value. Finally, another IRB command prompt is displayed, indicating that Ruby is ready for another command.

Here is another example of how to work with IRB:

```
irb(main):002:0> puts "Hello World!"
Hello World!
=> nil
irb(main):003:0>
```

This example uses the `puts` command, which causes a line of text to be displayed on the console. The line of text is passed to the `puts` command as an argument. An **argument** is a piece of data passed to a command or program for processing as input. IRB responds by displaying `Hello World!`. Next, IRB displays a value of `nil`, indicating the result of the last expression that it processed.

The word `nil` is used to represent a Ruby value of nothing. Unlike most Ruby commands, the `puts` command always returns a value of `nil`.

23

As a new Ruby programmer, you are going to want to spend a lot of time working with IRB, experimenting with various language elements. You'll learn more about how to work with IRB in Chapter 2.

fxri–Interactive Ruby Help and Console

Windows users have an alternative to working with IRB: fxri–Interactive Ruby Help and Console. This graphical interface consists of three parts, as shown in Figure 1.9. On the left-hand side of the window is a list you can select from to learn more about various language elements. The upper-right side of the window displays syntactical information about the selected item. The lower-right side of the window provides access to the IRB command prompt, which you can work with exactly as if you have accessed IRB via the Windows command prompt.

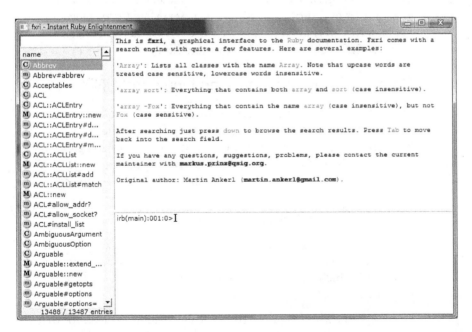

Figure 1-9 In addition to providing access to help information, fxri provides access to IRB

Developing Ruby Programs

Using the command prompt or IRB has certain advantages. To really take advantage of the programming language, however, you must learn how to create and execute Ruby programs. This will allow you to develop programs that can be executed over and over again. Ruby program files have .rb as their suffix.

24

The Mac OS X TextEdit application provides a number of advanced word processing features. To use TextEdit to save a Ruby program, you need to enable the Make Plain Text option located under TextEdit's Format menu before saving your program file. Alternatively, you can change TextEdit's default file settings so that it automatically saves all files as plain text files. Do this by clicking the TextEdit menu, selecting Preferences, then selecting Plain text under Format.

Creating Ruby Programs on Microsoft Windows

To create and save Ruby program files, you need a good text or program editor. If you are working on Microsoft Windows, you can use the Notepad text editor to create your program files. Alternatively, you can use the SciTE editor that comes installed with Ruby on Windows. SciTE is a generic code editor designed to facilitate the development of programs for a number of different programming languages.

Creating Ruby Programs on Mac OS X

Mac OS X users can use the TextEdit application to create and save Ruby programs. Alternatively, you can download and install any number of text or code editors, like TextMate (*http://www.macromates.com*) or Komodo IDE (*http://www.activestate.com*). Komodo IDE also runs on Windows and Linux.

Creating Ruby Programs on Linux and UNIX

Linux and UNIX programmers can always use the vi editor to create and save Ruby programs. Unless you already have experience with vi and have a personal affinity for it, however, you are probably going to want to use something else. One alternative is KATE (KDE Advanced Text Editor). KATE is a free text editor available at *http://kate-editor.org/*.

Using a Cross-Platform Ruby Editor

If you are going to be developing Ruby programs for execution on more than one type of operating system, you might want to look into FreeRIDE, which you can download for free at *http://rubyforge.org/projects/freeride/*.

FreeRIDE, shown in Figure 1.10, is a Ruby-specific code editor that supports a number of advanced features, including statement color-coding (where language keywords and data are displayed in different colors to help make the program code more readable) and the ability to execute Ruby programs without having to leave the text editor and switch over to the command prompt. To learn more about FreeRIDE, go to *http://freeride.rubyforge.org/wiki/wiki.pl*.

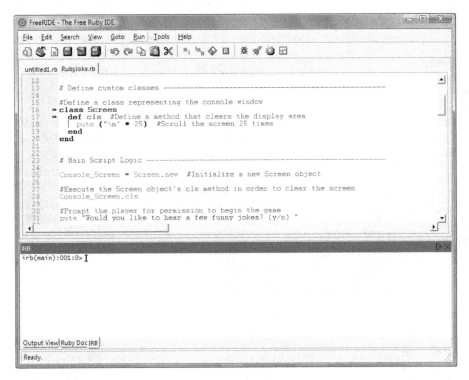

Figure 1-10 FreeRIDE is a Ruby program editor that works on Windows, Mac OS X, UNIX, and Linux

Creating Your First Ruby Program

The process involved in creating a Ruby program is really not very different from that of creating a text file or a spreadsheet. First, you open your text or code editor and create a new file. You are then ready to enter the code statements that will make up your Ruby program. Ruby programs may be many hundreds of lines long, or they may consist of a single statement.

You should create a folder where you can store all your Ruby programs. This will make them easy to find and manage.

For now, let's keep things simple by creating a Ruby program comprised of the following code statement:

```
puts "Hello World!"
```

This statement uses the **puts** command to display a text string. Now, save this file with a filename of HelloWorld.rb.

That's all there is to it. Your new Ruby program is ready for execution, as explained in the next section.

The file extension used to represent a Ruby program is .rb.

Running Your Ruby Program

In Microsoft Windows, the .rb file extension is automatically registered with the operating system when Ruby is installed, informing the operating system that any file with a .rb file extension is a Ruby program and should be processed by the Ruby interpreter. This allows you to run your Ruby programs from the Windows desktop by double-clicking on them.

Once you save your new Ruby program, you can run it from the command prompt. On Microsoft Windows, click Start > All Programs > Accessories > Command Prompt. This will open a Windows console window, giving you access to the command prompt. Once at the command prompt, navigate to the folder where you stored your new Ruby program file and type in the following command:

```
ruby HelloWorld.rb
```

Here, the name of the program to be executed is passed to the `ruby` command. Alternatively, you can run the program by specifying its full path and file name, as demonstrated here:

```
ruby c:\Ruby_Scripts\HelloWorld.rb
```

On Mac OS X, UNIX, and Linux, Ruby programs are run from the command prompt. As with Microsoft Windows, you do so by entering the `ruby` command, followed by the path and file name of the program, as demonstrated here:

```
ruby /Ruby_Scripts/HelloWorld.rb
```

Here, a program named HelloWorld.rb, which is stored in the Ruby_Scripts folder, is executed.

There is an alternative to running your Ruby programs this way.

The #!/usr/local/bin/ruby –w and #!/usr/bin/ruby –w statements are referred to as **shebang** statements. A shebang statement tells the operating system where to find Ruby.

On UNIX or Linux, include the following command as the first statement in your Ruby programs:

```
#!/usr/local/bin/ruby –w
```

On Mac OS X, make this your first statement:

```
#!/usr/bin/ruby –w
```

These statements tell the operating system where to find Ruby, and they direct Ruby to execute the contents of the program file. Including one in your program saves you the trouble of having to explicitly execute the `ruby` command every time you run the program. Notice that if you changed Ruby's default location during its installation, you will need to alter these commands. In addition to adding the command to your Ruby program, you must mark the Ruby program file as an executable file. You do this by using the `chmod` command, as demonstrated here:

```
chmod +x HelloWorld.rb
```

In the adjacent statement, applicable to UNIX, Linux, and Mac OS X, the .character (i.e., a single dot) was used to instruct the operating system to look in the current working directory for a file named HelloWorld.rb.

Once you have completed both these steps, you can execute your Ruby program by navigating to the directory where the file is stored and entering the following command at the command prompt:

```
$ ./HelloWorld.rb
```

Short Quiz

1. What is IRB? What is it used for?

2. How do you terminate an IRB session?

3. What does the term "nil" refer to in Ruby?

4. What is fxri?

5. What is the file extension assigned to Ruby programs?

Back to the Ruby Joke Game

It is time to work on this chapter's project, the Ruby Joke game. As you follow the steps required to create and execute this game, try not to worry too much about the program code you're asked to enter. For now, focus on the overall series of steps involved in creating and executing Ruby programs. You will learn the nuts and bolts of Ruby programming in later chapters.

Designing the Game

Developing the Ruby Joke game involves a specific series of steps. As you advance from step to step, be sure to pay careful attention. Do not skip any steps, and follow the instructions precisely, especially when typing the program's code statements. This will help you avoid errors and will make things go much more smoothly. Here is an outline of the steps involved, after which a detailed description of each step is provided, followed by the entire program.

1. Open your text or program editor and create a new file.

2. Add comment statements to the beginning of the program file to document the program and its purpose.

3. Define classes representing the computer screen.

4. Instantiate new objects used in the program.

5. Add the code statements that prompt the player for permission to continue.

6. Add the code statements that control the overall operation of the program.

7. Add the code statements that clear the display area.

8. Add the code statements that tell the game's first joke.

9. Add the code statements that tell the rest of the game's jokes.

10. Add the code statements that thank the player for playing.

Each of these steps is covered in detail in the sections that follow.

Step 1: Create a New Ruby File

Open your text or code editor and create a new file. Save the file with the name RubyJoke.rb. If you have created a folder to store all of your Ruby programs, store your new game program there.

Step 2: Document the Program and Its Purpose

You add comments to the beginning of a Ruby program so that you can later identify what the program is and does. Comments are ignored by the Ruby interpreter and therefore have no effect on the program's execution. In Ruby, a comment is coded as a line of text preceded by the # character.

You are ready to begin adding the code statements that will make up your program file. First, add the following statements to the beginning of the program file. These are comments, which provide information about the program and its purpose. This information may be useful to you later.

```
#-----------------------------------------------------------
#
# Script Name: RubyJoke.rb
# Version: 1.0
# Author: Jerry Lee Ford, Jr.
# Date: March 2010
#
# Description: This Ruby program tells a series of five jokes
#
#-----------------------------------------------------------
```

Step 3: Define a Class Representing the Computer Screen

Now that you've documented your program file, it's time to begin writing the code statements that will make your program do something. Type the following statements immediately after the comment statements you typed in the previous step:

```
class Screen
  def cls #Define a method that clears the display area
    puts ("\n" * 25) #Scroll the screen 25 times
  end
end
```

Without going too deeply into things at this point, these statements define a class named Screen that represents the console window in which the game will display. Within the definition of the class named

Screen, a method named cls is defined that, when executed, writes 25 blank lines to the console window, thus making it ready to display new text.

Step 4: Instantiate New Objects

The Screen class defined in Step 3 is only a template. Using that template, the first statement shown here creates, or instantiates, a new object based on that class. The object is assigned the name Console_Screen.

```
Console_Screen = Screen.new
Console_Screen.cls
```

The second statement executes the Screen class's cls method, clearing the display area. Add these two statements at the end of your program file as it currently exists.

Step 5: Prompt the Player for Permission to Continue

Before telling the game's first joke, the game prompts the player for permission to continue. Add the following statements to the end of the program file:

```
puts "Would you like to hear a few funny jokes? (y/n)"
answer = STDIN.gets
answer.chop!
```

The first statement causes a text message to be displayed asking for permission to tell some jokes and instructing the player to respond by typing either a y or n, which represents yes or no. The next two statements collect and format the input provided by the player.

Step 6: Outline the Program's High-Level Conditional Logic

Once the player's input has been collected, it must be analyzed. If the player entered a value of n, the game should invite the player to return and play later. If, on the other hand, the player enters a value of y, the game should start telling its jokes. In order to set up a high-level structure for managing this overall process, add the following statements to the end of your program file:

```
if answer == "n"

else

end
```

In the next several steps, you will be asked to type program statements within this block of code.

Remember, you have not learned anything about Ruby syntax or how to formulate Ruby statements yet, so do not be discouraged if the programming statements you are typing seem a little confusing. For now, focus your attention on the overall process of creating your first Ruby game.

29

Step 7: Clear the Screen

The next two statements invite the player to return and play the game
again another time. They should be executed if the player entered a
value of n when prompted to play the game. Therefore, you will need
to place these statements in the code block between the first and
second statements, as shown here in bold:

```ruby
if answer == "n"
  Console_Screen.cls
  puts "Sorry to hear that. Please return and play" +
    "again soon."
else

end
```

When executed, these two statements will call on the Screen class's
cls method to clear the screen and display a text message, encouraging the player to return and play again another time.

Step 8: Tell the First Joke

Now it is time to tell the game's first joke. Place the following statements
between the second and third statements of the code block (i.e., after
the else keyword and before the end keyword), as shown here in bold:

```ruby
if answer == "n"

else
  Console_Screen.cls

  puts "What is black and white and red all over?" +
    "(Press Enter)"
  pause = STDIN.gets

  puts "A messy penguin eating cherry pie! (Press Enter)"
  pause = STDIN.gets
end
```

These statements cause the display area to be cleared and display the
first joke's opening line. The program then pauses to give the player
a chance to read the set-up line. The program resumes execution as
soon as the player presses Enter, at which time the joke's punch line
is displayed. Then the program is halted to give the player a chance to
read it. Game play resumes when the player presses Enter.

Step 9: Tell the Remaining Jokes

Now it is time to tell the rest of the program's jokes. Place the
following statements between the second and third statements of the
code block, just after the statements that were added in Step 8, telling
the game's first joke.

```
Console_Screen.cls

puts "What is black and white and red all over?" +
   "(Press Enter)"
pause = STDIN.gets

puts "A sunburned penguin! (Press Enter)"
pause = STDIN.gets

Console_Screen.cls

puts "What is black and white and red all over?" +
   "(Press Enter)"
pause = STDIN.gets

puts " An embarrassed Dalmatian puppy! (Press Enter)"
pause = STDIN.gets

Console_Screen.cls

puts "What is black and white and red all over?" +
   "(Press Enter)"
pause = STDIN.gets

puts "A zebra with a scratched knee! (Press Enter)"
pause = STDIN.gets

Console_Screen.cls

puts "What is black and white and red all over?" +
   "(Press Enter)"
pause = STDIN.gets

puts "A skunk with diaper rash! (Press Enter)"
pause = STDIN.gets
```

There are four additional jokes included in this group of code
statements. Notice that the statements that tell each joke are nearly
identical, the only difference being that the text strings tell different
jokes.

Step 10: Thank the Player

You are almost done. All that remains is to clear the screen one last
time and thank the player. Add the following statements to the end of
the program file:

```
Console_Screen.cls

puts "Thanks for playing the Ruby Joke game!"
```

Running Your New Ruby Program Game

You have now completed building the Ruby Joke game. If you have not already done so, save your Ruby program. Next, you should review your program to ensure that it is complete, then execute it and test its execution.

Reviewing the Completed Program File

Because it involved numerous steps, you may have made mistakes. To allow you to check whether your Ruby program is properly written, here is a copy of the fully assembled game. Notice there are a number of additional comment statements in the program file, all marked with the # character. These are to help you understand everything that is going on within the program file.

```ruby
#------------------------------------------------------------
#
# Script Name: RubyJoke.rb
# Version: 1.0
# Author: Jerry Lee Ford, Jr.
# Date: March 2010
#
# Description: This Ruby program tells a series of five
#              jokes
#
#------------------------------------------------------------


# Define custom classes ------------------------------------

class Screen
  def cls #Define a method that clears the display area
    puts ("\n" * 25) #Scroll the screen 25 times
  end
end


# Main Script Logic ----------------------------------------

#Initialize a new Screen object
Console_Screen = Screen.new

#Execute the Screen object's cls method to clear the
#screen
Console_Screen.cls

#Prompt the player for permission to begin the game
puts "Would you like to hear a few funny jokes? (y/n)"

#Collect the player's response
answer = STDIN.gets
```

```
#Remove any extra characters appended to the string
answer.chop!

#Analyze the player's response
#See if the player elected not to play
if answer == "n"

  #Clear the display area
  Console_Screen.cls

  #Invite the player to return and play again
  puts "Sorry to hear that. Please return and play again" +
      "soon."

else

  #Clear the display area
  Console_Screen.cls

  #Display the beginning of the first joke
  puts "What is black and white and red all over?" +
      "(Press Enter)"

  #Force the player to press Enter to continue
  pause = STDIN.gets

  #Display the punch line
  puts "A messy penguin eating cherry pie! (Press Enter)"

  #Force the player to press Enter to continue
  pause = STDIN.gets

  #Clear the display area
  Console_Screen.cls

  #Display the beginning of the second joke
  puts "What is black and white and red all over?" +
      "(Press Enter)"

  #Force the player to press Enter to continue
  pause = STDIN.gets

  #Display the punch line
  puts "A sunburned penguin! (Press Enter)"

  #Force the player to press Enter to continue
  pause = STDIN.gets

  #Clear the display area
  Console_Screen.cls

  #Display the beginning of the third joke
  puts "What is black and white and red all over?" +
      "(Press Enter)"
```

```ruby
#Force the player to press Enter to continue
pause = STDIN.gets

#Display the punch line
puts "An embarrassed Dalmatian puppy! (Press Enter)"

#Force the player to press Enter to continue
pause = STDIN.gets

#Clear the display area
Console_Screen.cls

#Display the beginning of the fourth joke
puts "What is black and white and red all over?" +
    "(Press Enter)"

#Force the player to press Enter to continue
pause = STDIN.gets

#Display the punch line
puts "A zebra with a scratched knee! (Press Enter)"

#Force the player to press Enter to continue
pause = STDIN.gets

#Clear the display area
Console_Screen.cls

#Display the beginning of the fifth joke
puts "What is black and white and red all over?" +
    "(Press Enter)"

#Force the player to press Enter to continue
pause = STDIN.gets

#Display the punch line
puts "A skunk with diaper rash! (Press Enter)"

#Force the player to press Enter to continue
pause = STDIN.gets

#Clear the display area
Console_Screen.cls

puts "Thanks for playing the Ruby Joke game!"


end
```

Executing Your Program

All that remains is to run your Ruby Joke game. Access the operating-system command prompt and navigate to the folder where you saved your Ruby program. Type the following command, then press Enter:

```
ruby RubyJoke.rb
```

The game should run exactly as described at the beginning of the chapter. If you made a typo somewhere, however, you'll get an error message when you try to run your program. If this happens, review the error message carefully and look for any clues to what went wrong. If you are unable to figure out what went wrong based on the text of the error message, review your program file and look for mistyped or missing program statements. Once you have identified and corrected all your typing errors, try running your Ruby program again.

Summing Up

- Ruby is a modern, object-oriented programming language created by a Japanese computer scientist named Yukihiro Matsumoto.

- Ruby's development was influenced by Smalltalk, Perl, Python, C++, Lisp, and ADA.

- Ruby on Rails, sometimes referred to as Rails, is a web-based application development framework that supports web development using Ruby.

- Ruby is an interpreted programming language. Ruby programs are not converted into executable code until they are processed by a Ruby interpreter. An interpreter is an application that converts source code into a format that the operating system can execute.

- Ruby's object-oriented focus and its extensive set of classes and libraries provide it with capabilities that surpass most other programming languages.

- Ruby is a natural, English-like programming language. Unlike other programming languages, you can often tell exactly what a Ruby statement is doing just by looking at it.

- Ruby does not require programming statements loaded down with brackets and parentheses, nor does it require every statement to end with a semicolon. Ruby statements tend to be less wordy than those of other programming languages. The result is fewer mistakes when writing programs.

- A variable is a pointer to a location in memory where a piece of data is stored.

- Ruby is as powerful as any other modern programming language. Its programs are often used to tie applications together, getting them to work together and increase efficiency.

- Ruby views everything as an object. Qualities that describe or characterize an object, such as size or type, are referred to as object properties, which are stored as variables. Objects interact with one another using their own internal methods.

- Ruby can run directly on Microsoft Windows, Mac OS X, and multiple versions of UNIX and Linux, as well as many other operating systems.

- IRB stands for Interactive Ruby. It is used to submit Ruby statements for processing.

- Although you can use IRB on Microsoft Windows, a second option, known as fxri-Interactive Ruby Help & Console, is also available to Windows users. fxri is a graphics interface made up of three distinct parts.

- Ruby programs are saved as plain text files with a .rb file extension.

Comprehension Check

1. In what year was Ruby first released? Who was its creator?

2. Initially, Ruby's reception was somewhat lukewarm. That changed when what application was developed?

3. Which of the following is a feature of Ruby?

    a. It is an interpreted programming language.

    b. It is an object-oriented programming language.

    c. It uses English-like syntax.

    d. All of the above.

4. (True/False) With its devotion to object-oriented programming, Ruby has an extensive collection of classes and libraries that provide it with capabilities surpassing those of many other programming languages.

5. A reference to a location in memory where a piece of data is stored is referred to as a _____.

6. (True/False) Unlike most object-oriented programming languages, Ruby treats numbers as objects.

7. Ruby is a flexible programming language capable of performing which of the following types of tasks?

   a. Processing text files

   b. Network programming

   c. Application prototyping

   d. All of the above

8. (True/False) The purpose of IRB is to test the execution of Ruby programs.

9. _____ is a word that represents a value of nothing.

10. A _____ is a line of text, or a portion of a line, that is preceded by the # character. All text that follows the # character is ignored by the Ruby interpreter.

11. (True/False) Rather than integrating support for object-oriented programming long after the language was originally created, as is being done with Perl, Ruby was created from the ground up with object-oriented programming in mind.

12. Ruby is a modern, object-oriented programming language created by a Japanese computer scientist named Yukihiro Matsumoto, better known within the Ruby community as _____.

13. Ruby programs are not converted into executable code until you run them using a Ruby _____.

14. Which of the following commands can be used to determine if Ruby is installed on your computer?

    a. `ipconfig all`

    b. `ruby -v`

    c. `dir ruby`

    d. `ruby -verify`

15. Which of the following commands can be used to display a text string?

    a. puts

    b. show

    c. display

    d. pop

16. Which of the following operating systems support(s) Ruby?

    a. Microsoft Windows

    b. Mac OS X

    c. Linux

    d. All of the above

17. The _____ is an interface that allows you to interact with Ruby and execute as many statements as you want.

18. (True/False) Ruby programs run faster than compiled counterparts because they are compiled prior to execution.

19. (True/False) RubyGems is a package manager that provides a standard format for distributing Ruby programs.

20. _____ supports the development and execution of Ruby programs that can interact with the Microsoft .NET Framework.

Reinforcement Exercises

 Exercise 1-1

The following exercises are designed to further your understanding of Ruby programming by having you make improvements to the Ruby Joke game.

1. The jokes told by the Ruby Joke game are admittedly somewhat bland. Spice things up a bit by replacing the game's jokes with jokes that fit your own sense of humor. To do so, type over the text of each joke and punch line.

2. The Ruby Joke game does not take long for the player to complete, telling only five jokes. Add at least five additional jokes

to the game. To do this, copy and paste and then modify the code statements that tell one of the game's other jokes.

3. Change the message displayed at the end of the game so that, in addition to thanking the player, it displays a copyright statement and the URL of your website. To do this, add `puts` statements after the closing message. (Note: The copyright statement can be something as simple as "Copyright 2010." If you do not have a URL, make one up.)

4. The Ruby Joke game's program begins with a series of comment statements that document its name, version, author, date, and description. Expand upon this information by including the following additional information: website and last update. To do this, add two additional comments to the beginning of the program.

5. Each time the game executes, it clears the screen after each joke is told by executing the following statement:

```
Console_Screen.cls
```

Starting with the first joke, comment out each occurrence of this statement by preceding it with the # character (e.g., `#Console_Screen.cls`) to see what effect this has upon the game. Leave the last instance of this statement uncommented on.

Discovery Projects

 Project 1-1

Visit the Ruby Programming Language website located at *http://www. ruby-lang.org/en/*. Explore the site's Downloads, Documentation, and Libraries pages. Visit the Community page and browse Ruby's mailing lists and user groups and sign up for those that interest you.

 Project 1-2

Take some time to get comfortable with IRB. Open the command prompt and type `irb`. Next, execute the following statements and write down what happens:

- Type 5 * 5 + 3 and press Enter.

- Type a = 5 and press Enter. Type b = 10 and press Enter. Type c = a + b and press Enter. Type c and press Enter.

- Type `"Alexander".length` and press Enter.

- Type `x = 55` and press Enter. Then type `x` and press Enter.

- Type `rand(5)` and press Enter. Then press the up arrow key and press Enter.

- Type `a = "building"` and press Enter. Type `a` and press Enter. Type `a.reverse` and press Enter.

- Type `5.times do print "Hi there! " end` and press Enter.

Project 1-3

In addition to working with Windows, Mac OS X, Linux, and UNIX, Ruby works with different virtual machine environments. These include JRuby, a Java-based Ruby environment developed by Sun Microsystems, and Microsoft's IronRuby, which works with the Microsoft .NET Framework. Even if you do not plan to work with either of these environments, it is a good idea to have a working knowledge of them. Visit the JRuby home page located at *http://www.jruby.org/* to learn about JRuby. Visit the IronRuby home page located at *http://www. ironruby.net/* to learn about IronRuby. Write a one-page document summarizing the major features and benefits of each environment.

## CHAPTER 2

Interacting with Ruby

In this chapter, you learn how to:

- ◎ Open and work with IRB
- ◎ Access IRB online
- ◎ Use IRB to execute Ruby statements and scripts
- ◎ Use IRB to perform mathematical calculations
- ◎ Access Ruby documentation
- ◎ Create the Ruby Tall Tale game

Ruby is a robust programming language used all over the world to perform a wide range of tasks. Learning Ruby takes time. One of the best ways to learn more about Ruby is to experiment with the language using IRB, also known as Interactive Ruby. IRB shows you the results of Ruby statements and expressions that you have created and executed. Working with it will give you insight into the operation of Ruby keywords, operators, commands, and object-oriented programming methodology. This chapter provides you with an overview of IRB. You also learn how to access Ruby's documentation. And you learn how to create a new Ruby script, the Ruby Tall Tale game.

Project Preview: The Ruby Tall Tale Game

In this chapter, you create your second computer game, the Ruby Tall Tale game. By developing an interactive mad-lib-style storytelling game, you will learn how to collect and process player input. A mad-lib is a storytelling game in which player input is collected without telling the player the context in which the input will be used. Once collected, the player's input is plugged into the story's plot. As a result, the story that is ultimately told has unpredictable elements that will result in variations every time the game is played.

The game begins, as shown in Figure 2-1, by prompting the player for permission to begin the game.

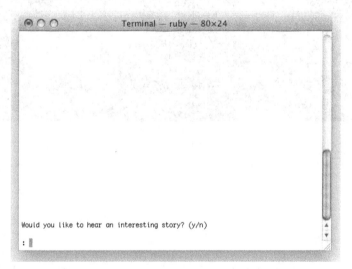

```
Would you like to hear an interesting story? (y/n)
: 
```

Figure 2-1 An invitation to play the Ruby Tall Tale game as it would appear on a Mac OS X screen

If the player decides not to play, the game displays the window shown in Figure 2-2, encouraging the player to play some other time.

Figure 2-2 The game encourages the player to play some other time

If, on the other hand, the player decides to play the game, the game displays the window shown in Figure 2-3, prompting the player to provide the first of five pieces of information.

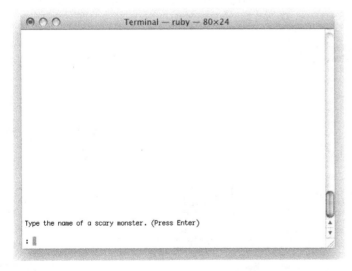

Figure 2-3 The player is asked to provide the first of five pieces of information

Once all the information has been provided, the game inserts the input into the story's plot and begins to tell its story, one paragraph at a time. Figure 2-4 shows an example of how the story's first paragraph might read.

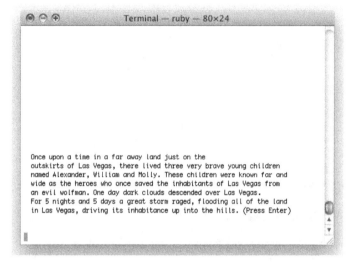

Figure 2-4   Like many stories, the Ruby Tall Tale game begins by setting the scene and introducing its heroes

The second paragraph of the story introduces the villain, as shown in Figure 2-5.

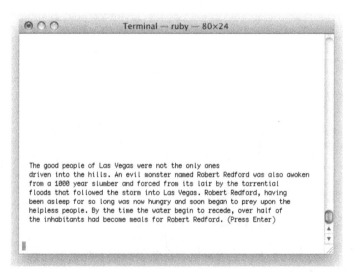

Figure 2-5   The story introduces the villain and establishes the need for heroes

In the third paragraph, the heroes arrive on the scene just in time to save the day, as shown in Figure 2-6.

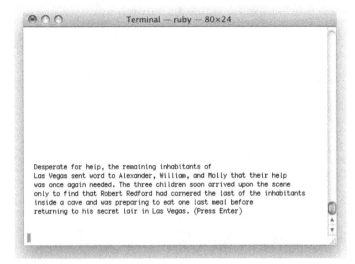

```
Terminal — ruby — 80×24




Desperate for help, the remaining inhabitants of
Las Vegas sent word to Alexander, William, and Molly that their help
was once again needed. The three children soon arrived upon the scene
only to find that Robert Redford had cornered the last of the inhabitants
inside a cave and was preparing to eat one last meal before
returning to his secret lair in Las Vegas. (Press Enter)
```

Figure 2-6   The story paints a picture of desperation and identifies the challenge its heroes face

Finally, the fourth paragraph brings the story to a happy conclusion, as shown in Figure 2-7.

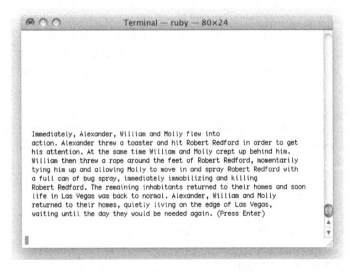

```
Terminal — ruby — 80×24




Immediately, Alexander, William and Molly flew into
action. Alexander threw a toaster and hit Robert Redford in order to get
his attention. At the same time William and Molly crept up behind him.
William then threw a rope around the feet of Robert Redford, momentarily
tying him up and allowing Molly to move in and spray Robert Redford with
a full can of bug spray, immediately immobilizing and killing
Robert Redford. The remaining inhabitants returned to their homes and soon
life in Las Vegas was back to normal. Alexander, William and Molly
returned to their homes, quietly living on the edge of Las Vegas,
waiting until the day they would be needed again. (Press Enter)
```

Figure 2-7   In the end, the people are saved and the heroes return to their homes

With the story now completed, the game pauses to thank the player for participating, then terminates, as shown in Figure 2-8.

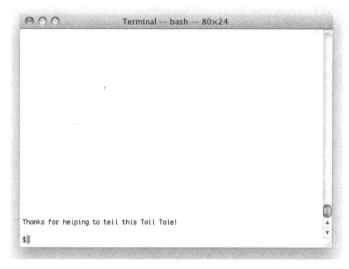

Figure 2-8   The game ends after thanking the player

Getting to Know IRB

Whether you are trying to learn auto mechanics or a new programming language, sometimes the best way to get started is to look under the hood and start tinkering. In programming terms, this means formulating and testing different programming statements to see what happens. An auto mechanic may have trouble finding a fully operational automobile to tinker on, but Ruby programmers don't have this problem. Every time Ruby is installed, it comes with a convenient and powerful tool called Interactive Ruby – IRB, for short.

IRB provides Ruby programmers with command-prompt access to a Ruby parser, which is a small command-line program that supports the real-time execution of Ruby commands, allowing programmers to write and test different parts of a computer program as they go along. Many programmers use IRB to try out a particular piece of code before adding it to a Ruby script. Programmers new to Ruby tend to spend many hours working with IRB from the command prompt, learning the basics of Ruby programming.

Starting an IRB Session

As you have already seen, you start IRB from the operating system's command prompt by typing irb and pressing Enter, as demonstrated here:

```
C:\>irb
irb(main):001:0>
```

That is how it looks on a computer running Microsoft Windows. When started this way, IRB displays a command prompt and waits for you to enter commands.

The irb command is actually quite flexible, allowing you to specify a number of different options using the following syntax:

irb [Options] [Script] [Arguments]

As shown here, IRB can process up to three types of input, labeled Options, Script, and Arguments. Note that the square brackets are used to signify that each of the three types of input is optional. You do not include the brackets in your command. Also note that each piece of input is separated by blank spaces.

Options represents any number of optional arguments supported by IRB, as outlined in Table 2-1. (An **argument** is a piece of data that is processed as input by IRB.) When supplied, options change the way the irb command is executed. **Script** represents the complete name and path of a Ruby script that you want IRB to run when it starts. **Arguments** represents a list of one or more additional pieces of data that the script processes as input when it executes.

Option	Description
-d	sets $DEBUG equal to true
-f	prevents the processing of ~/.irbrc
-I path	sets the $LOAD_PATH directory
-m	enables Math mode
-r module	loads module/s
--v	displays IRB version information
--back-trace-limit x	displays backtrace data using the last x number of entries
--inf-ruby-mode	configures IRB to run under Emacs
--inspect	formats output using Object#inspect
--irb_debug n	specifies the debug level
--noinspect	disables the default --inspect option
--noprompt	suppresses the display of the IRB command prompt
--noreadline	disables execution of the readline module
--prompt type	configures the IRB command prompt to one of the following: classic, null, xmp, simple, default, inf-ruby
--readline	loads the readline module
--simple-prompt	sets the IRB command prompt to simple
--tracer	configures IRB to display trace information
--version	displays IRB version information

Table 2-1   IRB Command-Line Options

To start IRB using options specified in Table 2-1, type irb followed by the code for that option. For example, to access information about which IRB version you're using, type irb –v, as shown here:

```
C:\>irb –v
```

In response, output similar to the following is displayed:

```
irb 0.9.5(05/04/13)
```

Working with Multiple IRB Sessions

If you open two separate IRB sessions, each exists independently of the other, and each maintains its own memory space. Therefore, any classes, methods, or variables you define in one IRB session will not be visible or accessible in the other.

You can start additional IRB sessions by opening another terminal or command-line session. You can also start them from within a current IRB session by typing the irb command. The new IRB session has an entirely new context, or execution environment, where you can make changes without affecting other IRB sessions, as shown here:

```
irb(main):001:0> irb
irb#1(main):001:0>
```

Here, the new IRB session is indicated by the presence of irb#1 at the beginning of the command prompt. Any objects you create within this new context are available only within that context. Typing exit will close the new (child) IRB session and restore the old (parent) IRB session, as shown here:

```
irb#1(main):001:0> exit
=> #<IRB::Irb: @context=#<IRB::Context:0x36c6c60>,⏎
   @signal_status=:IN_EVAL,⏎
   @scanner=#<RubyLex:0x36c6904>>
irb(main):002:0>
```

Instead of using the exit command, you may enter quit, irb_exit, or irb_quit to close an IRB session. You can also do it by pressing Ctrl+D.

When the parent IRB session is restored, any objects you previously defined within it are accessible. However, any objects you defined within the child session are not accessible. Similarly, the child session cannot make any changes that affect the parent session once it is restored.

Accessing IRB Online

If you don't have immediate access to IRB, perhaps because Ruby isn't installed on your computer, you can access it online. Go to *http://tryruby.org/* to access a web-enabled version of IRB available on the Try Ruby! web page. Notice the IRB command prompt. Figure 2-9 displays an online IRB session in action.

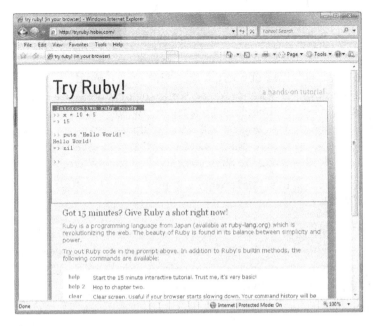

Figure 2-9   The Try Ruby! web page provides online access to IRB

As Figure 2.9 demonstrates, the Ruby expressions and statements you enter in the online IRB will be executed the same way they are processed by your computer's IRB.

Working with IRB

Using IRB, you can experiment with Ruby and learn how things work. Each time you start up a new Ruby session, IRB keeps track of any classes, objects, or variables that you define for as long as the current IRB session remains active. In the sections that follow, you will learn the fundamentals of how to work with IRB.

Executing Ruby Statements

Let's begin by executing a `print` statement, as shown in the following example:

```
irb(main):002:0> print "Welcome to Ruby"
Welcome to Ruby=> nil
irb(main):003:0>
```

Here, the `print` command, which causes a line of text to be displayed on the screen, is executed. The text string to be displayed is passed to the `print` command as an argument contained within double quotation marks. The next line shows the result returned by the print command. The value `nil` represents Ruby's interpretation of an unassigned value. Unlike the `print` command, most commands you execute using IRB will return a specific result.

When executed within a Ruby script, the `print` command displays a text string but does not advance the cursor to the next line. As a result, back-to-back `print` commands will display the two text strings as if they were a single contiguous string. Most of the time, you are probably going to want to display individual text strings on separate lines. You can do this using the `puts` command, as shown here:

```
irb(main):001:0> puts "Welcome to Ruby"
Welcome to Ruby
=> nil
irb(main):002:0>
```

As you can see, the `puts` command displays a line of text passed to it as an argument and then returns a value of `nil` after execution. The following example shows an expression that returns a result:

```
irb(main):002:0> puts 5 + 1
6
=> nil
```

Here, the `puts` command passes an expression of 5 + 1. IRB processes the expression, adding the numbers together. The result is then passed to the `puts` command as an argument. The `puts` command displays the resulting value, after which a value of `nil` is displayed.

Following Ruby's Syntax Rules

To work with different Ruby commands, keywords, and operators, you will have to learn how to follow specific syntactical rules. Failure to follow these rules when formulating script statements will result in errors that prevent your scripts from executing. Consider the following piece of script:

```
irb(main):005:0> put "Welcome to Ruby"
NoMethodError: undefined method 'put' for main:Object
        from (irb):5
irb(main):006:0>
```

As you work your way through this book, you will see hundreds of examples of properly formulated Ruby statements. When you are not sure about the rules for working with a specific Ruby method, you should check the script's documentation, as described later in this chapter.

50

Executing Incomplete Statements

IRB contains a Ruby parser. As a result, it can tell when the statements you enter are incomplete. If you press the Enter key without typing a complete statement, IRB displays a modified version of the command prompt that includes an asterisk character. This character serves as a visual indicator that IRB is waiting for you to finish typing the current statement, as shown here:

```
irb(main):001:0> 5 - 1 +
irb(main):002:0*
```

Once a complete statement has been entered, IRB processes the statement and redisplays its regular command prompt, as shown here:

```
irb(main):001:0> 5 - 1 +
irb(main):002:0* 4
=> 8
irb(main):003:0>
```

Using IRB to Test Ruby Scripts

You can also use IRB to execute Ruby scripts (or portions of Ruby scripts). For example, suppose you have downloaded a Ruby script from the Internet that contains a set of code statements for performing a particular task, and now you want to know how the code statements work. You can quickly find out by copying and pasting these statements into a new script and then executing it using the `load` method, as shown here:

```
load 'c:\Ruby_Scripts\RubyJoke.rb'
```

The `load` method lets you execute a Ruby script from the IRB. You must pass it a string containing the complete path and filename of the Ruby script you want to run. IRB will run the script, displaying the value returned by each statement as it executes.

If copying and pasting the script statements into a new script file is too much work, you can just copy and paste them directly to the IRB command prompt, and IRB will immediately execute them. For example, suppose you wanted to test the execution of the `Screen` class that was created as part of the Ruby Joke script back in Chapter 1, "Ruby Basics." You would copy and paste the following statements at the IRB command prompt:

```
class Screen
  def cls #Define a method that clears the display area
    puts ("\n" * 25) #Scroll the screen 25 times
  end
end
```

In response, IRB loads the class definition into the current IRB session and returns a value of `nil`, as shown here:

```
irb(main):001:0> class Screen
irb(main):002:1>    def cls #Define a method that clears ↵
                            #the display area
irb(main):003:2>        puts ("\n" * 25) #Scroll the ↵
                                         #screen 25 times
irb(main):004:2>    end
irb(main):005:1> end
=> nil
irb(main):006:0>
```

Instantiation is a term that describes the process used to create a new object. The object that is created is based on a predefined class definition. The object inherits all of the features of the class on which it is based. Therefore, if you were to create two different objects based on the same class definition, those two objects would be identical.

A class is a definition or template. Its statements execute when called upon to create a new `Screen` object. This is accomplished using the syntax outlined here:

```
variableName = ClassName.new
```

The first part of the line, *variableName*, is a placeholder representing any valid variable name you want to use to refer to the object being instantiated. The second part, *ClassName*, represents the name of the class being used as the basis for instantiating the object, and `new` is the name of the method that, when executed, creates the actual object.

At this point, you can tell IRB to instantiate an object based on the `Screen` class, as shown here:

```
Console_Screen = Screen.new
```

A **method** is a collection of statements defined within a class that can be used to interact with and control the operation of objects created based on that class.

Once instantiated, you can interact with the new object using the syntax shown here:

```
Console_Screen.cls
```

Here, the `Screen` class's `cls` method has been called upon to execute. When executed, this method displays 25 blank lines to the console screen, effectively clearing it and readying it for the display of new text.

Short Quiz

1. What is IRB, and how is it started?

2. List four commands that can be used to terminate an IRB session.

3. What is an expression?

4. What is the term that describes the process used to create new objects?

5. What `Screen` class method writes blank lines to the console screen?

52

Using IRB to Perform Mathematical Calculations

You can use IRB to experiment with various calculations to see how Ruby will handle them. You can also use IRB as a quick command-line calculator. Table 2-2 outlines the various operators that Ruby provides for performing mathematical calculations.

Operator	Name	Description
+	Addition	Adds two numbers
−	Subtraction	Subtracts one number from another
*	Multiplication	Multiplies two numbers
/	Division	Divides one number by another number
**	Exponentiation	Multiplies a number by itself a specified number of times
%	Modulus	Returns the remainder portion of a division operation

Table 2-2   Ruby Math Operators

Using IRB as a Calculator

Using the math operators listed in Table 2-2, you can formulate mathematical expressions of any level of complexity when writing Ruby statements. The following example calculates two numbers being added:

```
irb(main):001:0> 1 + 1
=> 2
irb(main):002:0>
```

Here, IRB has been used to add 1 + 1. After evaluating this expression, IRB displays the result and then redisplays its command prompt. The following set of examples shows how to work with each of the remaining operators shown in Table 2.2:

```
irb(main):002:0> 10 - 5
=> 5
irb(main):003:0> 3 + 2
=> 5
irb(main):004:0> 3 * 2
=> 6
irb(main):005:0> 8 / 2
=> 4
irb(main):006:0> 2 ** 3
8
irb(main):007:0> 7 % 2
=> 1
irb(main):008:0>
```

In addition to the rather simple examples shown here, you can create mathematical expressions of great complexity.

Accessing Methods Stored in the Math Module

In addition to the standard set of mathematical operator methods just discussed, Ruby provides you with access to a collection of mathematical methods stored in its Math module. A **module** is a structure used to store collections of classes, methods, and constants. A **constant** is a value that is defined within a program and cannot be changed. The Math module includes a number of methods that support advanced mathematical operations. For example, it includes a sqrt method, which determines the square root of any number, as shown here:

```
irb(main):005:0> Math.sqrt(16)
=> 4.0
```

Here, the square root of 16 has been calculated. The sqrt method's output is returned in the form of a floating-point number (i.e. a number that includes a decimal).

Make sure you type method names correctly; otherwise, you'll run into errors. For example, to call upon Math module methods, you must spell Math with an initial capital. If, instead, you spell it with all lowercase letters (math), you will get the following error:

```
irb(main):006:0> math.sqrt(16)
NameError: undefined local variable or method 'math'⏎
            for main:Object from (irb):6
irb(main):007:0>
```

Ruby's Math module provides you with access to numerous mathematical methods. These include acos(), which computes the arc cosine for a specified value, and cos(), which computes the cosine for a specified value. To learn more about the methods contained in Ruby's Math module, visit *http://www.ruby-doc.org/core/classes/Math.html.*

Operator Precedence

In mathematics, arithmetic operations are performed in a defined order called precedence. Ruby scripts adhere to these same rules. Exponentiation is performed first. Multiplication, division, and modulus division occur next. (All three have the same level of precedence.) Finally, addition and subtraction are performed. (Addition and subtraction have the same level of precedence.) Operators with the same level of precedence are performed from left to right.

The following example shows how Ruby's predetermined order of precedence works:

```
10 + 5 * 2 - 8 / 4 + 5**2
```

First, exponentiation is performed, so the value of 5**2 is calculated, resulting in a value of 25. Next, multiplication and division are performed from left to right, so 5 is multiplied by 2, resulting in a value of 10. Next, 8 is divided by 4, resulting in a value of 2. At this point, the expression logically could be rewritten as follows:

```
10 + 10 - 2 + 25
```

Next, addition and subtraction are performed from left to right. Therefore, 10 is added to 10, resulting in a value of 20. Next, 2 is subtracted from 20, yielding a value of 18, to which a value of 25 is added. The end result is 43, as shown here:

```
irb(main):001:0> 10 + 5 * 2 - 8 / 4 + 5**2
=> 43
irb(main):002:0>
```

Overriding Operator Precedence

Parentheses are used to override Ruby's predetermined order of precedence. Ruby processes mathematical expressions by first evaluating anything inside parentheses, then following the order of precedence to process the expression, as shown here:

```
irb(main):001:0> (4 + 7) * 3 - 7 / (2 + 5) ** 2
=> 33
```

Here, the expression is processed by IRB, resulting in a value of 33. First, the equations inside parentheses are processed, resulting in an expression that looks like this:

```
11 * 3 - 7 / 7 ** 2
```

Next, exponentiation is done, so 7 is squared, resulting in an expression that looks like this:

```
11* 3 - 7 / 49
```

By default, whenever two integers are divided in Ruby, the value that is returned is also an integer, the remainder being automatically truncated. Dividing 7 by 49 results in a value of .142857142857143. Since Ruby always returns an integer, a value of 0 is returned.

Multiplication and division are then performed, so 11 is multiplied by 3, and 7 is divided by 49, resulting in an expression that looks like this:

```
33 - 0
```

Finally, 0 is subtracted from 33, for a final result of 33:

```
33
```

Integers Versus Floating-Point Numbers

Ruby treats whole numbers as integers. Any operation performed using integers results in an integer value, and any remainder value is cast off. The following example shows how Ruby deals with a remainder when performing division using integers:

```
irb(main):001:0> 10 / 4
=> 2
irb(main):002:0>
```

As you can see, a value of 2 is returned instead of a value of 2.5. The other .5 is thrown away. That is how Ruby deals with integers. If you require a greater level of mathematical precision, you need to use floating-point numbers, which are numbers that include a decimal point. Consider the following:

```
irb(main):003:0> 10.0 / 4.0
=> 2.5
irb(main):004:0>
```

Because floating-point numbers have been specified with the use of a decimal point, a value of 2.5 is returned. You don't have to make both numbers floating-point numbers to ensure that Ruby performs floating-point division. All Ruby requires is that you include a decimal point in one of the numbers being calculated, as shown here:

```
irb(main):007:0> 10.0 / 4
=> 2.5
irb(main):008:0>
```

Accessing Ruby Documentation

Ruby provides an enormous collection of classes. Within these classes, there are thousands of methods, all of which come with Ruby when it is installed on your computer. There are too many of them to cover in a single book, but you can easily access the documentation for most of them via a system referred to as RDoc.

You can access RDoc online from a number of websites, most notably at *http://www.ruby-doc.org/*, as shown in Figure 2-10.

Figure 2-10 Accessing Ruby documentation at *www.ruby-doc.org*

You can also access Ruby documentation by using ri, a command-line Ruby documentation viewer. If you want to display information about a Ruby Numeric class, for example, you access the operating system's command prompt and type ri, followed by the name of the class, as shown in Figure 2.11.

Watch out for case sensitivity when working with ri. You must spell the name of the class with an opening capital letter. Specifying ri Numeric returns documentation for the Numeric class. However, specifying ri numeric returns an error.

```
C:\>ri Numeric
------------------------------------------------------------ Class: Numeric
     Numeric is a built-in class on which Fixnum, Bignum, etc., are
     based. Here some methods are added so that all number types can be
     treated to some extent as Complex numbers.

     ------------------------------------------------------------------

Includes:
---------
     Comparable(<, <=, ==, >, >=, between?)

Instance methods:
-----------------
     +@, -@, <=>, abs, angle, arg, ceil, coerce, conj, conjugate, div,
     divmod, eql?, floor, im, imag, image, integer?, modulo, nonzero?,
     polar, quo, real, remainder, round, singleton_method_added, step,
     to_int, truncate, zero?

C:\>_
```

Figure 2-11 Using ri to view documentation about Ruby's Numeric class

The documentation typically includes a description. When viewing the documentation for a Ruby class, the class's methods are also listed. You can also use `ri` to retrieve documentation for Ruby methods. For example, you would type `ri  Numeric.round` to display information about the `Numeric` class's `round` method, as shown in Figure 2-12.

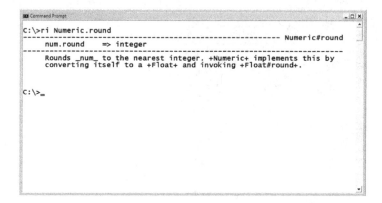

```
C:\>ri Numeric.round
---------------------------------------------------------- Numeric#round
     num.round    => integer
------------------------------------------------------------------------
     Rounds _num_ to the nearest integer. +Numeric+ implements this by
     converting itself to a +Float+ and invoking +Float#round+.


C:\>_
```

Figure 2-12 Using `ri` to display documentation about the `Numeric` class's `round` method

You don't always have to specify the name of the class in which a method is defined. In Ruby, a method may be defined in different classes. However, if a method is only defined in one class, you can view its documentation by simply typing `ri` followed by the name of the method. However, if the method is associated with more than one class, you will see a message similar to the following:

```
C:\>ri round
More than one method matched your request. You can refine
your search by asking for information on one of:

    Float#round, Integer#round, Numeric#round,
        REXML::Functions::round,
    Fox::FXGLViewer#getBackgroundColor,
    Fox::FXGLViewer#setBackgroundColor,
    Fox::FXTableItem#drawBackground,
    Windows::Window#GetForegroundWindow
```

As this example demonstrates, the `round` method is associated with many classes, including `Float`, `Integer`, `Numeric`, and `REXML`.

The `ri` tool is convenient and powerful. To learn more about it, type `ri` at the operating-system command prompt and press Enter. You will see the screen shown in Figure 2-13.

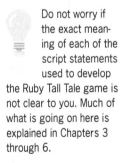

Figure 2-13   Viewing help documentation for `ri`

Short Quiz

1. What structure is used to store a collection of classes, methods, and constants?

2. What does the phrase "order of precedence" mean?

3. Can the order of precedence be altered? How?

4. What happens to the remainder part of an arithmetic equation in which one integer is divided by another integer?

5. Ruby supports thousands of methods that are included when it is installed on a computer. Access to documentation for these methods is provided via a tool referred to as _____.

Back to the Ruby Tall Tale Game

In this game, the player is prompted to answer a series of questions without being told how the answers will be used. Then the game incorporates the player's input into the plot of the game's story, which is displayed one paragraph at a time.

Do not worry if the exact meaning of each of the script statements used to develop the Ruby Tall Tale game is not clear to you. Much of what is going on here is explained in Chapters 3 through 6.

Designing the Ruby Tall Tale Game

As with Chapter 1's Ruby Joke game, the Ruby Tall Tale game is developed by following a series of steps, as outlined here. As you move from one step to the next, be sure to follow the instructions exactly.

1. Open your text or script editor and create a new file.
2. Add comment statements to the beginning of the script file to document the script and its purpose.
3. Define custom classes required by the game.
4. Prepare the game for play.
5. Add the code statements that outline the script's high-level conditional logic.
6. Add the code statements that terminate the game when the user decides not to play.
7. Prompt the player to provide story input for key story elements.
8. Assemble the game's story using the player's input.
9. Tell the game's story.
10. Thank the player for playing the game.

Each of these steps is covered in detail in the sections that follow.

Step 1: Create a New Ruby File

Open your text or script editor, and create a new Ruby script file. Name the file TallTale.rb, then save it in whatever location you've chosen for storing your Ruby script files.

Step 2: Document the Script and Its Purpose

Add the following statements to the beginning of the script file. These comment statements provide information about the script and its purpose.

```
#-------------------------------------------------------------
#
# Script Name: TallTale.rb
# Version:     1.0
# Author:      Jerry Lee Ford, Jr.
# Date:        April 2010
#
# Description: This Ruby script demonstrates how to
# collect and process user input through the
# development of an Interactive storytelling game.
#
#-------------------------------------------------------------
```

Step 3: Define Custom Classes

The Ruby Tall Tale game includes two classes. The script statements that make up these two classes are shown next. They should be added to the end of the script file.

```ruby
class Screen

 def cls
   puts ("\n" * 25)
   puts "\a"
 end

end

class Tale

 attr_accessor :monster, :villain, :object, :place,
    :location

 attr_accessor :P1, :P2, :P3, :P4

 def tell_Story(paragraph)
   puts paragraph
 end

end
```

The first class is named **Screen**. It contains a method named **cls**. When executed, the **cls** method clears the console window by writing 25 blank lines. The method then causes an audible beep sound to be played, notifying the player that the game window has been cleared.

The second class is named **Tale**, and it defines properties representing key components of the game's storyline. The **:monster**, **:villain**, **:object**, **:place**, and **:location** properties represent pieces of input that will be collected from the player when the game executes, and **:P1**, **:P2**, **:P3**, and **:P4** will be used to store the paragraphs that make up the game's storyline. The **Tale** class also includes a method named **tell_Story**, which displays any text that is passed to it as an argument.

Step 4: Prepare the Game for Execution

You need to clear the screen by instantiating a **Screen** object and then executing the **Screen** class's **cls** method. To do so, add the following statements to the end of the script file:

```ruby
Console_Screen = Screen.new

Console_Screen.cls

print "Would you like to hear an interesting story?" +
   "(y/n)\n\n: "
```

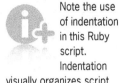

Note the use of indentation in this Ruby script. Indentation visually organizes script statements and makes them easier to read and understand.

61

An **escape character** is a two-character sequence made up of the \ character followed by a letter, another \ character, or a double-quote. You will learn more about escape characters in Chapter 3, "Working with Strings, Objects, and Variables."

```
answer = STDIN.gets
answer.chomp!
```

Once the `cls` method has been executed, the player is invited to play the game and instructed to reply by choosing y or n. The player's response is retrieved using the `STDIN` class's `gets` method and assigned to a variable named `answer`.

Step 5: Outline the Script's High-Level Conditional Logic

Now that you have the player's response, add the following lines, which analyze the player's input, to the end of the script file:

```
if answer == "n"

else

end
```

The rest of the script statements will be embedded within these statements. The ones you embed between the first two statements will execute when the player chooses n when invited to play the game. The ones you embed between the last two statements will execute when the player responds with anything other than n when invited to play the game.

As written, the game only asks for responses of y or n. If the player responds by entering anything other than one of these two letters, the game will treat the response as if a y was entered.

You will learn the ins and outs of applying conditional logic in Chapter 4, "Implementing Conditional Logic."

Step 6: Prematurely Terminating Game Execution

The following pair of statements clears the console screen and displays a text string that encourages the player to return and play the game another time. These statements are executed when the player chooses not to play. The statements should therefore be placed between the `if` statement and the `else` statement that you added to the script file in the preceding step.

```
Console_Screen.cls

puts "Okay, perhaps another time.\n\n"
```

Step 7: Collect Player Input

The rest of the statements are added between the `else` statement and the `end` statement. Add the following statements:

```
Story = Tale.new

Console_Screen.cls

print %Q{Type the name of a scary monster. (Press Enter)
\n\n: }
```

```
monster = STDIN.gets
monster.chomp!

Console_Screen.cls

print %Q{Who is your favorite movie star? (Press Enter)
\n\n: }
villain = STDIN.gets
villain.chomp!

Console_Screen.cls

print %Q{Type in the name of a thing. (Press Enter)\n\n: }
object = STDIN.gets
object.chomp!

Console_Screen.cls
print %Q{Enter the name of a good hiding place. (Press Enter)
    \n\n: }
place = STDIN.gets
place.chomp!

Console_Screen.cls
print %Q{Enter the name of a popular vacation site. ↵
    (Press Enter)\n\n: }
location = STDIN.gets
location.chomp!
```

The first statement instantiates an object based on the Tale class, which means that the object inherits the class's methods and properties. The console window is cleared, and a text string displays that poses a question to the player. The player's input is stored in a variable named monster. Four additional questions display, and the player's responses are recorded in separate variables.

Step 8: Build the Game's Story

The next set of statements assigns each of the game's four paragraphs to different properties belonging to the Story object. Each paragraph is written as a large text string. Variables have been embedded inside the text string and will be replaced by their assigned values. The process of replacing variables with their values is referred to as **variable substitution**. Add the following statements immediately after the statements that were added in Step 7:

```
Story.P1 = %Q{ Once upon a time in a far away land, just on the
outskirts of #{location}, there lived three very brave young
children named Alexander, William, and Molly. These children
were known far and wide as the heroes who once saved the
inhabitants of #{location} from an evil #{monster}. One day
dark clouds descended over #{location}. For 5 nights and 5 days
a great storm raged, flooding all of the land in #{location},
driving its inhabitants up into the hills. (Press Enter)

}
```

Story.P2 = %Q{ The good people of #{location} were not the only ones driven into the hills. An evil monster named #{villain} was also awoken from a 1,000 year slumber and forced from its lair by the torrential floods that followed the storm into #{location}. #{villain}, having been asleep for so long, was now hungry and soon began to prey upon the helpless people. By the time the water began to recede, over half of the inhabitants had become meals for #{villain}. (Press Enter)

}

Story.P3 = %Q{ Desperate for help, the remaining inhabitants of #{location} sent word to Alexander, William, and Molly that their help was once again needed. The three children soon arrived on the scene only to find that #{villain} had cornered the last of the inhabitants inside a #{place} and was preparing to eat one last meal before returning to his secret lair in #{location}. (Press Enter)

}

Story.P4 = %Q{ Immediately, Alexander, William, and Molly flew into action. Alexander threw a #{object} and hit #{villain} to get his attention. At the same time, William and Molly crept up behind him. William then threw a rope around the feet of #{villain}, momentarily tying him up and allowing Molly to move in and spray #{villain} with a full can of bug spray, immediately immobilizing and killing #{villain}. The remaining inhabitants returned to their homes and soon life in #{location} was back to normal. Alexander, William, and Molly returned to their homes, quietly living on the edge of #{location}, waiting until the day they would be needed again. (Press Enter)

}

You can enclose text strings inside double quotation marks, but you can also embed them within %Q{ and } characters. In addition, you can perform variable substitution within the strings by placing the variable name inside #{ and } characters. You will learn the specifics of how this works in Chapter 3, "Working with Objects, Strings, and Variables."

Step 9: Tell the Game's Story

Now that the story's plot has been mapped out, it is time to begin telling the story to the player. Add the following set of statements immediately after the preceding set of statements (inside the else and end lines):

```
Console_Screen.cls
Story.tell_Story Story.P1
STDIN.gets

Console_Screen.cls
Story.tell_Story Story.P2
STDIN.gets
```

64

```
Console_Screen.cls
Story.tell_Story Story.P3
STDIN.gets

Console_Screen.cls
Story.tell_Story Story.P4
STDIN.gets
```

These statements are grouped into four nearly identical sets. Each set begins by calling on the **Screen** class object's **cls** method to clear the console window. Next, the **Tale** class's **tell_Story** method is called and passed a paragraph to display. The **STDIN** class's **gets** method is then run in order to pause the execution of the script until the player presses Enter.

Step 10: Thank the Player

To thank the player for playing the Ruby Tall Tale game, add the following statements to the previous set of statements (inside the **else** and **end**):

```
Console_Screen.cls
puts "Thanks for helping to tell this Tall Tale!\n\n"
```

These two statements clear the console window and display a closing message thanking the player for playing the game.

Running Your New Ruby Script Game

Save your Ruby script. You have now completed building the Ruby Tall Tale game. To allow you to check whether your script is properly written, here is a copy of the fully assembled game. Notice there are a number of additional comment statements. These are to help you understand everything that is going on within the script file.

```
#-----------------------------------------------------------
#
# Script Name: TallTale.rb
# Version: 1.0
# Author: Jerry Lee Ford, Jr.
# Date: April 2010
#
# Description: This Ruby script demonstrates how to
# collect and process user input through the
# development of an interactive storytelling game.
#
#-----------------------------------------------------------
```

```ruby
# Define custom classes ------------------------------------
#Define a class representing the console window
class Screen

  def cls #Define a method that clears the display area
    puts ("\n" * 25) #Scroll the screen 25 times
    puts "\a" #Make a little noise to get the player's
              #attention
  end

end

#Define a class representing the game's story
class Tale

  #Define class properties representing story elements
  attr_accessor :monster, :villain, :object, :place,
    :location

  #Define class properties representing story paragraphs
  attr_accessor :P1, :P2, :P3, :P4

  #Define a method to be used to display story paragraphs
  def tell_Story(paragraph)
    puts paragraph
  end

end


# Main Script Logic --------------------------------------

Console_Screen = Screen.new #Initialize a new Screen
                            #object

#Execute the Screen object's cls method in order to clear
#the screen
Console_Screen.cls

#Prompt the player for permission to begin the game
print "Would you like to hear an interesting story? (y/n)" +
  "\n\n: "

answer = STDIN.gets #Collect the player's response
answer.chomp! #Remove any extra characters appended to
              #the string


#Analyze the player's response
if answer == "n" #See if the player elected not to play

  Console_Screen.cls #Clear the display area
```

```
    #Invite the player to return and play again
    puts "Okay, perhaps another time.\n\n"

else

    Story = Tale.new #Instantiate a new story object

    ###############################################
    # It is time to start collecting player input #
    ###############################################

    Console_Screen.cls #Clear the display area

    #Prompt the player to provide some input
    print %Q{Type the name of a scary monster. (Press Enter)
\n\n: }
    monster = STDIN.gets #Force the player to press Enter
                         #to continue
    monster.chomp! #Remove any extra characters appended
                   #to the string

    Console_Screen.cls #Clear the display area

    #Prompt the player to provide some input
    print %Q{Who is your favorite movie star? (Press Enter)
\n\n: }
    villain = STDIN.gets #Force the player to press Enter
                         #to continue
    villain.chomp! #Remove any extra characters appended
                   #to the string

    Console_Screen.cls #Clear the display area

    #Prompt the player to provide some input
    print %Q{Type in the name of a thing. (Press Enter)
\n\n: }
    object = STDIN.gets #Force the player to press Enter
                        #to continue
    object.chomp! #Remove any extra characters appended
                  #to the string

    Console_Screen.cls #Clear the display area

    #Prompt the player to provide some input
    print %Q{Enter the name of a good hiding place.
(Press Enter)\n\n: }
    place = STDIN.gets #Force the player to press Enter to
                       #continue
    place.chomp! #Remove any extra characters appended
                 #to the string

    Console_Screen.cls #Clear the display area
```

```
#Prompt the player to provide some input
print %Q{Enter the name of a popular vacation site.↵
    (Press Enter)\n\n: }
location = STDIN.gets #Force the player to press
                        #Enter to continue
location.chomp! #Remove any extra characters appended
                #to the string


##############################################
# It is time to start telling the story #
##############################################

#Display the first paragraph of the story
Story.P1 = %Q{ Once upon a time in a far away land, just on
the outskirts of #{location}, there lived three very brave
young children named Alexander, William, and Molly. These
children were known far and wide as the heroes who once
saved the inhabitants of #{location} from an evil
#{monster}. One day dark clouds descended over #{location}.
For 5 nights and 5 days a great storm raged, flooding all
of the land in #{location}, driving its inhabitants up
into the hills. (Press Enter)

}

#Display the second paragraph of the story
Story.P2 = %Q{ The good people of #{location} were not
the only ones driven into the hills. An evil monster
named #{villain} was also awoken from a 1,000 year
slumber and forced from its lair by the torrential
floods that followed the storm into #{location}.
#{villain}, having been asleep for so long, was now
hungry and soon began to prey upon the helpless
people. By the time the water began to recede, over
half of the inhabitants had become meals for
#{villain}. (Press Enter)


}

#Display the third paragraph of the story
Story.P3 = %Q{ Desperate for help, the remaining inhabitants
of #{location} sent word to Alexander, William, and Molly that
their help was once again needed. The three children soon
arrived on the scene only to find that #{villain} had cornered
the last of the inhabitants inside a #{place} and was preparing
to eat one last meal before returning to his secret lair in
#{location}. (Press Enter)

}

#Display the fourth paragraph of the story
Story.P4 = %Q{ Immediately, Alexander, William, and Molly
```

flew into action. Alexander threw a #{object} and hit
#{villain} to get his attention. At the same time, William
and Molly crept up behind him. William then threw a rope
around the feet of #{villain}, momentarily tying him up and
allowing Molly to move in and spray #{villain} with a full can
of bug spray, immediately immobilizing and killing #{villain}.
The remaining inhabitants returned to their homes and soon
life in #{location} was back to normal. Alexander, William,
and Molly returned to their homes, quietly living on the edge
of #{location}, waiting until the day they would be needed
again. (Press Enter)

```
}

Console_Screen.cls #Clear the display area
Story.tell_Story Story.P1 #Tell the story's first
                          #paragraph
STDIN.gets #Force the player to press Enter to continue

Console_Screen.cls #Clear the display area
Story.tell_Story Story.P2 #Tell the story's second
                          #paragraph
STDIN.gets #Force the player to press Enter to continue

Console_Screen.cls #Clear the display area
Story.tell_Story Story.P3 #Tell the story's third
                          #paragraph
STDIN.gets #Force the player to press Enter to continue

Console_Screen.cls #Clear the display area
Story.tell_Story Story.P4 #Tell the story's fourth
                          #paragraph
STDIN.gets #Force the player to press Enter to continue

end
```

All that remains is to run your Ruby Tall Tale game and see what happens. Access the operating system command prompt, and navigate to
the folder where you saved your Ruby script. Type the following command, then press Enter:

```
ruby TallTale.rb
```

The game should run exactly as described at the beginning of the
chapter. If you made a typo somewhere, however, you'll get an error
message when you try to run your script. If this happens, review the
error message carefully and look for any clues to what went wrong. If
you are unable to figure out what went wrong based on the text of the
error message, review your script file and look for mistyped or missing script statements. Once you have identified and corrected all your
typing errors, try running your Ruby script again.

Summing Up

- IRB provides Ruby programmers with command-line access to a Ruby parser. Many programmers use IRB to test a particular piece of code before adding it to a Ruby script.

- You start IRB from the operating system's command prompt by entering irb and pressing Enter.

- If you open up two separate IRB sessions, each session maintains its own separate memory space. Therefore, any classes, methods, or variables you define in one IRB session will not be visible or accessible in another session.

- Go to *http://tryruby.org/* to access a web-enabled version of IRB available on the Try Ruby! web page.

- The print command displays a line of text to the screen.

- nil is a value that represents Ruby's interpretation of an unassigned value.

- The puts command displays text strings on separate lines.

- The new command is used to define a new object.

- Instantiation is a term that describes the process used to create a new object. The object inherits all the features of the class on which it is based.

- You can use IRB to experiment with various calculations to see how Ruby handles them.

- A module is a structure used to store collections of classes, methods, and constants.

- In addition to the standard set of mathematical operator methods, Ruby provides a collection of mathematical methods stored in its Math module.

- Ruby evaluates arithmetic operations in an order of precedence, starting with exponentiation. You can use parentheses to override Ruby's default order of precedence.

- In Ruby, any operation performed using only integers results in an integer value, whether there would normally be a remainder or not.

- For a greater level of mathematical precision, use floating-point numbers (numbers that include a decimal point).

- Thousands of methods are included when Ruby is installed on your computer.

- You can access Ruby documentation for classes and methods at a number of websites, most notably *http://www.ruby-doc.org/*.

- You can also access Ruby documentation on your computer by using `ri`, a command-line Ruby documentation viewer.

Comprehension Check

1. Every Ruby installation comes with a convenient and powerful tool called _____, which stands for Interactive Ruby.

2. The _____ command displays a line of text on the screen and moves the cursor down to the beginning of the next line.

3. Objects:

   a. are created through a process known as instantiation.

   b. are created based on a predefined class definition.

   c. inherit all the features of the class upon which they are based.

   d. all of the above.

4. An individual IRB session maintains its own separate _____. As a result, any classes, methods, or variables that are defined in one IRB session will not be visible or accessible in another IRB session.

5. Which of the following math operators returns the remainder portion of a division operation?

   a. *

   b. ?

   c. **

   d. %

6. What is the name of the module that contains methods that support advanced mathematical operations?

   a. `Division`

   b. `Math`

   c. `Arithmetic`

   d. `IRB`

7. What command opens a new IRB session and displays IRB's version information?

8. Arithmetic operations are performed based on a predetermined order of precedence. Which of the following choices correctly outlines Ruby's order of precedence?

    a. Exponentiation > multiplication/division/modulus > addition/subtraction

    b. Addition/subtraction > multiplication/division/modulus/exponentiation

    c. Multiplication/division/modulus > exponentiation > addition/subtraction

    d. None of the above

9. Access to online documentation for most of Ruby's methods is provided via a tool referred to as _____.

10. (True/False) Ruby documentation can be accessed on your computer using ri, which is a command-line Ruby documentation viewer.

11. In addition to using the exit command, you can close an IRB session using which of the following commands?

    a. quit

    b. irb_exit

    c. irb_quit

    d. All of the above

12. Which of the following refers to a series of language keywords, operators, and variables that, when processed, returns a result?

    a. Statement

    b. Comment

    c. Expression

    d. None of the above

13. (True/False) Unlike other programming languages, Ruby does not impose any syntactical rules upon the formulation of code statements.

14. (True/False) While IRB is effective at testing the execution of individual Ruby statements, it cannot be used to execute entire Ruby scripts.

15. The term _____ is used to describe the process whereby a new object is created.

16. A _____ is a structure used to store collections of classes, methods, and constants.

17. What characters can be used to override the order of precedence?

    a. (and)

    b. { and }

    c. # and #

    d. All of the above

18. The round method rounds off a numerical value. Which of the following classes supports this method?

    a. float

    b. integer

    c. numeric

    d. All of the above

19. After evaluating the following expression, what value would Ruby generate?

    4 + 7 * 3 − 7 / 2 + 25

    a. 27

    b. 0

    c. 47

    d. None of the above

20. (True/False) The ** (exponentiation) method is used to return the remainder portion of a division operation.

Reinforcement Exercises

 Exercise 2-1

The following exercises are designed to further your understanding of Ruby programming by challenging you to make improvements to the chapter's game project, the Ruby Tall Tale game.

1. As currently designed, the Ruby Tall Tale game collects from the player five pieces of information that are used as input in the creation of the game's story. As a result, there is a limit to how dynamic the story can be. Review the story, and look for opportunities to replace other keywords with user input.

   To implement this challenge, you will have to add programming logic that prompts the player for additional input and then incorporates that input into the story's text via embedded variables.

2. As a programmer, it is important to take credit for your hard work. Add a paragraph to the end of the story that provides the player with a little information about the game and its author. Add your URL as well. If you do not have a URL, use your school's URL.

   To implement this modification, add a fifth paragraph to the end of the story and then add statements to the end of the script that display the paragraph and pause execution to give the player a chance to read it.

3. Add a transitional message between the collection of story input and the telling of the story that lets the player know that input collection is done and that the game is ready to tell the story. To do so, you need to clear the console window and then display the transitional text.

4. Modify the program so that the message that's displayed when the player elects not to play the game is also displayed at the end of the story. To do so, insert additional text messages using `puts` statements just before the `else` keyword in the Main Script Logic section.

5. As currently written, the game prompts the player to enter n to quit and y to play. If n is entered, the game halts. However, if anything else is entered, or if the Enter key is pressed with nothing entered, the game resumes. Change the game so that it can only be played when the player enters y. Do this by replacing the first set of script statements that follows with the second set of script statements that follows.

Replace this:

```
answer = STDIN.gets #Collect the player's response
answer.chop! #Remove any extra characters appended to
             #the string

#Analyze the player's response
if answer == "n" #See if the player elected not
                 #to play
```

With this:

```
loop do

    #Execute the Screen object's cls method in order to
    #clear the screen
    Console_Screen.cls

    #Prompt the player for permission to begin the game
    print "Would the player like to hear a interesting story" +
        "(y/n)\n\n: "

    $answer = STDIN.gets #Collect the player's response
    $answer.chop! #Remove any extra characters appended
                  #to the string

    break if $answer == "y" || $answer == "n"

end

#Analyze the player's response
if $answer == "n" #See if the player elected not
                  #to play
```

Discovery Projects

 Project 2-1

Ruby is supported by an extensive collection of documentation made available via RDoc. Visit *http://www.ruby-doc.org/* and become acquainted with the help and documentation made available through this community-driven site.

To make sure you are equally comfortable accessing documentation via ri, use ri to display and review information about the following classes:

- Math
- Numeric
- String

Print off screen prints showing the output for each of these classes.

Project 2-2

One of the most convenient ways of exchanging information about Ruby is through a mailing list. There are a number of them dedicated to Ruby. Sign up with one or more of these mailing lists, and take advantage of them as you work through the course.

Two such mailing lists are ruby-talk and ruby-doc. To join ruby-talk, send an email to ruby-talk-ctl@ruby-lang.org and enter the following line as the text message in the body portion of your email, replacing FirstName and LastName with your name:

Subscribe FirstName LastName

To join ruby-doc, send an email to ruby-doc-ctl@ruby-lang.org and enter the following line as the text message in the body portion of your email, replacing FirstName and LastName with your name:

Subscribe FirstName LastName

Print off screen prints when signing up for these two mailing lists.

Project 2-3

The irb command can be configured using the command-line options shown in Table 2-1. Using the information provided there, perform the following tasks:

1. Configure and start a new IRB session that does not display a prompt.

2. Configure and start a new IRB session that displays a simple (>>) prompt.

3. Execute an irb command that displays IRB version information.

Capture screen prints showing the output for each of these tasks.

## CHAPTER 3

Working with Strings, Objects, and Variables

In this chapter, you learn:

◎ How to create and format text strings

◎ Options for manipulating string contents

◎ How to work with `String` class methods

◎ The principles of object-oriented programming

◎ How to convert from one class to another

◎ How to store and retrieve data

◎ How to store data that does not change

◎ How to create the Ruby Virtual Crazy 8-Ball game

The first two chapters focused on Ruby's overall capabilities. They showed how to experiment with Ruby using IRB, and they reviewed the basic steps for creating and executing Ruby scripts. This chapter digs deeper into the language to show how things work. It addresses numerous object-oriented programming techniques, including the steps involved in defining custom classes. Once you define these classes, you can use them as a template for instantiating new objects. This chapter also reviews the creation and manipulation of strings, as well as the storage and retrieval of object data using variables.

Project Preview: The Ruby Virtual Crazy 8-Ball Game

In this chapter, you learn how to create a new computer game called the Ruby Virtual Crazy 8-Ball game. In developing this Ruby script, you learn how to work with text strings, objects, and variables. You also learn how to generate random numbers, which are used as the basis for providing randomly selected answers to a player's questions.

The game begins by displaying the welcome screen shown in Figure 3-1. To begin, the player presses Enter.

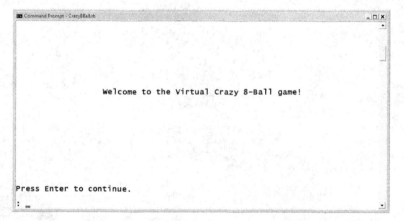

Figure 3-1   The welcome screen for the Ruby Virtual Crazy 8-Ball game

Next, the game poses a question, instructing the player to respond with y or n, as shown in Figure 3-2.

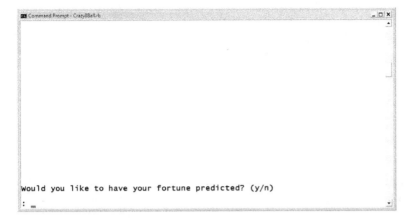

Figure 3-2 The game requires the player to agree to play

If the player responds with anything other than y or n, the game redisplays the screen shown in Figure 3-2. If the player responds by typing n, the game displays the screen shown in Figure 3-3.

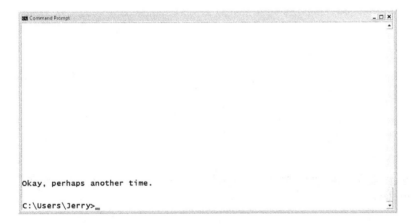

Figure 3-3 The game invites the player to return and play again

If the player responds with y, the game prompts the player to ask it a question and press Enter, as shown in Figure 3-4, where the player asks the question "Will I ever be rich?"

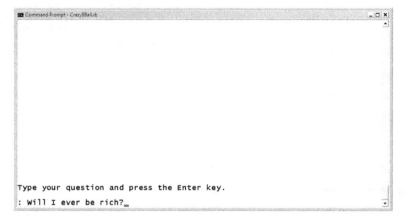

Figure 3-4 The game prompts the player to ask it a question

The game then answers the player's question by displaying one of six randomly selected answers, as shown in Figure 3-5.

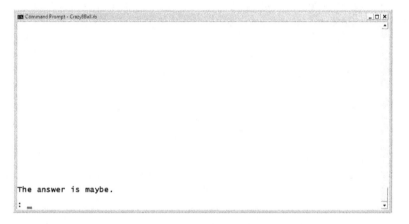

Figure 3-5 The game provides a randomly selected answer to the player's question

When the player presses Enter, the game invites the player to ask a new question, as shown in Figure 3-6.

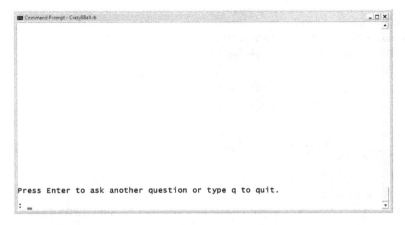

Figure 3-6 The player has the option of asking another question or typing q to quit the game

The last screen displayed thanks the player for playing the game, as shown in Figure 3-7.

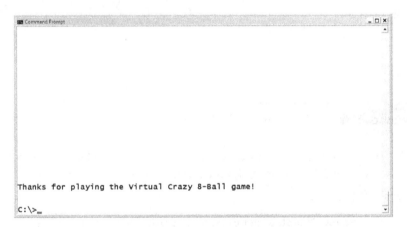

Figure 3-7 The Ruby Virtual Crazy 8-Ball game has ended

Creating and Formatting Text Strings

As you are no doubt aware by this point in the book, text plays a big role in most Ruby scripts, especially when communicating with users. Text can consist of letters, numbers, special characters, even blank spaces. So far, all the text strings you have worked with in this book have been enclosed within double quotation marks, as shown here:

```
"Sample text string"
```

You can also create a text string within a Ruby script by enclosing it within single quotation marks, as shown here:

```
'Sample test string'
```

Deciding whether to use double-quote or single-quote strings is a matter of personal preference, although there are some things you can do with text strings enclosed within double quotes that you can't do using single quotes. For example, double-quote strings can perform escaping and variable substitution operations using #{}. Single-quote strings do not support either of these operations.

Modifying Text String Format

Using escape characters within double-quote text strings, you can exercise detailed control over the way Ruby displays the strings. An escape character is a two-character sequence usually made up of the \ character followed by a letter. Table 3-1 provides a list of the various escape characters.

Option	Description
\b	Backspace
\f	Formfeed
\n	New line
\r	Return
\s	Space
\t	Tab

Table 3-1   String Escape Substitution Characters

To help you understand how to work with escape characters, here are a few examples. Consider the following statement:

```
puts "1 2 3 4 5"
```

When executed, this statement results in the following output:

```
1 2 3 4 5
```

Now consider this statement, which reformats the previous statement by embedding a series of \t escape characters:

```
puts "\t1 \t2 \t3 \t4 \t5"
```

When executed, the statement now results in the following output:

```
        1       2       3       4       5
```

As you can see, the \t escape character allows you to perform tab operations. Now consider the following statement, which reformats the first statement by embedding a series of \n escape characters:

```
puts "\n1 \n2 \n3 \n4 \n5"
```

The \n escape character is the equivalent of a new-line operation. When executed, the statement results in the following output:

```
1
2
3
4
5
```

The \r escape character executes a carriage return, and the \n escape character executes a line feed. The \t escape character moves the cursor to the next tab stop, which is predefined as eight spaces.

String Interpolation

String interpolation, also referred to as variable substitution, is the process of substituting the value of an expression or variable inside a string. It is performed by embedding a text string within other strings using the #{} characters. To see how this works, look at the following statements:

```
totalScore = 100
puts "Game over. Your score is #{totalScore}."
```

When executed, these two statements produce the following output:

```
Game over. Your score is 100.
```

As you can see, the value stored in the totalScore variable has been inserted into a specified location in the text string. Interpolation also works with expressions. Consider the following example:

```
totalScore = 100
bonusPoints = 50
puts "Game over. Your score is #{totalScore + bonusPoints}."
```

When executed, these statements result in the following output.

```
Game over. Your score is 150.
```

As you can see, Ruby added the values of totalScore and bonusPoints, then substituted the total value into the text string where specified by the expression.

Manipulating String Contents

Ruby provides you with many different options for working with strings. You can compare two different strings to see if they are the same. You can concatenate them (link them together) to create new strings. You can multiply them, creating repeated instances of a string. You can compare one string to another to see if they match. You can spread text strings out over multiple lines. You can also use

Regular expressions are covered in Chapter 7, "Working with Regular Expressions."

84

Ruby's support for regular expressions to search strings and modify their content.

Concatenating Text Strings

String concatenation is the process of joining two strings together to form a new string. It is performed using the string class's + method. To see how concatenation works, consider the following example:

```
totalScore = 100
puts "Game over. Your score is " + totalScore.to_s + "."
```

Here, a string has been created by joining three smaller strings. The first string is "Game over. Your score is ". The second string converts the numeric value of totalScore into a string using the to_s method. The third string is ".". When executed, the statement results in the following output:

```
Game over. Your score is 100.
```

Notice the inclusion of an extra blank space at the end of the first text string. This prevents the first and second text strings from running together when displayed. Also notice the use of the to_s method. This is used to convert a numeric value, allowing it to be treated like a string.

Here is another example of how to concatenate strings. This time, the \n escape character has been included to control the format of the resulting new string.

```
story = "Welcome to Principles of Ruby Programming"
author = "by Jerry Lee Ford, Jr."
puts story + "\n\n" + author
```

When executed, these statements result in the following output:

```
Welcome to Principles of Ruby Programming

by Jerry Lee Ford, Jr.
```

Here, a new string is created by adding together two new-line escape characters and a string variable. The string is then displayed.

Multiplying Text Strings

You can also create new strings by multiplying existing strings. This is done using the String class's * method. Consider the following example:

```
x = "Happy birthday to you. " * 3
puts x
```

Here, the text string "Happy birthday to you. " is repeated three times, as shown here:

```
Happy birthday to you. Happy birthday to you. Happy↵
    birthday to you.
```

Comparing Text Strings

Another commonly performed string operation is to compare two strings to see whether they are the same. This is done using the equality operator (==). You have seen examples of string comparisons numerous times in this book. For example, consider the following statements:

```
puts "Would you like to hear a few funny jokes? (y/n) "
answer = STDIN.gets
answer.chop!

if answer == "n" #See if the player elected not to play
```

Here, the player is prompted to enter a value of y or n. The player's input is then captured as answer, which is then used in the last statement to determine whether the value of answer is equal to n.

String comparisons are performed using the == (comparison) operator, not the = (assignment) operator. Because they look similar, they can get mixed up, resulting in an error.

Creating Multiline Text Strings

You can create text strings by embedding text within quotation marks, as we discussed. You can also create text strings by embedding a sequence of characters within the %q{ and } characters or the %Q{ and } characters. Embedding text within the %q{ and } characters creates a string that is equivalent to a single-quote string. Embedding characters within the %Q{ and } characters creates a string that is equivalent to a double-quote string.

The advantage of using the %q{ and } and %Q{ and } characters instead of quotation marks is that these characters can be used to specify strings that span multiple lines, as shown here:

```
story = %Q{Once upon a time there were three children↵
    named Alexander, William, and Molly.}
```

With the %q{ and } and the %Q{ and } characters, there is no practical limit to the length of the text strings you create. A key difference between these two string characters is that the %Q{ and } characters recognize embedded escape characters and also allow string interpolation. The %q{ and } characters do not allow either of these operations.

When creating multiline text strings, you can replace the opening and closing brackets with any matching set of characters you want. The following example uses the %q[and] characters to define a string:

```
story = %q[Once upon a time there were three ↵
    children named Alexander, William, and ↵
    Molly.]
```

The important thing to remember when deciding which characters to use is to not choose characters that also appear within the string text; otherwise, the program will not work correctly.

Short Quiz

1. (True/False) Strings can consist of letters, numbers, and special characters, but not blank spaces.

2. The process of joining two strings together to form a new string is called _____.

3. (True/False) By embedding escape characters within double-quote strings, you can exercise detailed control over the way Ruby displays the strings.

4. You can convert a numeric value to a string value using which of the following methods?

   a. to_t

   b. to_s

   c. to_text

   d. conv_s

5. String comparisons are performed using which of the following operators?

   a. =

   b. equals

   c. ==

   d. None of the above

Working with String Class Methods

Ruby's String class gives you access to a number of additional string-manipulation methods, as shown in Table 3-2.

Method	Description
capitalize	capitalizes the first letter of a string
downcase	converts a string to all lowercase letters
chop	removes the last character from a string
length	returns an integer representing the number of characters in a string
next	replaces the next letter in a string with the next letter in the alphabet
reverse	reverses the order of characters in a string
swapcase	reverses the case of each letter in a string
upcase	converts a string to all uppercase letters

Table 3-2   Some of the Methods Belonging to the String Class

What follows are a few examples of how to work with String class methods.

The first example uses the String class's length method:

```
irb(main):028:0> story = "Once upon a time"
=> "Once upon a time"
irb(main):029:0> puts story.length
16
=> nil
irb(main):030:0>
```

Here, the String class's length method is used to display the number of characters, including blank spaces, that make up the string stored in the story variable.

In the next example, the upcase method is used to convert the content of the string to all uppercase characters:

```
irb(main):030:0> story = "Once upon a time"
=> "Once upon a time"
irb(main):031:0> puts story.upcase
ONCE UPON A TIME
=> nil
irb(main):032:0>
```

In the next example, different string methods are combined:

```
irb(main):001:0> story = "Once upon a time"
=> "Once upon a time"
irb(main):002:0> puts story.reverse.upcase
EMIT A NOPU ECNO
=> nil
irb(main):003:0>
```

Refer to RDoc to learn more about the methods associated with the String class.

Here, the reverse and upcase methods are joined together and executed. The reverse method reverses the order of all the characters in the string, and the upcase method converts them to all uppercase.

Object-Oriented Programming

Traditionally, programs have been developed using logical procedures that take input, process it, and generate output. Ruby, however, is an object-oriented programming (OOP) language. It is organized around objects instead of actions, data instead of logic. In OOP languages, objects are not objects in the way we usually think of them. Instead, they are self-contained entities made up of computational procedures (called methods) and data (called properties) that contain information about the objects.

Objects are instantiated based on classes. A class is an outline or blueprint that defines the methods and properties that together form an object. For example, you could define an automobile class and use it to create any number of objects, each of which would represent an individual automobile.

Defining a New Class

Ruby scripts use objects to represent things like files, folders, and network resources. They also use objects to represent real-world things like people, automobiles, and animals. Once you've defined objects, you can interact with them and define relationships among them.

What follows is the syntax for defining objects as a class:

```
class ClassName
  statements
end
```

Here, class is a keyword that tells Ruby a new class is being defined, and ClassName is the name assigned to the new class. (You must capitalize the first letter of every class definition.) On the second line, statements is a placeholder that identifies where you will add script statements that define class properties and methods. On the third line, end is a keyword that identifies the end of the class definition.

The following statements define a class named Automobile:

```
class Automobile

end
```

A class definition is a template that can be used to instantiate (create) individual objects. In the case of the preceding example, the class represents an automobile. The keyword end marks the end of the class definition.

Defining Class Properties

Within the definition of a class, you can add one or more attributes associated with that class. For example, you might want to add attributes such as model and color to the Automobile class. Class attributes, more commonly referred to as class properties, are defined using the keyword attr_accessor and the following syntax:

```
attr_accessor :attribute1, :attribute2,...
```

The keyword attr_accessor identifies a list of one or more object properties. Each property is preceded by the colon character. Successive properties are separated from each other with a comma. There is no limit to the number of properties you can add. The following example shows how to assign two properties to the Automobile class:

```
class Automobile
  attr_accessor :model, :color
end
```

The first property specifies the model or type of automobile being added, and the second property specifies the color of the automobile.

Instantiating and Interacting with New Objects

Within the Automobile class, you can instantiate (create) new objects using the following syntax:

```
variableName = ClassName.new
```

Here, variableName refers to the name of a variable that is used to store the object and refer to it. ClassName is the name of the class being used to create the new object. new is a method that initiates the creation of the new object. Using the above syntax, you can create a new object as shown here:

```
superCar = Automobile.new
```

When executed, this statement creates a new object named superCar using the Automobile class as its template. Once instantiated, you can assign values to the object's properties, as shown here:

```
superCar.model = "Edsel"
superCar.color = "Red"
```

Once you define object property values, you can refer to them, as shown here:

```
puts "Super car is the car of tomorrow. It is based " +
    "on the original #{superCar.model} design."
```

When executed, this statement displays the text string shown here:

```
Super car is the car of tomorrow. It is based on the
original Edsel design.
```

If you want, you can modify the value assigned to a property by reassigning another value, as shown here:

```
superCar.model = "Mustang"
```

Defining Class Methods

In order to control your objects, you need to define class methods. You can then use the methods to programmatically interact with any object you instantiate. Ruby methods are defined using the following syntax:

```
def methodname(arguments)
    Statements
end
```

Here, def is a keyword that denotes the beginning of a method. methodname is the name to be assigned to the new method. arguments is a comma-separated list of parameters passed to the method for processing. Within the method, the parameters are treated as local variables (variables accessible only within the method). Statements is a placeholder representing one or more statements that will be executed whenever the method is called.

Here is an example of how a custom method is defined:

```
class Automobile

  attr_accessor :model, :color

  def honk
    puts "Honk!!!"
  end
end
```

Here, a method named honk is defined within a class named Automobile. As with properties, you can interact with object methods by specifying the name of the class, followed by a period and then the name of the method.

The following statements show how to create a new object based on the Automobile class and how to execute the class's honk method:

```
myCar = Automobile.new
myCar.honk
```

Inheritance

One of the primary benefits of object-oriented programming is that it allows programmers to create classes (and therefore objects) based on real-life things like automobiles, tools, people, or anything else you can imagine. In real life, objects have relationships with other objects. For example, you inherited certain traits from your father. And your children, should you have children, will inherit certain traits from you. You may also share attributes with a brother or sister.

Ruby allows you to use one class definition as the basis for creating another class definition via a process called inheritance. In this case, the new "child" class is created as a copy of the original "parent" class. You can create as many child instances as you want. If necessary, you can modify the characteristics of the child class.

Thanks to inheritance, you can define classes that model real-life concepts. For example, you might define a generic automobile class that defines all the basic properties associated with a car and that includes all the methods required to control a car. Then you can use this class as a template for creating a whole series of child subclasses, each of which might represent an individual make and model of a car. What follows is an example of a class definition for a car:

```
class Automobile

    attr_accessor :model, :color

    def honk
        puts "Honk!!!"
    end
end
```

Here, an `Automobile` class is defined that contains two property definitions, `model` and `color`, and a method named `honk`. If you want, you can use the `Automobile` class as the basis for defining a new class. One way of doing this would be to copy and paste the `Automobile` class and then rename it, as shown here:

```
class Edsel

    attr_accessor :model, :color

    def honk
        puts "Honk!!!"
    end
end
```

Creating a new class in this manner is highly inefficient because it results in two identical sets of code that must be maintained. Should you later want to make a change in the class by adding another property, you would have to make the modification twice, once for the Automobile class and once for the Edsel class. A much better way of doing this would be to base the new Edsel class on the Automobile class, taking advantage of object inheritance, as shown here:

```
super class Edsel < Automobile
```

```
end
```

Here the **superclass** operator is used to create a new class named Edsel, which is modeled on the Automobile class. The Edsel class inherits all of the properties and methods of the Automobile class. Not only does this approach require less code, it reduces the chances of making typing errors. And if you later decide to make a change that will affect all the car-related classes, all you have to do is make the change in the Automobile class; any child classes (or subclasses) will automatically inherit the change as well. There is no limit to the number of child classes you can create from a parent class. Therefore, if you need to expand your product line to include a second type of car, you can easily do so, as shown here:

```
class Mustang < Automobile
```

```
end
```

Here, a new Mustang class is created. It automatically inherits all the properties and methods of the Automobile class.

Ruby allows you to modify a child class so as to differentiate it from the parent class. For example, take a look at the following statements:

```
class Explorer < Automobile
  attr_accessor :transmission
  def breaks
    puts ". . . screech!"
  end
end
```

Here, a new Explorer class has been defined based on the Automobile class. In addition to inheriting all of the Automobile class's properties and methods, the Explorer class has been modified to include a new property and a new method unique to it.

Converting from One Class to Another

In Ruby, numbers and strings are both treated as objects. Ruby supports a number of different numeric classes, including Fixnum, Integer, Bignum, and Float. Ruby automatically determines what numeric class a number should be assigned based on its value.

Implicit Class Conversion

For the most part, you do not need to concern yourself with the class that Ruby has assigned to a given number. However, you may come across situations where you need to convert an object from one class to another. In some situations, Ruby implicitly handles object conversion for you. Consider the following example:

```
irb(main):001:0> x = 10
```

Here, a variable named x has been assigned a value of 10. In response, Ruby creates a new object based on the Fixnum class. To verify this, you can execute the class method, which retrieves an object's class name, as shown here:

```
irb(main):002:0> x.class
=> Fixnum
```

As you can see, x is assigned to the Fixnum class. However, if you reassign a value too large to fit into that class, Ruby will automatically, or implicitly, convert x to Bignum, as shown here:

```
irb(main):007:0> x = 1000000000000000
=> 1000000000000000
irb(main):008:0> x.class
=> Bignum
```

If you then assign a string as the value of x, Ruby will again change the object's class, as shown here:

```
irb(main):009:0> x = "Hello"
=> "Hello"
irb(main):010:0> x.class
=> String
```

Explicit Class Conversion

In addition to implicitly coercing an object from one class to another, Ruby allows you to explicitly coerce an object from one class to another. You might need to do this if you have written a script that collects and processes user input. By default, Ruby will treat any input provided by the user as a string, even if the input was a number, as in the following example:

```
irb(main):001:0> answer = STDIN.gets
10
=> "10\n"
```

This example collects user input by executing the STDIN class's gets method. This method pauses the console session and waits for the user to provide input, which is then assigned the specified variable.

In this example, the value entered by the user is the number 10. Ruby automatically appends the \n characters to the end of the user's input when the Enter key is pressed. To remove the trailing \n characters and ensure that the value assigned to answer is exactly what the user entered, execute the following command:

```
irb(main):002:0> answer.chop!
=> "10"
```

As this example shows, you can easily remove the end-of-line marker (\n) from the answer variable using the chop! method. When executed, this method removes the last character from a specified string. If the string ends with the \n characters, the chop! method will remove both characters.

If you try to perform addition using numeric input collected from the user, you will run into an error, because Ruby cannot implicitly convert strings to numbers. Here is an expanded version of the previous example:

```
irb(main):001:0> answer = STDIN.gets
10
=> "10\n"
irb(main):002:0> answer.chop!
=> "10"
irb(main):003:0> x = 5 + answer
TypeError: String can't be coerced into Fixnum
        from (irb):3:in '+'
        from (irb):3
irb(main):004:0>
```

As shown here, a numeric value of 5 cannot be added to a string value of "10."

To prevent this type of error from occurring and to get the results you expect, you can explicitly force the conversion of an object's type by using various conversion methods. For example, you could use the to_i method to return the value stored in answer as an integer, as shown here:

```
irb(main):005:0> x = 5 + answer.to_i
=> 15
irb(main):006:0>
```

As you can see, once the object's type has been explicitly converted, the error no longer occurs, and the expected result is generated. If you prefer, you can use the to_f method to convert a string of "10" to a floating-point number, as shown here:

```
C:\>irb
irb(main):001:0> answer = STDIN.gets
10
=> "10\n"
```

```
irb(main):002:0> answer.chop!
=> "10"
irb(main):003:0> x = 5 + answer.to_f
=> 15.0
irb(main):004:0>
```

As you can see, this time Ruby has generated a floating-point value
as the result. Going in the opposite direction, you can use the to_s
method to convert a numeric value to a string. For example, consider
the following statements:

```
irb(main):001:0> x = 5
=> 5
irb(main):002:0> y = 4
=> 4
irb(main):003:0> z = x + y
=> 9
```

Here, two variables are defined and assigned values of 5 and 4, which
are then added together and assigned to a variable named z. Using
the to_s method, you can instruct Ruby to treat the values assigned
to x and y as strings instead of numeric values, as shown here:

```
irb(main):004:0> z = x.to_s + y.to_s
=> "54"
irb(main):005:0>
```

This time, instead of adding two numeric values together, Ruby
coerces x and y into strings and concatenates the strings to form a
new string that is assigned to a variable named z. If you use the class
method to check on the z variable's class type, you will see that it has
been set to String.

```
irb(main):006:0> z.class
=> String
irb(main):007:0>
```

Storing and Retrieving Data

When working with numbers, strings, and other types of objects, you
may want to store their values so you can later reference and modify
them. This is done with variables. Variables point to the locations in
memory where objects are stored. The objects may be numbers, text, or
any custom objects you have defined. For example, the following statement defines a variable named x and assigns it an integer value of 10:

```
x = 10
```

Likewise, the following statement assigns a text string to a variable
named y:

```
y = "Well, hello there."
```

Variables are an essential part of any Ruby script, which is why you have already seen them used many times in this book. Now it is time to learn more about how to create and work with them.

Naming Variables

In Ruby, variable names are case sensitive. This means that, to Ruby, `totalcount` and `TotalCount` are two separate variables, since one has capital letters and the other doesn't. Ruby has a couple of rules regarding the naming of variables:

- Variable names must begin with a letter or an underscore character.

- Variable names can only contain letters, numbers, and underscore characters.

By these rules, Ruby would regard each of the following variable names as valid:

- `Totalscore`

- `totalScore`

- `total_score`

- `Total_Score`

- `x`

- `TotalTimes2`

On the other hand, Ruby would not regard the following variable names as valid:

- `total score` (blank spaces not allowed)

- `@totalScore` (special characters not allowed)

- `total-score` (only letters, numbers, and underscore characters allowed)

- `2TimesLucky` (beginning with a number not allowed)

Variable Assignments

In Ruby, variables are assigned values with the `equals assignment` operator (=), as shown here:

```
x = 10
```

Here, an integer value of 10 has been assigned to a variable named x. You also use the `equals assignment` operator to modify a variable's value by assigning it the results of an expression, as shown here:

```
x = 1
x = x + 1
```

Here, a variable named x is assigned an initial value of 1. Then the value assigned to x is modified by assigning it the value returned from the expression x + 1. As a result, the value of x is raised by an increment of 1.

Raising a variable's value by an increment is a common task. To make it easier to perform, use the += operator, as shown here:

```
x += 1
```

The += operator, sometimes called the arithmetic assignment operator, provides a shorthand way of raising a variable's value a specified amount. When using this operator, the + character is always specified first, followed immediately by the = character, with no blank spaces in between. In the previous example, the value of x is raised by an increment of 1.

Variable Scope

In Ruby, access to a variable depends on the scope that has been set for that variable. The term "scope" refers to the areas within a script where a variable can be seen and accessed. Ruby supports four different scopes, as outlined in Table 3-3.

Type	Opening Character(s)	Description
Local	a-z and _	Scope is limited to each iteration loop, module, class, and method in which it is defined or to the entire script if the variable is defined outside of one of the structures.
Instance	@	Scope is limited to the scope associated with the object itself.
Class	@@	Scope is limited to objects of a particular class.
Global	$	Scope has no limit, allowing the variable to be accessed throughout the script.

Table 3-3 Variable Scopes

In Ruby, variable scope is indicated by the characters at the beginning of the variable's name. A variable name that begins with the $ character signifies a global variable. A variable name that begins with a lowercase letter or the underscore character signifies a local variable.

Local variables are variables that have a limited scope. For example, if a variable name begins with a lowercase letter and the variable is defined inside a method, the variable is accessible only within that method. In the following statements, a method named Add_Stuff accepts two arguments, x and y, that are local variables within the method and, therefore, not accessible outside of the method.

```
def Add_Stuff(x, y)
    puts x + y
end
```

If you type this example into IRB and execute it by passing the method arguments 3 and 4, a result of 7 will be displayed, as shown here:

```
irb(main):004:0> Add_Stuff(3, 4)
7
```

However, if you attempt to access the x or the y variable from outside of the method, as shown here, an error will occur:

```
irb(main):005:0> puts x
NameError: undefined local variable or method 'x' for
    main:Object from (irb):5
```

Global variables can be accessed from anywhere within a Ruby script and are created by making the first character of the variable name a $, as shown here:

```
$x = 1000
```

The $x variable will be accessible from anywhere within the Ruby script it is defined in. You will see an example of how to use global variables later in this chapter, when you create the Ruby Virtual Crazy 8-Ball game.

Storing Data That Does Not Change

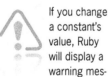
If you change a constant's value, Ruby will display a warning message while allowing the script to continue running. In this way, Ruby is different from most other programming languages, which generate an error message and halt the program's execution.

To use a value that is not subject to change, you need to define it as a constant. A constant is very much like a variable, the differences being that constant names begin with a capital letter and generate warning messages if you change their values during script execution.

The following expression shows how to define a constant and assign it a value:

```
irb(main):001:0> Pi = 3.14
=> 3.14
```

Here, a constant named `Pi` has been defined and its value set to 3.14 using the = operator.

Once you define the value assigned to the constant, you can reference it as needed. If you forget that you are working with a constant and change the value that is assigned to it, Ruby will generate a warning message while allowing the script to continue running.

```
irb(main):002:0> Pi = 3.1415
(irb):2: warning: already initialized constant Pi
=> 3.1415
```

Short Quiz

1. (True/False) Ruby is not an object-oriented programming language.

2. A _____ definition is a template that can be used to create or instantiate individual objects.

3. A _____ is a container used to group classes, methods, and constants.

   a. Module

   b. Property

   c. Method

   d. Super class

4. In addition to implicitly coercing Ruby to change an object's data type from one class to another, you can _____ coerce it to do so.

5. Which of the following methods can be used to remove the end-of-line marker from the end of a text string?

   a. `cut!`

   b. `capture!`

   c. `substr!`

   d. `chop!`

Back to the Ruby Virtual Crazy 8-Ball Game

It is time to develop this chapter's game project, the Ruby Virtual Crazy 8-Ball game. As you follow the development of this script file, be sure to focus on the use of text strings, variables, classes, and objects. Pay particularly close attention to the way the script interacts with and controls objects once they have been instantiated.

Designing the Game

The development of the Ruby Virtual Crazy 8-Ball game is completed in 10 steps, as outlined here:

1. Open your text or script editor, and create a new file.

2. Add comment statements to the beginning of the script file to document the script and its purpose.

3. Define a class representing the terminal window.

4. Define a class representing the game's virtual 8-Ball window.

5. Instantiate custom script objects.

6. Display a greeting message.

7. Get confirmation before continuing game play.

8. Analyze the player's reply.

9. Manage early game termination.

10. Process and respond to player questions.

Follow these steps carefully, and do not skip any steps or parts of steps. Specifically, look for typos, and make sure you do things in the correct order.

Step 1: Create a New Ruby File

Open your text or script editor, and create a new Ruby script file. Save the file with the name Crazy8Ball.rb, and store it in the folder with your other Ruby scripts.

Step 2: Document the Script and Its Purpose

Add the following comment statements to the new script file. These comments describe the game and its purpose.

```
#----------------------------------------------------------------
#
# Script Name: Crazy8Ball.rb
# Version:     1.0
# Author:      Jerry Lee Ford, Jr.
# Date:        April 2010
#
# Description: This Ruby script demonstrates how to work
#              with variables. It generates random
#              numbers to create a fortune-telling game
#              that provides randomly selected answers
#              to the player's questions.
#----------------------------------------------------------------
```

You can modify the documentation to suit your own needs. You might want to consider including your URL if you have a website, or you might want to record any changes, game instructions, or anything else you think would be useful.

Step 3: Define a Screen Class

Define the first of two custom classes used by the script. The first class is named Screen. It closely resembles the Screen class used in Chapter 2. However, this version of the Screen class includes a new method definition.

```
# Define custom classes ---------------------------------

#Define a class representing the console window
class Screen

  def cls #Define a method that clears the display area
    puts ("\n" * 25) #Scroll the screen 25 times
    puts "\a" #Make a little noise to get the player's
              #attention
  end

  def pause #Define a method that pauses the display area
    #Execute the STDIN class's gets method to pause
    #script execution until the player presses Enter
    STDIN.gets
  end
```

As shown here, all class names must be capitalized. The first method defined within this class is the cls method. It contains two statements. The first statement writes 25 blank lines to the console window, clearing the screen. The second statement processes a string containing the \a escape character, which makes a beep sound, thus notifying the player each time the terminal screen is cleared. The second method pauses the display area, preventing text from scrolling off the screen before the player has had time to read it.

Step 4: Define a Ball Class

Define the second of two classes used by the script. The second class is named Ball. It serves as a template that the script uses to instantiate an object that represents a virtual 8-Ball. As such, the class defines a number of properties and methods required to operate and interact with the 8-Ball.

```ruby
#Define a class representing the 8-Ball
class Ball

  #Define class properties for the 8-Ball
  attr_accessor :randomNo, :greeting, :question, :goodbye

  #Define a method to be used to generate random answers
  def get_fortune
    randomNo = 1 + rand(6)

    #Assign an answer based on the randomly generated
    #number
    case randomNo
      when 1
        $prediction = "yes"
      when 2
        $prediction = "no"
      when 3
        $prediction = "maybe"
      when 4
        $prediction = "hard to tell. Try again"
      when 5
        $prediction = "unlikely"
      when 6
        $prediction = "unknown"
    end

  end

  #This method displays the 8-Ball greeting message
  def say_greeting
    greeting = "\t\t Welcome to the Virtual Crazy 8-Ball" +
    "game\n\n\n\n\n\n\n\n\n\n\n\n\nPress Enter to " +
    "continue. \n\n: "
    print greeting
  end

  #This method displays the 8-Ball's primary query
  def get_question
    question = "Type your question and press the Enter⏎
      key. \n\n: "
    print question
  end

  #This method displays the 8-Ball answers
  def tell_fortune()
    print "The answer is " + $prediction + ". \n\n: "
  end

  #This method displays the 8-Ball's closing message
  def say_goodbye
    goodbye = "Thanks for playing the Virtual Crazy" +
      "8-Ball game!\n\n"
    puts goodbye
  end

end
```

The class definition begins by specifying four class properties. The randomNo property stores a random number between 1 and 6. The greeting property stores a text string containing the game's welcome message. The question property stores a text string to notify the player when it is time to ask a question. The goodbye property stores a text string that represents the game's closing message.

In addition to the four class properties, the class defines five methods. The first method, get_fortune, is responsible for randomly selecting one of six possible answers to the player's questions. It does this using the rand method, which retrieves a random number in the form of an integer.

The random number, stored in randomNo, is used in a case code block that assigns a text string representing one of six 8-Ball answers to the $prediction global variable. A case code block is a structure for implementing conditional logic. It compares a single value, in this case randomNo, to a series of possible matching values, as specified by one or more when statements. You will learn more about how to work with the case code block in Chapter 4, "Implementing Conditional Logic."

The next method defined is the say_greeting method, which assigns a text string to the class's greeting property and uses the puts method to display that string. The get_question method comes next. It assigns a text string to the class's question property and uses the print method to display that string. The tell_fortune method is then defined. It accepts a single argument, which is assigned to a local variable named randomAnswer. This variable is used to formulate a text statement that is displayed using the print method. The last method defined is the say_goodbye method, which assigns a text string to the class's goodbye property and uses the print method to display that string.

The rand method returns a random integer between 0 and the specified upper limit. Therefore, in the first statement of the get_fortune method, rand(6) returns a number that is greater than 0 and less than 6. Adding 1 to this number results in a range from 1 to 6.

103

Step 5: Instantiate New Objects

Instantiate both of the custom classes you just defined by adding the following statements to the end of the script file:

```
# Main Script Logic --------------------------------------

Console_Screen = Screen.new #Initialize a new Screen object
Eight_Ball = Ball.new #Initialize a new Ball object
```

As you can see, a single object is instantiated for each class using the new method. A variable named Console_Screen is used to represent the Screen object, and a variable named Eight_Ball is used to represent the Ball object.

Step 6: Greet the Player

It is time to work with the script's objects to interact with and control both the screen and the 8-Ball. To begin, add the following statements to the end of the script file:

```
Console_Screen.cls #Clear the display area

#Call method responsible for greeting the player
Eight_Ball.say_greeting

Console_Screen.pause #Pause the game
```

The first statement executes the Screen class's cls method to clear the display area. The second statement executes the Ball class's say_greeting method to display a greeting message. The third statement uses the Screen class's pause method to pause the game and give the player a chance to review the greeting message.

Step 7: Prompt for Confirmation to Continue

Next, the game sets up a loop that asks for confirmation of the player's intention to play. A loop is a set of statements that repeatedly executes a preset number of times or until a specified condition occurs.

Within the loop, the player is prompted to enter a value of y or n. If the player enters anything other than y or n, the loop repeats, prompting the player again. Once a response of y or n is entered, the loop stops executing. The script statements for performing this task are shown next and should be added to the end of the script file.

```
answer = "" #Initialize variable that is used to control
            #the game's first
            answer = ""

#Loop until the player enters y or n and do not accept any
#other input.
until answer == "y" || answer == "n"

  Console_Screen.cls #Clear the display area

  #Prompt the player for permission to begin the game
  print "Would you like to have your fortune predicted?⏎
    (y/n)\n\n: "

  answer = STDIN.gets #Collect the player's response
  answer.chop! #Remove the last character appended to
              #the string

end
```

The first statement initializes a variable that is used to control the execution of the loop that follows, in which a series of script statements has been embedded. The loop executes until the player enters a value of y or n when asked for confirmation. By using a loop to control the execution of the embedded statements, you are able to validate the player's input. If the player responds by typing anything other than a y or n, the loop executes again, prompting the player to provide valid input.

Step 8: Analyze the Player's Response

It is time to analyze the input the player has provided. This is done by adding the following conditional logic statements to the end of the script file:

```
#Analyze the player's response
if answer == "n" #See if the player elected not to play

else #The player has elected to play the game

end
```

The rest of the statements in the script will be either embedded within these two statements or placed immediately after them. They control the high-level conditional logic for the script. The statements embedded between the first two statements execute when a reply of n is given to the invitation to play the game. The statements embedded between the last two statements will execute when a reply of y is given.

Step 9: Manage Early Termination of the Game

To allow for the possibility that the player will reply with a value of n, add the following statements between the opening if statement and the else statement that you added to the script file in the previous step:

```
Console_Screen.cls #Clear the display area

#Invite the player to return and play again
puts "Okay, perhaps another time. \n\n"
```

These statements clear the screen and display a text message that encourages the player to return and play another time.

Step 10: Respond to Player Questions

Finally, add the following statements between the else and the end statements:

```
#Initialize variable that is used to control the game's
#primary loop
gameOver = "No"

#Loop until the player decides to quit
until gameOver == "Yes"

   Console_Screen.cls #Clear the display area
   #Call upon the method responsible for prompting the
   #player to ask a question
   Eight_Ball.get_question
```

```
#Call upon the method responsible for generating
#an answer
Eight_Ball.get_fortune

Console_Screen.pause #Pause the game


Console_Screen.cls #Clear the display area

#Call upon the method responsible for telling the player
#the 8-Ball's answer
Eight_Ball.tell_fortune

Console_Screen.pause #Pause the game

Console_Screen.cls #Clear the display area

#Find out if the player wants to ask another question
print "Press enter to ask another question or type q" +
   "to quit. \n\n: "

answer = STDIN.gets #Collect the player's response
answer.chop! #Remove the last character appended to
             #the string

#Analyze the player's response
if answer == "q" #See if the player elected not to play
  gameOver = "Yes" #The player wants to quit
end

end

Console_Screen.cls #Clear the display area

#call upon the method responsible for saying goodbye to ↵
   the player
Eight_Ball.say_goodbye
```

This final set of statements is responsible for managing the overall play of the game. First, a variable named gameOver is defined and assigned an initial value of "No." This variable is used to control the execution of the loop that follows. The loop contains the script statements that prompt the player to ask the 8-Ball a question and then call upon the various object methods, as required, to execute Screen and Ball methods that control Screen and Ball interaction.

Upon each execution of the loop, the Ball class's get_question method is executed. This method displays a message that prompts the player to enter a question. Next, the get_fortune method is executed. This method randomly selects the 8-Ball's answer, which is then displayed by calling on the tell_fortune method. Finally, a message is displayed that instructs the player to either press the Enter key to ask another question or type q and press Enter to end the game. The player's response is collected and assigned to the answer variable. The String class's chop! method is executed to remove the end-of-line character from the end of the variable's value, after which the value is analyzed to determine whether it is equal to q. If it is, the value of gameOver is set equal to "Yes", resulting in the end of the loop. Otherwise the value of gameOver remains unchanged, and the loop executes again.

Once the loop finishes executing, it is time to bring the game to a close. This is done by the last three statements, which clear the screen and display a closing message that thanks the player for playing.

Running Your New Ruby Script Game

Save your Ruby script. If you typed the code statements correctly, the program should work as expected. If you run into any errors, read the error messages carefully to ascertain what went wrong. If necessary, review the script and look for mistyped or missing statements.

Summing Up

- Text plays a big role in many Ruby scripts, especially when communicating with users.

- Ruby recognizes a number of escape characters that can be used to provide detailed control over the display of text.

- Using variable interpolation, programmers can substitute the value of an expression or a variable within a string.

- Using the + string method, you can concatenate two strings to form a larger string.

- Using the * method, you can multiply a string a specified number of times.

- Use the == operator to compare two values to see if they are equal.

- Use the %q{ and } characters or the %Q{ and } characters to generate multiline strings.

- The String class provides access to numerous methods that can be used to manipulate text strings.

- Ruby is an object-oriented programming language. Objects are self-contained entities that include information about themselves in the form of properties and contain program code stored in methods.

- In Ruby, you can formulate customized classes from which new objects can be instantiated.

- Inheritance is the process of creating a class based on an existing class. The child class can be further customized as necessary.

- A module is a container used to group classes, methods, and constants.

- Ruby supports a number of different numeric classes, including Fixnum, Integer, Bignum, and Float. Ruby implicitly manages the assignment of class type to numeric values. If necessary, Ruby also allows programmers to explicitly coerce class type using conversion methods like to_i and to_f.

- There are strict rules to follow when defining variable names.

- Variable value assignments are made using the = method (not the == method).

- Ruby restricts access to variables by enforcing different levels of variable scope, as specified by the first character(s) in the variable's name.

- Data that is known at design time and does not change during script execution should be stored in a constant.

Comprehension Check

1. Which of the following escape characters can be used to insert a tab within a text string?

   a. \s

   b. \t

   c. \n

   d. \b

2. The process of inserting the value of an expression or variable inside a string is called _____.

3. Concatenation, the process of joining or merging two strings to form a new string, is performed using which of the following methods?

   a. con

   b. &

   c. _

   d. +

4. Which of the following is a true statement about objects?

   a. Objects contain information about themselves using properties.

   b. Objects provide program code stored in methods that can be used to interact with and manipulate themselves.

   c. Objects are self-contained.

   d. All of the above

5. The method that initiates the creation of a new object is called _____.

6. A _____ points to the location in memory where objects are stored.

7. Which of the following rules must be followed when formulating variable names?

   a. They must begin with a letter or an underscore character.

   b. They can only contain letters, numbers, and underscore characters.

   c. They cannot include blank spaces.

   d. All of the above

8. Variable value assignments in Ruby are made using which of the following operators:

   a. ==

   b. =

   c. !=

   d. equals

9. (True/False) In Ruby, a variable with a name that begins with the $ character is a global variable.

10. _____ are values that begin with a capital letter and cannot be changed during program execution.

    a. Variables

    b. Constants

    c. Arrays

    d. Objects

11. A commonly performed string operation is the comparison of two strings to see whether they are identical (equal). This is done using which of the following operators?

   a. =

   b. ==

   c. <>

   d. None of the above

12. (True/False) When creating multiline text strings, you can replace the opening and closing brackets with any matching set of characters you want.

13. Which of the following methods removes the last character from a string?

   a. chop!

   b. next

   c. reverse

   d. None of the above

14. Which of the following methods converts a string to all uppercase characters?

   a. capitalize

   b. reverse

   c. upcase

   d. All of the above

15. Object properties are implemented as _____.

   a. Methods

   b. Embedded class data

   c. Variables

   d. None of the above

16. The code defined within an object definition that is used to interact with and control an object is referred to as object _____.

   a. Properties

   b. Methods

c. Functions

d. None of the above

17. The process of creating a new object is referred to
    as _____.

18. The _____ method reverses the order of all the
    characters in a string.

19. Which of the following is a valid variable name?

    a. `Player1 Score`

    b. `#TotalPoints`

    c. `1stPlayerScore`

    d. None of the above

20. _____ include information about themselves in
    the form of properties, and they provide program code stored
    as methods for interacting with and manipulating themselves.

Reinforcement Exercises

The following exercises are designed to further your understanding of
Ruby programming by challenging you to make improvements to the
chapter's game project, the Ruby Virtual Crazy 8-Ball game.

1. Modify the Ruby Virtual Crazy 8-Ball game so that, in
   addition to welcoming the player at the beginning of the
   game, it displays instructions for how to play. Implement this
   challenge by modifying the text that is displayed by the `Ball`
   class's `say_greeting` method.

2. The Ruby Virtual Crazy 8-Ball game responds to player
   questions by randomly selecting and displaying one of six
   answers. Make the game more unpredictable by expanding
   the list of possible answers from six to 10. Implement this
   challenge by expanding the number of `when` statements from
   six to 10 in the `Ball` class's `get_fortune` method. Make sure
   you also modify the `get_fortune` method so that it generates
   its random number within a range of one to 10.

3. The Ruby Virtual Crazy 8-Ball game allows the player to
   submit blank questions by simply pressing the Enter key.
   Disable this behavior, forcing the player to type something
   before pressing Enter.

Hint: Modify the `Ball` class's `get_question` method as shown here, and delete the first `Console_Screen.pause` statement that is executed near the end of the script, just after the `get_fortune` method is executed.

```
#This method displays the 8-Ball's primary query
def get_question

  reply = ""

  #Loop until the player enters something
  until reply != ""
    Console_Screen.cls  #Clear the display area
    question = "Type your question and press the Enter ↵
      key. \n\n: "
    print question
    reply = STDIN.gets  #Collect the player's question
    reply.chop!  #Remove any extra characters
  end

end
```

4. Modify the game so that it displays your name and your school's URL in addition to a message thanking the player for playing the game. To implement this challenge, modify the `Ball` class's `say_goodbye` method by adding the specified text.

5. Modify the game so that the player sees the same closing information regardless of when the game ends. To do so, the `Ball` class's `say_goodbye` method will have to be called if the player decides not to play the game.

Discovery Projects

Project 3-1

Table 3.2 introduced you to a number of methods belonging to the `String` class. Using these methods, you can manipulate text strings in a variety of ways. However, the eight methods listed in the table barely scratch the surface. The Ruby `String` class supports over 100 different `String` class methods. To familiarize yourself with Ruby's string manipulation capabilities, visit *http:/www.ruby-doc.org/core/classes/String.html*.

Project 3-2

In addition to the `String` class methods, Ruby provides access to a collection of string escape substitution characters that can be used to exercise detailed control over the presentation of text output. Table 3.1 listed a number of escape characters, after which examples were given of how to work with the \t and \n characters. To become more familiar with these very important tools, open IRB and work with each of them. In addition, visit *http://www.ruby-forum.com/* and do a search on "Escape Characters." Review the forum posts.

Project 3-3

This chapter has introduced you to the four types of variable scope that Ruby supports. To learn more, visit http://*www.techotopia.com* and do a search on "Ruby Variable Scope." When reviewing the material on global variables, pay special attention to the discussion covering predefined global variables. These contain information about the Ruby environment. Write a one-page paper comparing and contrasting the advantages and disadvantages of each type of scope.

## CHAPTER 4

Implementing Conditional Logic

In this chapter, you will learn how to:

- ◎ Use conditional logic to create adaptive scripts
- ◎ Perform alternative types of comparisons
- ◎ Use conditional logic modifiers
- ◎ Work with the `if` and `unless` expressions
- ◎ Use `case` blocks to analyze data
- ◎ Use the ternary operator
- ◎ Nest conditional statements
- ◎ Combine and negate logical comparison operations
- ◎ Create the Ruby Typing Challenge game

It is virtually impossible to create Ruby scripts of any level of complexity without performing some conditional analysis. Conditional analysis is the evaluation of a piece of data, followed by a choice between different actions, only one of which is executed, depending on the result of the analysis. This might involve examining something, such as player input or the value of a randomly generated number. To help you perform a conditional analysis, Ruby provides access to a number of conditional expressions, modifiers, and logical operators that compare different values and control the conditional execution of script statements. This allows you to create Ruby scripts that can alter their execution based on the data they are presented with, and it results in adaptive scripts that can handle many different types of situations.

Project Preview: The Ruby Typing Challenge Game

In this chapter, you create a computer game called the Ruby Typing Challenge game, which evaluates the accuracy of the player's typing skills. Writing the Ruby script will show you how to apply conditional logic to analyze user input.

The game begins by displaying the welcome screen shown in Figure 4-1.

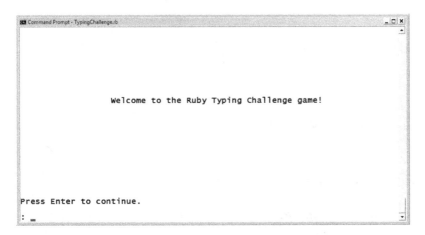

Figure 4-1 The welcome screen for the Ruby Typing Challenge game

Next, the game prompts the player for permission to begin the test, as shown in Figure 4-2. The player is instructed to respond with a y or n.

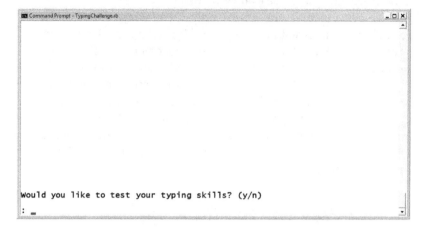

Figure 4-2 The game requires the player to agree to play

If the player types n and presses Enter, the screen shown in Figure 4-3 displays and the game ends.

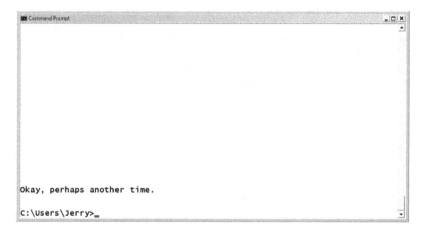

Figure 4-3 The player has elected not to take the test

If, on the other hand, the player elects to take the typing test, the instructions shown in Figure 4-4 display.

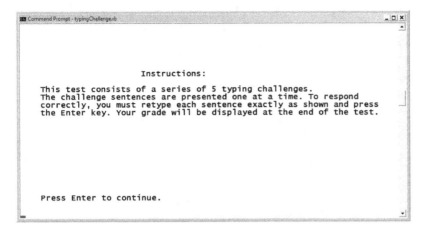

Figure 4-4 Instructions explain how to take the test

Next, the first of five sentences is presented, as shown in Figure 4-5. The player must type the sentence exactly as shown and then press Enter.

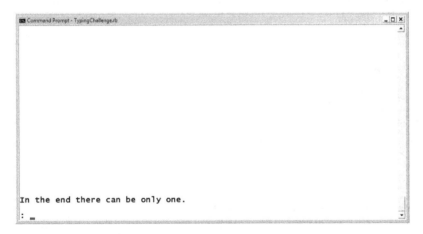

Figure 4-5 The first typing challenge

As soon as the player presses Enter, the game determines whether the player's sentence exactly matches the game's sentence. If the player's input is identical to the game's sentence, the screen shown in Figure 4-6 displays. If the player makes one or more typing mistakes, a message displays, notifying the player of the failure to correctly type the sentence.

Figure 4-6 The player has correctly typed the challenge sentence

The game's sentences grow longer as the test progresses. Once the player has typed all five sentences, the game calculates the player's score and displays a message indicating whether or not the player has passed the test, as shown in Figure 4-7.

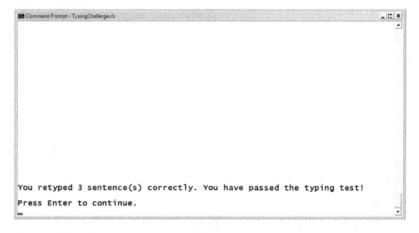

Figure 4-7 The player has passed the test

Once the player presses Enter, a message displays, thanking the player for taking the typing test, as shown in Figure 4-8.

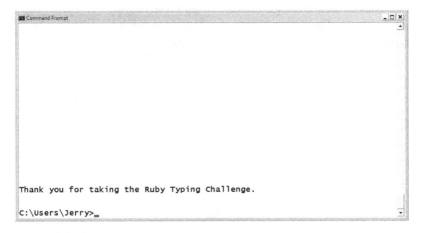

```
Command Prompt                                                    _ □ ×




Thank you for taking the Ruby Typing Challenge.

c:\Users\Jerry>_
```

Figure 4-8 The game ends after thanking the player for taking the test

Using Conditional Logic to Create Adaptive Scripts

Using Ruby, you can create scripts that consist of a series of statements executed in sequential order, without any alteration in the logical flow. While these may perform simple tasks well enough, they're not suited to complex tasks. Some level of conditional execution is almost always required—for example, if you prompt the player for permission to start the game and then either end or continue the game based on the player's response.

People use conditional logic all the time. For example, they wake up every morning and decide whether or not to go to work. Based on that decision, different courses of action are taken. See Figure 4-9, which visually outlines the conditional logic involved in selecting from two alternatives.

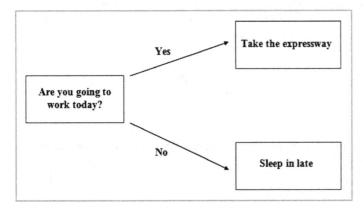

Figure 4-9 The conditional logic involved in selecting from two alternatives

This same conditional logic can be applied in developing a computer program or script. See Figure 4-10, which visually outlines the logic involved in responding to the player's decision whether or not to play a game.

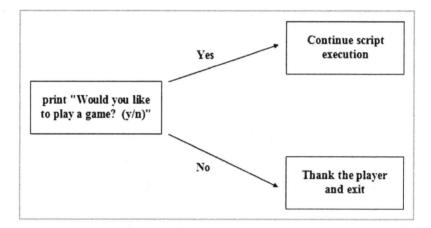

Figure 4-10 The conditional logic involved in determining whether or not to play the game

Figures 4-9 and 4-10 are examples of simple flowcharts. A **flowchart** graphically represents some or all of a script's logical flow. Prior to beginning work on a program or script, programmers will often create a flowchart to outline the overall design of the logic involved. This allows them to focus on the overall process required to create the program, and it helps them identify logical errors in the program's design before investing time in program development and testing.

Flowcharts are often used in large projects involving the combined efforts of many programmers. They help clarify the division of work and ensure that all the programmers understand where the part of the project they're working on fits into the overall scheme.

As you can see, Figure 4-10 outlines two distinct courses of action, of which only one will be followed, based on the user's decision whether or not to play the game. The logic outlined in the flowchart can be directly translated into script statements, as shown here:

```
puts "Would you like to play a game? (y/n)"
answer = STDIN.gets
answer.chop!

if answer == "n"
  puts "Sorry to hear that. Please return and play again" +
      "soon."
else
  puts "OK, let's play!"
  .
  .
  .
end
```

Here, the `puts` method is passed a text string containing a message that prompts the player to enter y or n, indicating whether or not game play should begin. The player types the appropriate response and presses Enter.

The key point to understand is that conditional programming logic hinges on an evaluation of whether a tested condition is true or false. Based on the result of the analysis, the appropriate set of program statements is then executed.

Ruby provides several options for applying conditional logic, each one designed for a specific type of situation:

- `if` modifier—appended to the end of Ruby statements to conditionally control the execution of the statement when the tested condition evaluates as true

- `unless` modifier—appended to the end of Ruby statements to conditionally control the execution of the statement when the tested condition evaluates as false

- `if` expression—creates complex conditional evaluations spread out over multiple lines that execute one or more statements when the tested condition evaluates as true

- `unless` expression—creates complex conditional evaluations spread out over multiple lines that execute one or more statements when the tested condition evaluates as false

- `case` expression—compares a value to a series of conditional tests to determine if one of the tests evaluates as true

- ternary operator—facilitates the inclusion of a conditional expression within a statement

Performing Alternative Types of Comparisons

Up to this point, all the comparison operations have used the `==` comparison operator. Like other modern programming languages, however, Ruby provides a whole range of comparison operators. Instead of a comparison test that evaluates whether one value is equal to another, you might set one up that evaluates whether one value is greater than or less than another. Table 4-1 provides a list of the comparison operators Ruby supports. The rest of the chapter shows you how to work with them.

Operator	Description
==	equal to
!=	not equal to
<	less than
<=	less than or equal to
>	greater than
>=	greater than or equal to

Table 4-1   Ruby Comparison Operators

Conditional Logic Modifiers

One quick and easy way Ruby allows you to integrate conditional logic into your scripts is through the use of conditional logic modifiers. By appending one of these modifiers to the end of a Ruby statement, you can conditionally control the execution of the statement.

The if Modifier

Using the if modifier, you can attach a conditional test to the end of a Ruby statement to conditionally control its execution. The conditional test consists of the if keyword followed by an expression that contains a comparison operator, as shown in the following example:

```
print "Enter your age and press Enter: "
answer = STDIN.gets
answer.chop!

puts "You must be 18 or older to play this game!" if ↵
    answer.to_i < 18
```

Here, the user is prompted to enter her age. The entered value is then analyzed to determine whether it is less than 18. If it is, the **puts** statement with the appended modifier is executed. However, if the entered value is 18 or greater, the **puts** statement is not executed.

The unless Modifier

The unless modifier is the opposite of the if modifier. It allows you to conditionally execute a statement when a conditional test evaluates as false. There is nothing you can accomplish with the unless modifier that you cannot accomplish with the if modifier. Therefore, its use is really just a matter of preference.

To see how the `unless` modifier is used, look at the following example:

```
print "Enter your age and press Enter: "
answer = STDIN.gets
answer.chop!

puts "You must be 18 or older to play this game!" unless↵
    answer.to_i > 17
```

As you can see, this example is nearly identical to the previous one, except that, instead of the `if` modifier, the `unless` modifier is used. In addition, the `less than` comparison operator is replaced by the `greater than` operator, and the number 18 is replaced by the number 17. Both examples produce the same result.

Working with `if` and `unless` Expressions

Using `if` and `unless` expressions, you can spread conditional statements over multiple lines. The resulting conditional tests are more powerful than their modifier equivalents, and by grouping together and controlling the execution of large numbers of statements, you will render your scripts easier to read and maintain.

Creating `if` Expressions

Unlike `if` modifiers, `if` expressions can control the execution of more than one statement. The `if` expression supports a very flexible syntax that allows you to use it in a number of different ways. Here is a high-level outline of the `if` expression's syntax:

```
if condition then
    statements
elsif condition then
    statements
.
.
.

else
    statements
end if
```

Here, *condition* refers to an expression that is to be tested, *statements* refers to one or more script statements that are to be conditionally executed, `elsif` is a keyword that, when specified, allows additional conditional tests to be performed, and `else` is a keyword that, when specified, allows you to identify an alternate set of programming statements to be executed when none of the preceding conditions evaluates as true.

Replacing if Modifiers with if Expressions

To better understand how to work with this powerful and extremely useful expression, you need to see examples of it in use. Earlier in this chapter, the following example was presented to demonstrate the use of the if modifier:

```
print "Enter your age and press Enter:   "
answer = STDIN.gets
answer.chop!

puts "You must be 18 or older to play this game!" if↵
   answer.to_i < 18
```

Using the if expression, this example could be rewritten as follows:

```
print "Enter your age and press Enter:   "
answer = STDIN.gets
answer.chop!

if answer.to_i < 18 then
   puts "You must be 18 or older to play this game!"
end
```

As you can see, this version is longer than the version that uses the if modifier. Using the if expression, however, you can include any number of statements within the opening if and closing end statements, allowing you to conditionally control their execution, as shown here:

```
if answer.to_i < 18
   puts "You must be 18 or older to play this game!"
   puts "Goodbye."
   exit
end
```

Notice the use of the exit method in this example. The exit method, which is provided by the kernel class, terminates the execution of a Ruby script.

Creating Single Line if Expressions

The if expression's flexible syntax allows for many formats. The following example demonstrates how to format an if expression that fits on a single line:

```
x = 10
if x == 10 then puts "x is equal to 10" end
```

In this format, the if expression is very similar to the if modifier. The difference is that the conditional check is performed at the beginning of the statement instead of at the end.

Using the else Keyword to Specify Alternative Actions

In addition to executing one or more script statements when a test condition is evaluated as true, an if expression can be modified to execute one or more alternative statements when a test condition is evaluated as false. To accomplish this, add the keyword else to the expression, as shown here:

```
x = 10
if x == 10 then
  puts " x is equal to 10"
else
  puts " x does not equal 10"
end
```

Here, one of two `puts` statements executes, depending on whether or not the value assigned to x is equal to 10.

125

Checking Alternative Conditions

There will be times when you need to examine a series of conditions to find out which one of them evaluates as true. One way of accomplishing this is to define a series of statements, as shown here:

```
if x == 10 then puts "x is 10" end
if x == 15 then puts "x is 15" end
if x == 20 then puts "x is 20" end
if x == 25 then puts "x is 25" end
```

The objective of these statements is to find out which of four possible values has been assigned to x. If you prefer, you can use the `if` expression's keyword `elsif` to accomplish the same thing, as shown here:

```
if x == 10 then puts "x is 10"
elsif x == 15 then puts "x is 15"
elsif x == 20 then puts "x is 20"
elsif x == 25 then puts "x is 25"
end
```

Though similar, the two preceding examples have subtle differences. In the first example, every statement gets executed. In the second example, the statements get executed until a match is found, after which no more statements are executed. If you need to, you can reformat your conditional logic to allow for the execution of more than one statement when a matching condition is found. To do so, place all of the statements to be executed on their own lines, as shown here:

```
if x == 10 then
  puts "x is 10"
  puts "10 is a low number"
elsif x == 15 then
  puts "x is 15"
  puts "15 is a medium number"
elsif x == 20 then
  puts "x is 20"
  puts "20 is a high number"
elsif x == 25 then
  puts "x is 25"
  puts "25 is a very high number"
end
```

You can also use the else keyword to provide an alternative course of action, should none of the preceding tests evaluate as true, as shown here:

```
if x == 10 then puts "x is 10"
elsif x == 15 then puts "x is 15"
elsif x == 20 then puts "x is 20"
elsif x == 25 then puts "x is 25"
else puts "The value of x is unknown"
end
```

Creating unless Expressions

The unless expression is the opposite of the if expression. It executes statements if the tested condition evaluates as false. As such, there is nothing you can accomplish with an if expression that you cannot accomplish with an unless expression. Consider the following if expression:

```
print "Enter your age and press Enter:   "
answer = STDIN.gets
answer.chop!

if answer.to_i < 18
  puts "You must be 18 or older to play this game!"
end
```

To convert it to an unless expression, just replace the if keyword with the unless keyword, and replace the < operator with the > operator, as shown here (notice that the number 18 has been replaced with the number 17):

```
print "Enter your age and press Enter:   "
answer = STDIN.gets
answer.chop!

unless answer.to_i > 17
  puts "You must be 18 or older to play this game!"
end
```

Whether to use an if expression or an unless expression is a matter of personal preference.

Short Quiz

1. (True/False) The kernel class's exit method is used to prevent the termination of a Ruby script.

2. (True/False) The else keyword can be used to specify that an alternative set of programming statements be executed when none of the preceding conditions evaluates as true.

3. (True/False) A major limitation of the if expression is that it can only be used with a single statement.

4. Flowcharts are often used in large programming projects to:

   a. graphically represent a script or program's logical flow.

   b. help coordinate the efforts of multiple programmers working on the same project.

   c. provide a high-level outline of the overall logic required to create a script or program.

   d. All of the above

5. Which of the following is an advantage of using a conditional modifier when performing conditional logic?

   a. It facilitates the development of compact statements.

   b. It allows more than one condition to be evaluated.

   c. It can be used to control the execution of one or more statements.

   d. All of the above

Using case Blocks to Analyze Data

To compare a series of expressions against a separate expression to see whether any of the expressions being evaluated results in an equivalent value, you can use the case block. You can accomplish the same thing with an if expression that contains a series of elsif statements, but the case block is better suited for situations where you need to compare a single value to a range of possible matches. The syntax for the case block is outlined here:

```
case expression
  when value
    statements
       .
       .
       .
  when value
    statements
  else
    statements
end
```

As you can see, the case block includes one or more when statements. The evaluated *expression* is compared to the values associated with one or more when statements. If a match occurs with one of the when

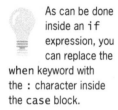

As can be done inside an `if` expression, you can replace the `when` keyword with the `:` character inside the `case` block.

statements, any statements associated with that `when` statement are executed. If none of the `when` statements match the value of the expression being evaluated, the statements belonging to the `else` statement (if present) are executed.

To see how to set up a `case` block, look at the following statements:

```
x = 10

case x

  when 1
    puts "*"
  when 5
    puts "*****"
  when 10
    puts "**********"
  else
    puts "No stars"

end
```

Here, the value assigned to x is compared to a series of values specified in a `case` block. Since the value of x is 10, the `puts "**********"` statement will be executed. Had none of the `when` statements contained a matching value, the `puts` statement associated with the `else` keyword would have executed. In most cases, you will find that it takes fewer lines of code to set up a `case` block than it does to set up an equivalent `if` expression using multiple `elsif` keywords.

If you want, you can omit the specification of an expression on the open `case` statement when setting up a `case` block, as shown here:

```
puts "\nWelcome to the vacation calculator!\n\n"

print "How many years have you worked for the company?" +
    "\n\n: "
answer = STDIN.gets
answer.chop!
answer = answer.to_i

case
  when (answer.between?(1, 5))
    puts "You are entitled to 1 week of vacation per" +
      "year."
  when (answer.between?(6, 10))
    puts "You are entitled to 2 weeks of vacation per" +
      "year."
  when (answer.between?(11, 15))
    puts "You are entitled to 3 weeks of vacation per" +
      "year."
  when (answer.between?(16, 20))
    puts "You are entitled to 4 weeks of vacation per" +
      "year."
  else
```

Notice the use of the `between?` method in each of this example's expressions. Each of Ruby's numeric classes supports this method, which returns a value of `true` or `false`, depending on whether or not a number is within a specified range.

```
    puts "You are entitled to 5 weeks of vacation per" +
        "year."
end
```

Here, an expression has been specified for each when statement. The statement belonging to the first expression that evaluates as true is executed, and the rest are skipped.

Using the Ternary Operator

The ternary operator (?:) is yet another way to set up conditional logic. It allows you to compare the values of two different expressions and make a variable assignment as a result of that comparison. The syntax required to work with the ternary operator is as follows:

```
variable = condition ? true_result : false_result
```

Here, *variable* is the value returned when the statement executes, *condition* is the expression that is evaluated, *true_result* is the value returned if the expression evaluates as true, and *false_result* is the value returned if the expression evaluates as false. For a better understanding of how to work with the ternary operator, look at the following example:

```
print "\n\nEnter your age and press Enter:   "
answer = STDIN.gets
answer.chop!
answer = answer.to_i

result = answer < 18 ? "denied!" : "approved!"

puts "\n\nYour access has been " + result + "\n\n"
```

Here, the user is prompted to enter his age. The statement that contains the ternary operator evaluates the expression answer < 18. If the user enters a value of 17 or less, the expression evaluates as true, and a value of "denied!" is assigned to a variable named result. If the user enters a value of 18 or more, the expression evaluates as false, and a value of "approved!" is assigned to result.

Nesting Conditional Statements

There may be times when you need to perform a more complicated analysis than can be accomplished using a single conditional modifier or expression. For example, you may need to perform one conditional evaluation based on the result of another conditional evaluation. One way to do this is by embedding one conditional statement within another in a process called **nesting**. To get a better understanding of how nesting works, look at the following example:

```
redStatus = "Go"
blueStatus = "Go"
greenStatus = "Go"
```

```
if redStatus == "Go" then
  if blueStatus == "Go" then
    if greenStatus == "Go" then
      puts "All systems are go. Prepare for launch!"
    end
  end
end
```

Although there is no limit to how deeply you can nest conditional statements within one another, going more than two or three deep will result in script code that is difficult to read and maintain.

Here, a series of three if expressions has been set up. If the first expression evaluates as false, the remaining if expressions are skipped. Otherwise, the second if expression is executed. If the second if expression evaluates as false, the third if expression is skipped. Otherwise, it is executed. Nesting also works with unless expressions.

Combining and Negating Logical Comparison Operations

Like most modern programming languages, Ruby supports the use of a number of logical, or Boolean, operators. These operators are listed in Table 4-2.

Operator	Description	Example
and	evaluates as true if both comparisons evaluate as true	x > 1 and x < 10
&&	evaluates as true if both comparisons evaluate as true	x > 1 && x < 10
or	evaluates as true if either comparison evaluates as true	x = 1 or x = 10
||	evaluates as true if either comparison evaluates as true	x = 1 || x = 10
not	reverses the value of a comparison	not (x > 5)
!	reverses the value of a comparison	! (x > 5)

Table 4-2   Ruby Boolean Operators

As you can see, the and and && operators are all but identical. The only difference is that the and operator has a higher level of precedence than the && operator. Likewise, the or and || operators are all but identical, the only difference being precedence, the or operator having higher precedence than ||. The and and && operators evaluate the second conditional expression only if the first conditional expression is true. The or and || operators evaluate the second operand only if the first operand is false.

To give you a better understanding of how to work with these operators, here are a few examples. The first example uses the && operator:

```
print "Enter your age and press Enter:  "
reply = STDIN.gets
reply.chop!
reply = reply.to_i

puts "You are eligible to play this game!" if reply >= 18 ↵
    && reply <= 65
```

Here, the if modifier at the end of the last statement uses the && operator to determine whether the value assigned to reply is both 1) greater than or equal to 18 and 2) less than or equal to 65. If both expressions evaluate as true, the puts statement executes. Otherwise, the puts statement is skipped.

You can enclose expressions within parentheses to make them easier to understand, as shown here:

```
puts "You are eligible to play this game" if (reply ↵
    >= 18) && (reply <= 65)
```

The following example uses the || operator:

```
print "What is your rank?:  "
rank = STDIN.gets
rank.chop!
rank = rank.to_i

puts "Access is permitted." if rank == 1 || rank == 3
```

Here, the last statement uses the || operator to determine if the value assigned to rank is either equal to 1 or equal to 3. If one (or both) of these expressions evaluates as true, the puts statement executes. If neither expression evaluates as true, the puts statement is skipped.

The following example demonstrates how to work with the ! operator, which negates or reverses the value returned from a conditional expression:

```
randomNo = 1 + rand(10)

print "What number am I thinking of? \n\n:  "
answer = STDIN.gets
answer.chop!

puts "Wrong! My number was " + randomNo.to_s if ! (answer. ↵
    to_i == randomNo)
```

Here, the rand method generates a random number from 1 to 10 and assigns it to a variable named randomNo. The user is prompted to guess what the random number is, and the player's answer is converted into an integer and compared to the value of randomNo. If these two values are not equal, the puts statement executes. Otherwise, it does not execute.

Short Quiz

1. (True/False) A case block is better suited than an if expression in situations where you need to compare a single value to a range of possible matches.

2. Ruby's numeric classes support the _____ method, which returns a true or false value depending on whether an evaluated numeric value is within a specific range.

3. Placing one or more conditional programming statements within another conditional programming statement is referred to as _____.

4. (True/False) Ruby enforces a strict limit on how deeply you can nest conditional programming statements, with a maximum of five levels.

5. Which of the following is a valid Ruby Boolean operator?

   a. and

   b. &

   c. between!

   d. All of the above

Back to the Ruby Typing Challenge Game

It is time to develop this chapter's game project, the Ruby Typing Challenge game. As you create this script, focus on the conditional expression's role in evaluating the player's typing accuracy.

Designing the Game

The development of the Ruby Typing Challenge game is completed in 13 steps, as outlined here:

1. Open your text or script editor and create a new file.

2. Add comment statements to the beginning of the script file to document the script and its purpose.

3. Define a Screen class representing the console window.

4. Define a Test class representing the typing test.

5. Develop a method in the Test class that displays a greeting message.

6. Develop a method in the Test class that displays test instructions.

7. Develop a method in the Test class that presents typing challenge sentences.

8. Develop a method in the Test class that displays test results.

9. Initialize script objects.

10. Prompt the player for permission to start the typing test.

11. Develop the overall programming logic responsible for analyzing the player's response.

12. Manage early game termination.

13. Execute methods required to deliver the typing test.

Follow along carefully, and do not skip any steps or parts of steps.

Step 1: Create a New Ruby File

Open your text or script editor and create a new Ruby script file. Save the file with the name TypingChallenge.rb and store it in the folder with your other Ruby scripts.

Step 2: Document the Script and Its Purpose

Add the following comment statements to the new script file. These comments provide a description of the script and its purpose.

```
#------------------------------------------------------------
#
# Script Name: TypingChallenge.rb
# Version:     1.0
# Author:      Jerry Lee Ford, Jr.
# Date:        March 2010
#
# Description: This Ruby script demonstrates how to apply
#              conditional logic in order to analyze user
#              input and control script execution through
#              the development of a computer typing test
#              that evaluates the player's typing skills.
#
#------------------------------------------------------------
```

Step 3: Define a Class Representing the Console Window

Define a class named Screen by adding the following statements to the end of the script file:

```
# Define custom classes ------------------------------------

#Define a class representing the console window
class Screen

  def cls   #Define a method that clears the display area
    puts ("\n" * 25)   #Scroll the screen 25 times
    puts "\a"   #Make a little noise to get the player's
                #attention
  end

  def pause     #Define a method that pauses the display area
    STDIN.gets  #Execute the STDIN class's gets method to
                #pause script execution until the player
                #presses the Enter key
  end
```

The first method defined in the class is the cls method. It contains two statements. The first statement writes 25 blank lines to the console window to clear the screen. The second statement processes a string containing the \a escape character, which makes a beep sound, thus notifying the player each time the console screen is cleared.

Step 4: Define a Class Representing the Typing Test

Define a class named **Test** by adding the following statements to the end of the script file:

```
#Define a class representing the typing test
class Test

end
```

Step 5: Define the *display_greeting* Method

Define the first of four methods belonging to the **Test** class by inserting the following statements between the class's opening and closing statements:

```
#This method displays the Typing Challenge greeting
#message
def display_greeting

  Console_Screen.cls #Clear the display area

  #Display a welcome screen
  print "\t\t  Welcome to the Ruby Typing Challenge game!" +
  "\n\n\n\n\n\n\n\n\n\n\n\nPress Enter to " +
            "continue. \n\n: "

Console_Screen.pause         #Pause the game

end
```

This method, named display_greeting, displays the game's welcome screen.

Step 6: Define the *display_instructions* Method

Define the second of four methods belonging to the Test class by adding the following statements at the end of the class definition, immediately after the display_greeting method:

```
#Define a method to be used to present test instructions
def display_instructions

  Console_Screen.cls        #Clear the display area
  puts "\t\t\tInstructions:\n\n"  #Display a heading

  #Display the game's instructions
  put %Q{    This test consists of a series of 5 typing
  challenges. The challenge sentences are presented
  one at a time. To respond correctly, you must retype
  each sentence exactly as shown and press the Enter
  key. Your grade will be displayed at the end of the test.
  \n\n\n\n\n\n\n\n\n
  Press Enter to continue.\n\n}

  Console_Screen.pause      #Pause the game

end
```

This method, named display_instructions, displays a text string containing instructions for playing the game.

Step 7: Define the *present_test* Method

Define the third of four methods belonging to the Test class by adding the following statements at the end of the class definition:

```
#Define a method to be used to present typing challenges
def present_test(challenge)

  Console_Screen.cls        #Clear the display area
  print challenge + "\n\n: "  #Display the challenge sentence
  result = STDIN.gets  #Collect the player's input
  result.chop!          #Remove the end of line marker

  #Analyze the player input and see if it is correct
  if challenge == result then
```

```
      #Keep track of the number of correctly retyped
      #challenge sentences
      $noRight += 1
      Console_Screen.cls        #Clear the display area
      #Keep the player informed
      print "Correct!\n\nPress Enter to continue."
      Console_Screen.pause         #Pause the game

   else

      Console_Screen.cls        #Clear the display area
      #Keep the player informed
      print "Incorrect!\n\nPress Enter to continue."
      Console_Screen.pause         #Clear the game

   end

end
```

This method, named **present_test**, is responsible for displaying
sentences passed to it as string arguments and for collecting and storing player input. An **if** expression has also been defined to analyze
whether the player's input matches the original sentence. If it does,
the value of **$noRight** is incremented by one to keep track of the
number of correctly typed sentences, and a text string is displayed
that notifies the player that the sentence was typed correctly.

If the player has made an error when typing the sentence, the value of
$noRight is not incremented, and a different text string is displayed,
notifying the player of the mistake.

Step 8: Define the **determine_grade** Method

Define the final method belonging to the **Test** class by adding the
following statements at the end of the class definition:

```
#Define a method to be used to display test results
def determine_grade

   Console_Screen.cls          #Clear the display area

   #To pass the test the player must correctly retype 3
   #sentences
   if $noRight >= 3 then

      #Inform the player of the good news
      print "You retyped " + $noRight.to_s + " sentence(s)" +
         "correctly. "
      puts "You have passed the typing test!\n\nPress Enter" +
         "to continue."

   else  #The player has failed the test
```

```
#Inform the player of the bad news
print "You retyped " + $noRight.to_s + " sentence(s)" +
    "correctly. "
puts "You have failed the typing test!\n\nPress Enter⏎
    to continue."

    end

end
```

This method, named determine_grade, is responsible for determining whether the player has passed the typing test. To pass, the player
must correctly type at least three sentences. To determine the player's
score, an if expression has been set up to evaluate whether the value
assigned to $noRight is greater than or equal to three. If it is, a text
string is displayed notifying the player of a passing grade.

If the value of $noRight is not greater than or equal to three, the else
portion of the if expression is executed, informing the player of a
failed test.

Step 9: Instantiate Script Objects

Instantiate instances of the Screen and the Test classes by adding the
following statements at the end of the script file:

```
# Main Script Logic ------------------------------------

#Initialize global variable that will be used to keep
#track of the number of correctly retyped sentences
$noRight = 0

Console_Screen = Screen.new  #Instantiate a new Screen
                             #object
Typing_Test = Test.new       #Instantiate a new Test
object

#Execute the Test object's display_greeting method
Typing_Test.display_greeting
```

In addition to instantiating the Console_Screen and Typing_Test
objects, these statements instantiate a global variable named $noRight,
which will be used both to keep track of the number of correctly typed
sentences and to execute the Test class's display_greeting method.

Step 10: Get Permission to Begin the Test

Include programming logic that prompts the player for permission
to begin the test by adding the following statements at the end of the
script file:

```
#Execute the Screen object's cls method in order to clear
    the screen
Console_Screen.cls
```

```
#Prompt the player for permission to begin the test
print "Would you like to test your typing skills? (y/n)" +
    "\n\n: "

answer = STDIN.gets  #Collect the player's response
answer.chop!  #Remove any extra characters appended to
              #the string

#Loop until the player enters y or n and do not
#accept any other input.
until answer == "y" || answer == "n"

  Console_Screen.cls  #Clear the display area

  #Prompt the player for permission to begin the test
  print "Would you like to test your typing skills? (y/n)" +
      "\n\n: "

  answer = STDIN.gets #Collect the player's response
  answer.chop! #Remove any extra characters appended
               #to the string

end
```

Step 11: Develop the Controlling Logic Required to Administer the Test

All that remains to be done is to develop the controlling logic responsible for analyzing the player's response when prompted for permission to begin the test. Add the following statements at the end of the script file:

```
#Analyze the player's response
if answer == "n"  #See if the player elected not to play

else  #The player wants to take the test

end
```

You will need to embed the code statements from Step 12 within the first part of the above if expression, and you will need to embed the code statements from Step 13 at the end of the if expression (between the else and end statements).

Step 12: Manage Early Game Termination

The following script statements are executed if the player responds with a value of n when prompted for permission to start the typing test. Place them between the opening if statement and the else statement that you added in the previous step.

```
Console_Screen.cls #Clear the display area
```

```
#Invite the player to return and play again
puts "Okay, perhaps another time.\n\n"
```

These statements clear the screen and display a text message encouraging the player to take the test some other time.

Step 13: Execute the Typing Test

The final set of script statements is responsible for administering the typing test. Embed it within the bottom half of the if expression you added in Step 11, following the else keyword.

```
#Execute the Test object's display_instructions method
Typing_Test.display_instructions

#Display typing challenges and grade each answer by calling on
#the Test object's present_test method
Typing_Test.present_test "In the end there can be only" +
    "one."
Typing_Test.present_test "Once a great plague swept" +
    "across the land."
Typing_Test.present_test "Welcome to Principles of Ruby ↵
    Programming."
Typing_Test.present_test "There are very few problems in ↵
    the world that enough M@Ms cannot fix."
Typing_Test.present_test "Perhaps today is a good day to ↵
    die. Fight beside me and let us die together."

#Notify the player of the results by executing the Test
#object's determine_grade method
Typing_Test.determine_grade

Console_Screen.pause        #Pause the game

Console_Screen.cls #Clear the display area
#Thank the player for taking the typing test
puts "Thank you for taking the Ruby Typing Challenge.\n\n"
```

As you can see, these statements make a series of calls to methods belonging to the Typing_Test and Console_Screen objects. First, the display_instructions method is called, followed by five separate calls to the present_test method. Each of these five passes a different text string to the method, which displays the sentence and prompts the player to retype it. Next, the determine_grade method is called. It determines whether the player has passed or failed the test. Finally, the screen is cleared, and a message is displayed thanking the player for playing the Ruby Typing Challenge game.

Running Your New Ruby Script Game

Save your Ruby script. If you typed the code statements correctly, the program should work as expected. If you run into any errors, read the error messages carefully to ascertain what went wrong. If necessary, review the script and look for mistyped or missing statements.

Summing Up

- Ruby scripts may consist of a series of statements executed in sequential order.

- Sequential scripts are not well suited to tasks with any level of complexity.

- A flowchart graphically represents all or some of a script's logical flow.

- Conditional programming logic is based on an evaluation of whether a tested condition is true or false.

- Ruby supports a number of constructs that implement conditional logic, including the if modifier, unless modifier, if expression, unless expression, case block, and the ternary operator.

- Ruby comparison operators include the following: ==, !=, <, <=, >, and >=.

- The if modifier is appended to the end of a statement and conditionally controls the statement's execution.

- The unless modifier is appended to the end of a statement and performs the opposite function of the if modifier, conditionally executing a statement when the tested condition evaluates as false.

- The if expression conditionally controls the execution of other statements, depending on whether an evaluated condition is true or false.

- The unless expression performs the opposite evaluation of the if expression.

- The case block evaluates a single value against a series of possible matching expressions.

- The ternary operator facilitates the inclusion of a conditional expression within another expression.

- By adding the elsif keyword to a conditional evaluation, you can define additional conditional tests to be performed.

- By adding the else keyword to a conditional evaluation, you can specify an alternative set of code statements to be executed if a condition evaluates as false.

- Ruby numeric classes support the between? method, which returns a Boolean value based on whether or not a number is within a specified range.

- The ternary operator (?:) is used to evaluate the value of two different expressions and make a variable assignment based on that comparison.

- To generate more complex logic, conditional statements can be nested within one another.

- There is no limit to how deeply you can nest conditional statements within one another.

- Ruby supports a collection of logical, or Boolean, operators, including the following: and, &&, or, ||, not, and !.

Comprehension Check

1. As a programming tool, flowcharts have the following benefits:

    a. They help outline the overall design of the logic involved.

    b. They help clarify the division of work among programmers in large projects.

    c. They help identify logical errors before investing time in program development and testing.

    d. All of the above

2. Which of the following is not a comparison operator supported by Ruby?

    a. =

    b. !=

    c. <=

    d. >

3. The `kernel` class's _____ method terminates the execution of a Ruby script.

    a. `end`

    b. `terminate`

    c. `exit`

    d. None of the above

4. Which of the following options allows you to analyze more than one value or expression against a range of different matches?

    a. A `case` block

    b. An `if` expression that makes repeated use of the `elsif` keyword

    c. Nested conditional statements

    d. All of the above

5. (True/False) The primary advantage of working with the `if` expression is its ability to control the execution of more than one code statement based on a conditional analysis.

6. (True/False) The `else` keyword allows programmers to specify an alternative set of statements that will be executed if a conditional statement is evaluated as true.

7. What is the primary difference between the `or` operator and the `||` operator?

    a. The `||` operator has a higher degree of precedence than the `or` operator.

    b. There is no difference. They are identical.

    c. The `or` operator has a higher degree of precedence than the `||` operator.

    d. None of the above

8. (True/False) The `and` operator and the `&&` operator evaluate the second operand only if the first operand is evaluated as true.

9. (True/False) An advantage of using conditional modifiers instead of conditional expressions is that they allow you to write script that is more compact.

10. The _____ operator evaluates the value of two expressions and makes a variable assignment based on that comparison.

11. (True/False) A `case` block is best suited to the analysis of two expressions or values.

12. The _____ method is used to determine whether a numeric value falls within a specified range.

13. (True/False) As a rule, you shouldn't nest conditional statements within one another more than two or three layers deep.

14. (True/False) The `elsif` keyword enables programmers to evaluate additional conditional tests.

15. (True/False) A disadvantage of using a `case` block instead of an `if` expression with the `elsif` keyword is that a `case` block generally requires more lines of code and is more difficult to read.

16. Which comparison operator is used to determine if one value is less than or equal to another?

    a. `<=`

    b. `>=`

    c. `==`

    d. `!=`

17. (True/False) The `unless` modifier performs the opposite type of evaluation to the `if` modifier.

18. An `if` statement code block begins with the `if` keyword and ends with which keyword?

    a. `?:`

    b. `exit`

    c. `end`

    d. None of the above

19. (True/False) Both the `=` operator and the `==` operator can be used to evaluate values in order to determine if they are equal.

20. Which of the following is true of `case` blocks?

   a. They are limited to the analysis of numeric data.

   b. They can accomplish the same types of comparisons as `if` expressions that use the `elsif` keyword.

   c. They support the use of the `else` keyword.

   d. All of the above

Reinforcement Exercises

The following exercises are designed to further your understanding of Ruby programming by challenging you to make improvements to the chapter's game project, the Ruby Typing Challenge game.

1. Make the game more difficult by increasing the number of typing challenges from five to 10. Modify the program so that it takes six correctly typed sentences to pass.

   To implement this challenge, copy the last of the five statements that generate the game's typing challenges and use it to add five additional challenges. You also need to modify the `display_instructions` method so that it tells the player there are 10 sentences instead of five. And you need to modify the `Test` class's `determine_grade` method so that it requires the player to type at least six sentences correctly in order to pass the challenge.

2. Rather than using a pass/fail grading system, modify the game to assign grades of A, B, C, D, and F to the player using a 10-point grading scale. Make sure you use the `case` statement when implementing your solution.

   To implement this challenge, modify the `Test` class's `determine_grade` method using a `case` code block. Assign an A for nine or 10 correctly typed sentences, a B for eight, a C for seven, a D for six, and an F for five or fewer.

3. Add an explanation of how the test is graded. To implement this challenge, modify the `test` class's `display_instructions` method and rewrite the text accordingly.

4. Provide immediate feedback for each mistyped sentence. To do so, modify the `Test` class's `present_test` method so that it informs the player a mistake has been made, then display the challenge sentence followed by the player's sentence so the player can determine where the error lies.

5. Modify the game so it rejects blank input—e.g., when the player presses Enter without typing a sentence. To implement this challenge, modify the Test class's present_test method, adding a loop with programming logic that analyzes player input and makes sure it does not consist of an empty string.

Discovery Projects

 ## Project 4-1

Programmers use flowcharts to graphically represent the organization of their scripts and programs before writing them. There are many software tools for creating flowcharts, such as Visio or even Microsoft Word. There are also a number of online services you can use, including *http://www.gliffy.com.* Go to this site and search for online flowcharting services. Sign up for one, and use it to develop a flowchart that outlines the programming logic used in the Ruby Typing Challenge.

 ## Project 4-2

Table 4-1 lists a number of commonly used comparison operators, but these are not the only ones Ruby supports. To learn more about Ruby comparison operators, visit *http://www.tutorialspoint.com/ruby/ruby_operators.htm* and review the complete list, along with the descriptions of what they do.

 ## Project 4-3

Understanding the various nuances of conditional programming logic is key to becoming a good programmer. To help reinforce the material presented in this chapter, visit *http://www.techotopia.com/index.php/Ruby_Essentials* and review the material that addresses the if statement, the case statement, and the ternary operator.

## CHAPTER 5

Working with Loops

In this chapter, you gain an understanding of loops and learn how to:

- ◎ Use language constructs to create loops
- ◎ Use loop modifiers
- ◎ Execute looping methods
- ◎ Alter loop execution
- ◎ Create the Superman Movie Trivia Quiz

Loops are an essential part of most Ruby scripts. They allow you to repeat a set of statements as many times as necessary to perform a particular task. Using a minimal amount of code, loops facilitate the development of scripts that can process huge amounts of data. They are also used to collect any amount of user input. Ruby provides support for loops in a number of ways, including built-in language constructs, statement modifiers, and object methods. Ruby also provides commands for altering and controlling the execution of loops.

Project Preview: The Superman Movie Trivia Quiz

In this chapter, you create a computer game called the Superman Movie Trivia Quiz. Through the creation of an interactive quiz that evaluates the player's knowledge of the Superman movie series, this Ruby script demonstrates how to work with loops to collect player input.

The game begins by displaying the welcome message shown in Figure 5-1.

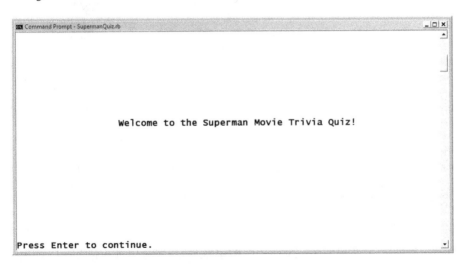

Figure 5-1 The welcome screen for the Superman Movie Trivia Quiz

After pressing Enter, the player is prompted for permission to begin the quiz, as shown in Figure 5-2.

148

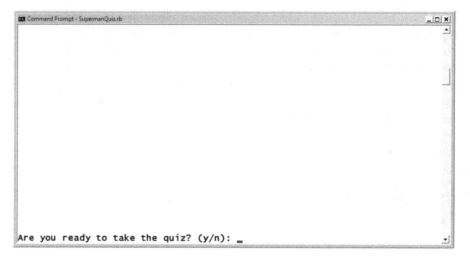

Figure 5-2   The player must decide to play before the quiz can begin

If the player decides not to play and enters a value of n, the message shown in Figure 5-3 displays, encouraging the player to take the quiz some other time.

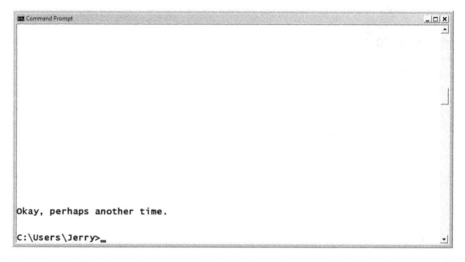

Figure 5-3   The player is encouraged to take the quiz some other time

If the player decides to take the quiz and enters a value of y, the instructions shown in Figure 5-4 are displayed, providing the player with an understanding of how the quiz will be administered.

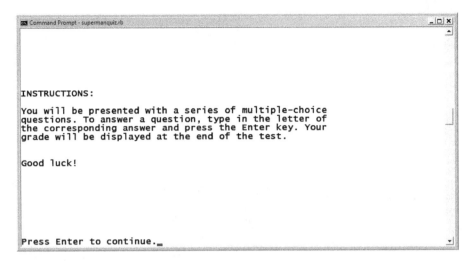

Figure 5-4 Instructions for how to play are provided

Next, the first of five questions is displayed, and the player is prompted to specify a letter representing one of four possible answers, as demonstrated in Figure 5-5.

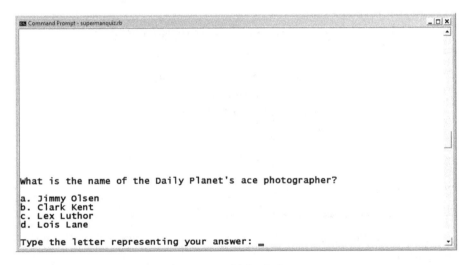

Figure 5-5 All the quiz questions are multiple choice

To advance to the next quiz question, the player must enter an a, b, c, or d and press Enter. Any other input is rejected. Once a valid answer has been provided, the game evaluates the player's input and displays the next quiz question. Once all the questions have been answered, the game displays a message indicating whether the player has passed or failed the quiz. If the player has passed, a ranking is assigned, as demonstrated in Figure 5-6.

150

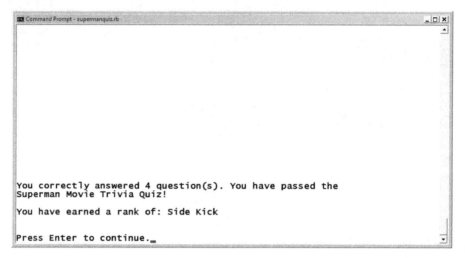

You correctly answered 4 question(s). You have passed the
Superman Movie Trivia Quiz!

You have earned a rank of: Side Kick

Press Enter to continue.

Figure 5-6 The player has passed the quiz by correctly answering four questions

After the player presses Enter, the screen shown in Figure 5-7 displays.

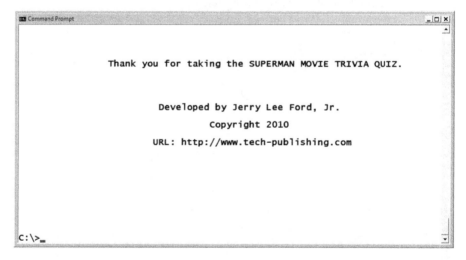

Thank you for taking the SUPERMAN MOVIE TRIVIA QUIZ.

Developed by Jerry Lee Ford, Jr.
Copyright 2010
URL: http://www.tech-publishing.com

Figure 5-7 The Superman Movie Trivia Quiz's closing screen thanks the player for taking the quiz

Understanding Loops

To process large amounts of data, you need to work with loops.
A **loop** is a set of statements that executes repeatedly. Loops facilitate
the processing of large text files or the collection of enormous
amounts of user input. They also allow you to develop scripts that can
repeat the execution of any number of commands.

Using loops, you can develop computer games that can be played over and over again. You can also develop programs that help process and validate user input, so that the script continues only if valid data has been entered. And you can do it using a minimal amount of code that can be executed as many times as necessary to accomplish a particular task. The reduced size of your Ruby scripts makes them easier to develop and maintain.

Ruby provides you with many different types of loops. They can be organized into the following three categories:

- Language constructs—commands provided as part of the core Ruby programming language

- Modifiers—commands appended to the end of a Ruby statement to control its repeated execution

- Methods—methods provided by objects that repeatedly execute

These three categories of loops will be examined in detail throughout the rest of this chapter.

Using Language Constructs to Create Loops

One way of incorporating loops into your Ruby program files is to work with the while, until, and for language constructs. These three loops are part of Ruby's core programming language. They are considered a little outdated by Ruby programmers who prefer to work with loop methods provided by various object classes. They are still widely used, however, and an understanding of how they work is fundamental to becoming a good Ruby programmer.

Working with while Loops

The while loop executes as long as a specified expression evaluates as true. Its syntax is as follows:

```
while Expression [ do | : ]
   Statements
end
```

Here, *Expression* is any valid Ruby expression, do and : are mutually exclusive (as indicated by the | character), meaning that you can use one or the other but not both, and *Statements* represents the statements you want the program to execute each time the loop repeats.

To get a feel for how to work with the `while` loop, look at the following example:

```
x = 1

while x <= 10 do
   puts x
   x += 1
end
```

Here, a variable named x is defined and assigned a value of 1. Next, a `while` loop is set up to run as long as the value of x is less than or equal to 10. The first statement in the loop prints the current value assigned to x, and the second statement increments the value of x by 1. As a result, this loop will display a list of numbers from 1 to 10, as shown here:

```
1
2
3
4
5
6
7
8
9
10
```

Watch out for endless loops. An **endless loop** is one that is set up in such a way that it never stops executing, thereby using up computer resources. If you execute a Ruby script with an endless loop, type Control-C to terminate its execution.

Working with `until` Loops

The `until` loop is pretty much the opposite of the `while` loop. It executes as long as the condition remains false and stops executing when the condition becomes true. The syntax for the `until` loop is as follows:

```
until Expression [ do | : ]
   Statements
end
```

Here, *Expression* refers to any valid Ruby expression, do and : are mutually exclusive, and *Statements* represents the statements you want the program to execute each time the loop repeats.

The `until` loop works very much like the `while` loop:

```
x = 1

until x > 10 do
   puts x
   x += 1
end
```

Here, a variable named x is defined and assigned a value of 1. Next, an until loop is set up to run until the value of x becomes greater than 10. The first statement in the loop prints the current value assigned to x, and the second statement increments the value of x by 1. This loop will display a list of numbers from 1 to 10, as shown here:

```
1
2
3
4
5
6
7
8
9
10
```

Working with for...in Loops

The for...in loop processes collections of data. The syntax for the for...in loop is as follows:

```
for Variable in Collection [ do | : ]
  Statements
end
```

Here, *Variable* represents a variable used by the loop to store the value of the item in the collection that is currently being processed, *Collection* is any valid Ruby expression that specifies the collection to be processed, do and : are mutually exclusive and must be left off if you decide to spread the loop over more than one line, and *Statements* represents the statements you want the program to execute each time the loop repeats.

To get a feel for how to work with the for...in loop, look at the following example:

```
MyList = ["Molly", "William", "Alexander", "Jerry", "Mary"]

for x in MyList
  print "Hi ", x, "!\n"
end
```

Here, an array named MyList is created and assigned a list of five names. Next, a for...in loop is set up to repeat once for each element stored in the array. Each time the loop repeats, or iterates, it prints a text string that displays the value of the array item currently being processed.

An **array** is an indexed collection of items stored as a list. You will learn how to create and work with arrays in Chapter 6, "Working with Collections of Data."

The preceding `for...in` loop will display the following output:

```
Hi Molly!
Hi William!
Hi Alexander!
Hi Jerry!
Hi Mary!
```

A `for...in` loop can also process a range of items. The range is expressed as two integer values separated by the `..` characters, as shown here:

```
for i in 1..5
    puts i
end
```

When executed, this example repeats five times, as specified by its beginning and ending range values, then displays the following output:

```
1
2
3
4
5
```

The Ruby range operator `..` allows you to display a range of consecutive letters or numbers. For example, `1..5` displays the following set of numbers: `1 2 3 4 5`. Likewise, `a..z` displays all the lowercase letters consecutively, from `a` to `z`.

Using Loop Modifiers

A loop modifier is an expression added to the end of a Ruby statement that causes the statement to be executed as a loop. It's perfect for situations where you only need to repeat the execution of a single statement. Ruby supports `while` and `until` loop modifiers.

The `while` Modifier

The `while` modifier evaluates a condition and executes an expression as long as the value of the condition remains true. The syntax for the `while` modifier is as follows:

Expression `while` *Condition*

Here, *Expression* is a Ruby statement you want conditionally executed, and *Condition* is a Boolean expression that, once evaluated, determines whether the opening expression is executed. To better understand how to work with the `while` modifier, look at the following example:

```
counter = 1
counter += 1 while counter < 10
puts counter
```

Here, a variable named `counter` is assigned a value of 1. Next, the value of `counter` is incremented by 1 if and only if the value assigned to `counter` is less than 10. The `while` modifier, attached to the second statement, repeats the statement over and over again, incrementing the value of `counter` repeatedly until `counter` becomes equal to 10, at which time the loop stops executing and the last statement executes, displaying the value of `counter`, which is 10.

The `until` Modifier

The `until` modifier is pretty much the opposite of the `while` modifier. It causes a statement to be repeatedly executed until a specified condition is evaluated as true. The syntax for the `until` modifier is as follows:

Expression until *Condition*

Here, *Expression* is a Ruby expression you want conditionally executed, and *Condition* is a Boolean expression that, once evaluated, determines whether the opening expression is executed. To better understand how to work with the `until` modifier, look at the following example:

```
counter = 1
counter += 1 until counter >= 10
puts counter
```

Here, a variable named `counter` is assigned a value of 1. Next, the value of `counter` is incremented by 1 repeatedly until the value of `counter` becomes equal to or greater than 10.

Short Quiz

1. (True/False) A loop is a set of statements that executes repeatedly.

2. Ruby supports three categories of loops. Which one of the following is not a Ruby-supported category?

   a. Methods

   b. Modules

   c. Modifiers

   d. Language constructs

3. (True/False) An endless loop is one that never stops executing.

4. Which of the following loops is provided as part of Ruby's core programming language?

   a. `while`

   b. `for`

   c. `until`

   d. All of the above

5. (True/False) Ruby's range operator (`..`) allows you to display a range of consecutive letters or numbers.

Executing Looping Methods

Ruby provides a number of looping methods in various classes. These methods simplify loop construction and reduce the chance of errors occurring when you work with Ruby's built-in language constructions (`while`, `until`, and `for...in`).

Working with the `each` Method

One commonly used looping method is the `each` method. It is used to process collections of data and is supported by a number of different Ruby classes, including the `Array`, `Dir`, `Hash`, and `Range` classes.

The syntax for the `each` method is as follows:

```
Object.each { |i| Statement }
```

Here, `Object` represents the object that the `each` loop operates on, `i` represents a variable used by the `each` loop to indicate the item currently being processed by the loop, and `Statement` represents a Ruby statement that is to be repeatedly executed.

This syntax outlines the use of the `each` method with a single Ruby statement. To use it with one or more statements, you may want to use the following syntax:

```
Object.each do |i|
  Statements
end
```

To better understand how to work with the `each` method, look at the following example:

```
MyList = ["Molly", "William", "Alexander", "Jerry", "Mary"]

MyList.each do |x|
  print "Hi ", x, "!\n"
end
```

Here, an array made up of five items is defined. Next, the Array class's **each** method is used to process and display each of the items stored in the array. The first time the loop executes, the value of the first array element ("Molly") is assigned to the x variable, which is then used inside the loop to display the element. The **each** method automatically iterates once for each item stored in the array, resulting in the following display of output:

```
Hi Molly!
Hi William!
Hi Alexander!
Hi Jerry!
Hi Mary!
```

Working with the `times` Method

The **times** method executes a code block a specific number of times. It is provided by the **Integer** class, and the syntax for it is as follows:

```
Integer.times { |i| Statement }
```

Here, *Integer* represents an integer value, and *i* represents an iterator. An **iterator** is a variable used as a counter to process the contents of a list of items. Here, *i* is used by the **times** method to indicate the count of the item currently being processed by the loop, and *Statement* represents a Ruby statement you want repeatedly executed.

This syntax outlines the use of the **times** method with a single Ruby statement. To use the **times** method with one or more statements, you may want to use the following syntax:

```
Integer.times do |i|
   Statements
end
```

To better understand how to work with the **times** method, look at the following example:

```
puts "Watch me count!"
10.times {|x| puts x}
```

Here, the **times** method is used to execute a statement 10 times. Upon each iteration of the loop, the value x is assigned an integer value representing the number of loop iterations, which is then displayed on the screen using the **puts** method. As shown below, x starts at 0 and ends at 9. The result is the display of the following output:

```
Watch me count!
0
1
2
3
4
5
6
7
8
9
```

You can rewrite this example using the multiline version of the `times` method's syntax, as shown here:

```
puts "Watch me count!"

10.times do
   |x| puts x
end
```

Working with the `upto` Method

The `upto` method is provided by the `Integer` class. As such, you can only use it to operate on integers. This method causes a loop to iterate a predetermined number of times. The syntax for a single-line version of the `upto` method is as follows:

```
Integer.upto(EndValue) { |i| Statement }
```

Here, *Integer* represents an integer value or variable, *EndValue* represents an integer that is passed to the `upto` method as an argument and tells the method how many times to iterate, *i* represents a variable used by the `upto` method to indicate the item currently being processed by the loop, and *Statement* represents a Ruby statement you want repeatedly executed.

The multiline version of this method's syntax is as follows:

```
Integer.upto(EndValue) do |i|
   Statements
end
```

To better understand how to work with the `upto` method, look at the following example:

```
1.upto(10) do |x|
   print x, ") Hello!\n"
end
```

Here, a loop is set up that executes 10 times (starting at 1 and ending at 10), as specified by the value that the integer and the argument (10) pass to the upto method. When executed, this example displays the following output:

```
1) Hello!
2) Hello!
3) Hello!
4) Hello!
5) Hello!
6) Hello!
7) Hello!
8) Hello!
9) Hello!
10) Hello!
```

Working with the downto Method

The downto method, which is provided by the Integer class, causes a loop to execute a predetermined number of times, starting at a specified integer value and counting down to whatever integer value is passed to it.

The syntax for the single-line version of the downto method is as follows:

```
Integer.downto(EndValue) { |i| Statement }
```

Here, *Integer* represents an integer value, *EndValue* is an integer that is passed to the downto method as an argument and tells the method how many times to iterate, *i* represents a variable used by the downto method to represent the item currently being processed by the method, and *Statement* represents a Ruby statement you want repeatedly executed.

The multiline version of this method's syntax is as follows:

```
Integer.downto(EndValue) do |i|
   Statements
end
```

To better understand how to work with the downto method, look at the following example:

```
5.downto(1) do |x|
   print x, ") Hello!\n"
end

puts "That's all folks!"
```

Here, a loop is set up that iterates five times. The first time the loop iterates, x is assigned a value of 5. Upon each subsequent iteration, the value of x is decreased by 1. The loop repeats over and over again (from 5 down to 1). When executed, this example generates the output shown here:

```
5) Hello!
4) Hello!
3) Hello!
2) Hello!
1) Hello!
That's all folks!
```

Working with the `step` Method

The `step` method sets up a loop that executes a given number of times. It works with the `Float` and `Integer` classes. The syntax for a single-line version of the `step` method is as follows:

```
Number.step(EndNumber, Increment) { |i| Statement }
```

Here, *Number* represents an integer or floating-point number, *EndNumber* specifies a value that, when passed, terminates the loop's execution, *Increment* specifies the value used to increment the loop each time it iterates, *i* represents a variable used by the `step` method to represent the item currently being processed by the method, and *Statement* represents a Ruby statement that you want repeatedly executed.

The multiline version of this method's syntax is as follows:

```
Number.step(EndNumber, Increment) do |i|
   Statements
end
```

To better understand how to work with the `step` method, look at the following example:

```
1.step(10,2) do |x|
   print x, ". Counting by 2\n"
end
```

Here, a loop is set up to execute five times. The first time the loop executes, the value of x is set to 1. The value of x is then incremented by 2 upon each subsequent iteration, resulting in the following output:

```
1. Counting by 2
3. Counting by 2
5. Counting by 2
7. Counting by 2
9. Counting by 2
```

The **step** method is quite flexible. For example, you can set it up to decrement instead of increment, as shown here:

```
50.step(10,-5) do |x|
  print x, ". I'm getting smaller!\n"
end
```

Here, the loop is set up to start at 50, decrementing by 5 upon each iteration until a value less than 10 is reached. As a result, the following output is displayed:

```
50. I'm getting smaller!
45. I'm getting smaller!
40. I'm getting smaller!
35. I'm getting smaller!
30. I'm getting smaller!
25. I'm getting smaller!
20. I'm getting smaller!
15. I'm getting smaller!
10. I'm getting smaller!
```

Working with the loop Method

The **loop** method belongs to the **Kernel** class. It is used to set up loops that run an undetermined number of times, which is useful when you do not know in advance how many times you want a loop to execute. The **loop** method has the following syntax:

```
loop { Statement }
```

Here, *Statement* represents a statement that is executed each time the loop iterates. To use the **loop** method with one or more statements, you may want to use the following syntax:

```
loop do
  Statements
end
```

Because loops created using the **loop** method run forever, you must provide a way to terminate them. This is done using the **break** command, which halts loop execution. To better understand how to work with the **loop** method, look at the following example:

```
counter = 1

loop do

  print counter.to_s + " "
  counter += 1
  break if counter == 10

end
```

Here, a variable named `counter` is assigned a value of 1. Next, a loop is set up using the `loop` method. Upon each iteration, the `print` method displays the current value assigned to `counter`. In addition, the value of `counter` is incremented by 1. At the end of each iteration of the loop, the last statement ensures that the loop has a way of terminating, executing the `break` command if the value of counter is equal to 10. When executed, this example generates the following output:

```
1 2 3 4 5 6 7 8 9
```

Altering Loop Execution

There may be times when you want to prematurely halt the execution of a loop. Ruby supplies a number of commands that alter loop execution. Descriptions of these commands are provided here:

- `break`—terminates the execution of a loop
- `redo`—repeats the current execution of a loop without evaluating its condition or iterating
- `next`—stops the current iteration of a loop and immediately begins a new iteration
- `retry`—restarts a loop from the beginning, resetting the value of the iterator

Prematurely Terminating Loop Execution

The `break` command allows you to terminate the execution of a loop at any time. To see how to use this command, look at the following example:

```
loop do

  print "Type q to quit this script. "

  answer = STDIN.gets
  answer.chop!

  break if answer == "q"

end
```

Here, a loop is set up that, by default, will repeat forever. Each time the loop executes, a message is displayed that prompts the user to type q to have the script quit. The user's response is captured and stored in a variable named `answer`. The last statement in the loop is set up to conditionally execute the `break` command based on whether the user provides the proper input.

Repeating the Current Execution of a Loop

The redo command causes a loop to repeat without evaluating its condition or iterating. Any statements that follow the redo command in the loop are skipped. You can use the redo command to force a loop to execute again if something occurs that you do not like. For example, if you've set up a loop to process user input and the user provides invalid input, the redo command will discard the input by forcing the loop to execute again. To see how this command works, look at the following example:

```
i = 1

loop do
  puts i
  redo if i == 3
  i += 1
end
```

Here, a loop is set up that will execute forever. Each time the loop repeats, the value of a variable named i is incremented by 1. The second statement within the loop conditionally executes the redo command when the value of i becomes 3. After the third iteration of the loop, therefore, the redo command is executed, which prevents the last statement in the loop from executing again, resulting in an endless stream of 3s. (The following output is arbitrarily halted after the display of the third "3.")

```
1
2
3
3
3
```

Skipping to the Next Iteration of a Loop

The next command stops the current iteration of the loop and immediately begins a new iteration. However, before the new iteration occurs, the loop condition is evaluated. Thus, the loop only executes again if the analysis of the loop condition permits it. To see how this command works, look at the following example:

```
for i in 1..5
  next if i == 3
  puts i
end
```

Here, a for...in loop is set up to execute over a range of numbers, starting at 1 and going through 5. Upon the third execution of the loop, when the value of i is equal to 3, the next command is executed. However, the loop continues executing two more times, resulting in the following output:

```
1
2
4
5
```

Restarting a Loop from the Beginning

The `retry` command restarts a loop from the beginning by resetting the loop's iterator to its starting value, as shown here:

```
for i in 1..5
  puts i
  retry if i == 3
end
```

Here, a `for...in` loop is set up that repeats for a range of numbers from 1 to 5. Each time the loop runs, the value of i is displayed. When the value of i becomes equal to 3, the `retry` command is executed, starting the loop over again. An endless loop has been created that repeatedly counts from 1 to 3, as shown here:

```
1
2
3
1
2
3
```

(This output is arbitrarily cut short. It would normally consist of endless repetitions of the series 1 2 3.)

Short Quiz

1. (True/False) The each method automatically repeats or iterates once for every item stored within an array.

2. (True/False) A loop created using the loop method executes only one time by default.

3. Ruby supplies a number of different methods for altering a loop's default execution. These methods include all of the following except:

   a. break

   b. next

   c. repeat

   d. retry

4. (True/False) An iterator is a variable used within a loop to keep track of the number of times the loop has repeated.

5. Which of the following methods can be used to restart a loop from the beginning?

   a. break

   b. next

   c. redo

   d. retry

Back to the Superman Movie Trivia Quiz

It is time to develop this chapter's game project, the Superman Movie Trivia Quiz. As you create this script, focus on using loops to prompt the player for permission to start the quiz, making sure only valid input is accepted.

Designing the Game

The development of the Superman Movie Trivia Quiz is completed in 12 steps, as outlined here:

1. Open your text or script editor, and create a new file.

2. Add comment statements to the beginning of the script file to document the script and its purpose.

3. Define a Screen class representing the terminal window.

4. Define a Quiz class representing the game's quiz.

5. Add a display_greeting method to the Quiz class.

6. Add a display_instructions method to the Quiz class.

7. Add a disp_q method to the Quiz class.

8. Add a determine_grade method to the Quiz class.

9. Add a display_credits method to the Quiz class.

10. Instantiate script objects.

11. Prompt the player for permission to begin the quiz.

12. Administer the quiz.

Follow along carefully, do not skip any steps, and look out for typos.

Step 1: Create a New Ruby File

Open your text or script editor, and create a new Ruby script file. Save the file with the name SupermanQuiz.rb, and store it in the folder with your other Ruby scripts.

Step 2: Document the Script and Its Purpose

Add the following comment statements to the new script file. These comments provide a description of the script and its purpose.

```
#------------------------------------------------------------
#
# Script Name: SupermanQuiz.rb
# Version:     1.0
# Author:      Jerry Lee Ford, Jr.
# Date:        March 2010
#
# Description: This Ruby script demonstrates how to work
#              with loops when collecting user input
#              through the creation of an interactive
#              quiz that evaluates the player's knowledge
#              of the Superman movie series.
#
#------------------------------------------------------------
```

Step 3: Define the *Screen* Class

The Superman Movie Trivia Quiz uses two custom classes, Screen and Quiz, each of which contains numerous methods for controlling the interaction with the user and executing the game. Define a new class named Screen by adding the following statements to the end of the script file:

```
# Define custom classes ------------------------------------

#Define a class representing the console window
class Screen

  def cls  #Define a method that clears the display area
    puts ("\n" * 25)  #Scroll the screen 25 times
    puts "\a"  #Make a little noise to get the player's
               #attention
  end

  def pause     #Define a method that pauses the display
                #area
    STDIN.gets  #Execute the STDIN class's gets method to
                #pause script execution until the player
                #presses the Enter key
  end

end
```

The first method defined in this class is the cls method. It contains two statements. The first statement writes 25 blank lines to the terminal window to clear the screen. The second statement processes a string containing the \a escape character, which makes a beep sound, thus notifying the player that the terminal screen has been cleared. The second method is used to pause the script's execution until the player presses Enter.

Step 4: Define the Quiz Class

The Quiz class contains the methods used to control the execution of the quiz. Define the Quiz class by adding the following statements to the end of the script file:

```
#Define a class representing the Superman Movie Trivia Quiz
class Quiz

end
```

Step 5: Define the display_greeting Method

Define the first of five methods belonging to the Quiz class by inserting the following statements between the class's opening and closing statements:

```
#This method displays the quiz's opening screen
def display_greeting

  Console_Screen.cls  #Clear the display area

  #Display welcome message
  print "\t\t  Welcome to the Superman Movie Trivia Quiz!" +
    "\n\n\n\n\n\n\n\n\n\n\n\n\nPress Enter to " +
    "continue."

  Console_Screen.pause      #Pause the game

end
```

This method, named display_greeting, displays the game's welcome screen.

Step 6: Define the *display_instructions* Method

Define the second of five methods belonging to the Quiz class by adding the following statements at the end of the class definition, immediately after the display_greeting method:

```
#Define a method to be used to present quiz instructions
def display_instructions

    Console_Screen.cls        #Clear the display area
    puts "INSTRUCTIONS:\n\n"   #Display a heading

    #Display the game's instructions
    puts "You will be presented with a series of " +
        "multiple-choice"
    puts "questions. To answer a question, type in " +
        "the letter of"
    puts "the corresponding answer and press the " +
        "Enter key. Your"
    puts "grade will be displayed at the end of the " +
        "test.\n\n\n"
    puts "Good luck!\n\n\n\n\n\n\n\n"
    print "Press Enter to continue."

    Console_Screen.pause        #Pause the game

end
```

This method, named display_instructions, displays a series of text strings containing instructions for taking the Superman Movie Trivia Quiz.

Step 7: Define the *disp_q* Method

The disp_q method presents the quiz questions and processes the player's answers. Define this third of five methods belonging to the Quiz class by adding the following statements to the end of the class definition:

```
#Define a method to be used to present and process quiz
#questions
def disp_q(question, q_A, q_B, q_C, q_D, answer)

    #Loop until the player inputs a valid answer
    loop do

        Console_Screen.cls        #Clear the display area

        #Format the display of the quiz question
        puts question + "\n\n"
        puts q_A
        puts q_B
        puts q_C
        puts q_D
```

```
  print "\nType the letter representing your answer: "

  reply = STDIN.gets   #Collect the player's answer
  reply.chop!          #Remove the end of line marker

  #Analyze the player's input to determine if it is
  #correct
  if answer == reply then

    #Keep track of the number of correctly answered
    #questions
    $noRight += 1

  end

  #Analyze the answer to determine if it was valid
  if reply == "a" or reply == "b" or reply == "c" or
     reply == "d" then

    break  #Terminate the execution of the loop

  end

  end

end
```

This method consists of a loop that repeatedly executes until the player provides a valid answer of a, b, c, or d to the current quiz question. Calling statements pass a series of arguments to the method. The first argument is a text string that represents the quiz question. The next four arguments are mapped to variables named q_A, q_B, q_C, and q_D, which represent the four possible answers to that question. The last argument specifies the answer to the question and is assigned to a variable named answer.

Once these assignments have been made, the screen is cleared, and then the quiz question is displayed. The player's answer is captured and stored in a variable named reply. Next, an if statement is set up to see if the value of reply is equal to the value assigned to answer, which means the player has correctly answered the question. If this is the case, the value of $noRight is incremented by 1 to keep track of the number of correctly answered questions.

The last set of statements conditionally examines the player's input to make sure it is valid (e.g., the player entered a, b, c, or d and nothing else). If it is valid, the break command is executed, terminating the execution of the loop.

Step 8: Define the *determine_grade* Method

The determine_grade method determines whether the player has passed the quiz. Define this fourth of five methods belonging to the Quiz class by adding the following statements to the end of the class definition:

```
#Define a method to be used to grade and display quiz
#results
def determine_grade

   Console_Screen.cls        #Clear the display area

   #To pass the test, the player must correctly answer at
   #least 3 questions
   if $noRight >= 3 then

      #Inform the player of the good news and assign a
      #ranking
      print "You correctly answered " + $noRight.to_s + "↵
         question(s). "
      puts "You have passed the \nSuperman Movie Trivia" +
         "Quiz!\n\n"
      puts "You have earned a rank of: Good Citizen" if↵
         $noRight == 3
      puts "You have earned a rank of: Side Kick"↵
         if $noRight == 4
      puts "You have earned a rank of: Superhero"↵
         if $noRight == 5
      print "\n\nPress Enter to continue."

   else #The player has failed the quiz

      #Inform the player of the bad news
      print "You missed " + (5 - $noRight).to_s +
         " questions. "
      puts "You have failed the Superman Movie Trivia Quiz."
      puts "Perhaps you should watch the movies again before↵
         returning to"
      puts "retake the quiz"
      print "\n\nPress Enter to continue."

   end

   Console_Screen.pause        #Pause the game

end
```

To pass the quiz, the player must correctly answer at least three questions. The grade is determined by an if expression that evaluates the value assigned to $noRight. If the value is greater than or equal to three, a series of puts statements is executed, notifying the player of a passing grade. The puts statements also assign the player a ranking based on the number of questions answered correctly. A ranking of Good Citizen is assigned when the player answers at least three

questions correctly. A ranking of Side Kick is assigned when the
player answers four questions correctly. And a ranking of Superhero
is assigned when the player answers all five questions correctly.

If the value of $noRight is less than 3, however, the player is informed
of a failing grade and told how many questions were missed.

Step 9: Define the *display_credits* Method

The display_credits method displays information about the quiz
and its developer, including the developer's URL. Define this fifth
of five methods belonging to the Quiz class by adding the following
statements to the end of the class definition:

```
#This method displays the information about the Superman
#Movie Trivia Quiz
def display_credits

    Console_Screen.cls  #Clear the display area

    #Thank the player and display game information
    puts "\t\tThank you for taking the SUPERMAN MOVIE TRIVIA ⏎
        QUIZ.\n\n\n\n"
    puts "\n\t\t\t Developed by Jerry Lee Ford, Jr.\n\n"
    puts "\t\t\t\t Copyright 2011\n\n"
    puts "\t\t\tURL: http://www.tech-publishing.com\n\n\n\n\n ⏎
        \n\n\n\n\n\n"

end
```

Step 10: Instantiate Script Objects

Instantiate two objects named Console_Screen and SQ, based on the
Console_Screen and Quiz classes, by adding the following statements
to the end of the script file:

```
# Main Script Logic ------------------------------------

#Initialize global variable that will be used to keep
#track of the number of correctly answered quiz
#questions
$noRight = 0

Console_Screen = Screen.new  #Instantiate a new Screen
                             #object
SQ = Quiz.new     #Instantiate a new Quiz object

#Execute the Quiz class's display_greeting method
SQ.display_greeting
```

In addition to instantiating the Console_Screen and SQ objects, these
statements define a global variable named $noRight, which is used
both to keep track of the number of correctly answered questions and
to execute the Quiz class's display_greeting method.

Step 11: Get Permission to Start the Quiz

Set up the prompt for getting the player's permission to play the game by adding the following statements to the end of the script file:

```
answer = ""

#Loop until the player enters y or n and do not accept any
#other input.
loop do

  Console_Screen.cls  #Clear the display area

  #Prompt the player for permission to start the quiz
  print "Are you ready to take the quiz? (y/n): "

  answer = STDIN.gets #Collect the player's response
  answer.chop!   #Remove one character from the end of
                 #the string

  break if answer == "y" || answer == "n"

end
```

Here, a loop is set up to execute until the player provides a valid response (y or n), at which time the break command is executed to terminate the loop and continue the quiz.

Step 12: Administer the Quiz

All that remains is to supply the programming logic that either starts the quiz or terminates it (if the player has decided not to take it). Add the following statements to the end of the script file:

```
#Analyze the player's input
if answer == "n"  #See if the player elected not to take
                  #the quiz

  Console_Screen.cls  #Clear the display area

  #Invite the player to return and take the quiz some
  #other time
  puts "Okay, perhaps another time.\n\n"

else #The player wants to take the quiz

  #Execute the Quiz class's display_instructions method
  SQ.display_instructions

  #Execute the Quiz class's disp_q method and pass it
  #arguments representing a question, possible answers and
  #the letter of the correct answer
```

```
SQ.disp_q("What is the name of the Daily Planet's ace" +
 "photographer?", "a. Jimmy Olsen", "b. Clark Kent," +
 "c. Lex Luthor", "d. Lois Lane","a")

#Call upon the disp_q method and pass it the second
#question
SQ.disp_q("What is the name of Clark Kent's home town?",
 "a. Metropolis", "b. Gotham City", "c. Smallville",
 "d. New York", "c")

#Call upon the disp_q method and pass it the third
#question
SQ.disp_q("In which movie did Superman battle" +
"General Zod?", "a. Superman", "b. Superman II",
"c. Superman III",  "d. Superman IV", "b")

#Call upon the disp_q method and pass it the fourth
#question
SQ.disp_q("What is the name of Superman's father?",
    "a. Nimo", "b. Jarrell", "c. Lex Luthor", "d. Krypton", "b")

#Call upon the disp_q method and pass it the fifth
#question
SQ.disp_q("Where had Superman been at the start of " +
 "'Superman Returns'?", "a. Moon", "b. Fortress of Solitude",
 "c. Earth's Core", "d. Krypton", "d")

#Call upon the Quiz class's determine_grade method to
#display the player's grade and assigned rank
SQ.determine_grade

#Call upon the Quiz class's display_credits method to
#thank the player for taking the quiz and to display
#game information
SQ.display_credits
```

end

As you can see, these statements are controlled by a large if statement. The first part of the statement checks whether the player has responded with a value of n when prompted for permission to take the quiz. These statements clear the screen and then display a message that encourages the player to take the quiz another time.

If the player decides to take the quiz, the statements in the else portion of the if code block are executed. They consist of a series of calls to methods belonging to the SQ and Console_Screen objects. The first method called is the display_instructions method, followed by five calls to the disp_q method. Each of these five calls passes a different set of arguments, representing a quiz question, four multiple-choice answers, and the correct answer. Once all five quiz questions have been processed by the `disp_q` method, the `Quiz` class's `determine_grade` method is called. This method is responsible for determining whether the player passed the quiz. Finally, the `display_credits` method is called. This clears the screen and displays a message thanking the player for taking the quiz.

Running Your New Ruby Script Game

Save your Ruby script. If you typed the code statements correctly, the program should work as expected. If you run into any errors, read the error messages carefully to ascertain what went wrong. If necessary, review the script and look for mistyped or missing statements.

Summing Up

- Loops allow you to repeat a set of statements as many times as necessary to perform a particular task.

- Ruby provides access to many different types of loops. They can be organized into the following three categories: language constructs, modifiers, and methods.

- Ruby supports the `while`, `until`, and `for` loops as part of the core programming language.

- The `while` loop executes as long as a tested condition remains true.

- An endless loop is a loop set up in such a way that it never stops executing, unnecessarily using computer resources.

- The `until` loop executes until the tested condition becomes true.

- The `for...in` loop processes collections of data.

- An array is an indexed collection of items stored as a list.

- The Ruby range operator (`..`) allows you to display a range of consecutive letters or numbers.

- A `loop` modifier is an expression added to the end of a Ruby statement that causes the statement to be executed as a loop.

- The `while` modifier evaluates a Boolean expression and then executes the statement as long as the Boolean expression remains true.

- The `until` modifier causes a statement to be repeatedly executed until a specified condition is evaluated as true.

- The `each` method automatically iterates once for each item stored in an array.

- The `times` method executes a code block a specific number of times.

- An iterator is a variable used to process the contents of a list of items.

- The `upto` method causes a loop to iterate a predetermined number of times.

- The `downto` method causes a loop to iterate a predetermined number of times, starting at a specified integer value and counting down to whatever integer value is passed to it.

- The `step` method is used to set up loops that execute a given number of times, based on the start, end, and step values.

- Loops created using the `loop` method run forever unless you provide a way to terminate them.

- The `break` command terminates the execution of a loop.

- The `redo` command repeats the current execution of a loop without evaluating its condition and without iterating.

- The `next` command stops the current iteration of a loop and immediately begins a new iteration.

- The `retry` command restarts the loop from the beginning, resetting the value of the iterator to its initial value.

Comprehension Check

1. (True/False) A `loop` method is an expression added to the end of a Ruby statement to have the statement executed as a loop.

2. The _____ modifier causes a statement to be repeatedly executed until a specified condition evaluates as true.

3. Which of the following statements accurately identifies the `times` method?

    a. It iterates once for every item stored in a list.

    b. It executes repeatedly as long as a tested condition evaluates as true.

    c. It is used to execute a code block a specified number of times.

    d. None of the above

4. The **each** method is supported by which of the following Ruby classes?

   a. array

   b. dir

   c. range

   d. All of the above

5. The _____ command restarts a loop over from the beginning, resetting the value of the iterator.

6. Which of the following commands terminates the execution of a loop?

   a. break

   b. redo

   c. next

   d. retry

7. Ruby provides support for loops in which of the following ways?

   a. Statement modifiers

   b. Object methods

   c. Language constructs

   d. All of the above

8. (True/False) The **until** loop executes until a tested condition becomes false.

9. The _____ loop can process a range of items.

10. The _____ command stops the current iteration of a loop and begins a new iteration.

11. (True/False) The **while**, **for**, and **until** loops are sometimes regarded as outdated.

12. Which of the following commands repeats the current execution of a loop?

    a. `break`

    b. `redo`

    c. `next`

    d. `retry`

13. The _____ method iterates a predetermined number of times, starting at a specified integer value and counting down to whatever integer value is passed to it.

14. (True/False) The `while` loop executes for as long as a tested condition remains false.

15. The _____ method executes a code block a specified number of times.

16. Which of the following statements is true of loops?

    a. Loops facilitate the development of scripts that repeat key steps over and over.

    b. Loops provide a mechanism for processing enormous amounts of user input.

    c. Loops help reduce the size of scripts by using a minimal number of statements.

    d. All of the above

17. (True/False) The `each` method is designed to process collections of data.

18. Which of the following methods does not execute a loop a predetermined number of times?

    a. `each`

    b. `step`

    c. `times`

    d. All of the above

19. (True/False) The `for...in` loop processes collections of data, such as arrays or a range of values.

20. Which of the following methods belongs to the `Kernel` module and executes forever unless you find a way to terminate its execution.

    a. `loop`

    b. `step`

    c. `each`

    d. None of the above

Reinforcement Exercises

The following exercises are designed to further your understanding of Ruby programming by challenging you to make improvements to the chapter's game project, the Superman Movie Trivia Quiz.

1. Currently, the Superman Movie Trivia Quiz consists of five questions. Make the quiz more challenging by increasing its size to 10 questions. To implement this change, copy the last of the five statements that call on the `Quiz` object's `disp_q` method to pose a quiz question. Add five copies of the statement immediately after the copied statement's question (along with the corresponding answers). You will also have to adjust the way the method calculates the number of questions missed. To do so, modify the `determine_grade` method so that six or more questions must be correctly answered to pass the quiz.

2. Give players the opportunity to take the quiz again if they fail. To implement this change, add the appropriate statements in a loop within the script's Main Script Logic section (added to the program file in Step 10). Prompt the player to take the quiz again if fewer than six questions are answered correctly. If the player elects not to retake the quiz, terminate the execution of the loop and allow the quiz to end.

3. Modify the quiz so that if the player decides not to take the quiz, the game still displays the text displayed by the `display_credits` method. To implement this change, replace the statements at the end of the program file that invite the player to play again with a statement that executes the `Quiz` object's `display_credits` method.

4. Currently, players who fail the quiz are advised to watch all the Superman movies before retaking it. There's also a Wikipedia page that provides information about each Superman movie. Modify the game to provide players with this web page's URL (i.e., *http://en.wikipedia.org/wiki/ Superman_movies*). To implement this change, modify the statements in the Quiz object's determine_grade method that are responsible for displaying output text.

5. Currently, the quiz does not inform players about the grading scale. As such, they have no way of ascertaining how they are doing until the game ends and their grades are displayed. Modify the game so that the player has the option of reading about the grade scale.

   To implement this change, modify the Quiz object's display_instructions method by adding the programming logic needed to collect player input. Then add a new method named disp_scale to the Quiz object and program it to display the quiz's grading scale. Lastly, go back to the display_instructions method and add a statement that calls upon the disp_scale method whenever the player elects to view it.

Discovery Projects

 Project 5-1

Loops are very flexible and can be configured in various ways. To demonstrate this, modify the following pair of examples so that instead of counting from 1 to 10, they count from 10 to 1.

```
x = 1
while x <= 10 do
  puts x
  x += 1
end

x = 1
until x > 10 do
  puts x
  x += 1
end
```

Project 5-2

Loops are an effective means for processing the contents stored within arrays. In the following example, an array named MyList is defined. It contains five text strings representing individual names. The Array object's each method then loops through the array and displays each of its elements.

```
MyList = ["Molly", "William", "Alexander", "Jerry", "Mary"]

MyList.each do |x|
  print "Hi ", x, "!\n"
end
```

The Array object also supports a method called sort, which, as its name suggests, sorts the contents of an array. To learn more about this method, visit *http://ruby-doc.org/core/classes/Array.html*. After that, modify the previous example so that it sorts the contents of the array, then iterates through it and displays the sorted values.

Project 5-3

An endless loop is one that is set up in such a way that it never stops executing, thereby wasting computer resources. To learn more about endless loops, go to *http://en.wikipedia.org/wiki/Endless_loop*. After that, create an endless loop using either an until or a while loop. Submit a printed copy of your script file along with a paragraph explaining what makes the loop endless and what must be done to correct it.

## CHAPTER 6

Working with Collections of Data

In this chapter, you learn how to:

- ◎ Store and manipulate lists using arrays
- ◎ Replace and add array items
- ◎ Retrieve items from arrays
- ◎ Store and manipulate lists using hashes
- ◎ Add hash key-value pairs
- ◎ Delete hash key-value pairs
- ◎ Retrieve data stored in hashes
- ◎ Create the Ruby Number Guessing game

Variables are an excellent way to store and manage small amounts of information, but what if you need to work with dozens, hundreds, or even thousands of pieces of data, like you might find in a personal address book or a small database? This chapter demonstrates how to manage large groups of related data using arrays and hashes. With these tools, you can develop Ruby scripts capable of storing, retrieving, and manipulating huge amounts of data with a minimum of programming statements.

Project Preview: The Ruby Number Guessing Game

In this chapter, you create a computer game called the Ruby Number Guessing game. It challenges the player to guess a randomly generated number from 1 to 100 in as few tries as possible.

The game begins by displaying the welcome screen shown in Figure 6-1.

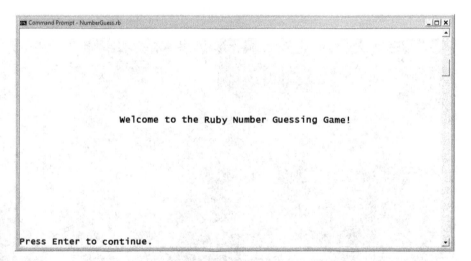

Figure 6-1   The welcome screen for the Ruby Number Guessing game

After pressing Enter, the player is prompted for permission to begin the game, as shown in Figure 6-2.

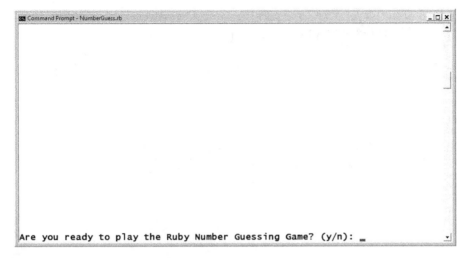

Figure 6-2 The game prompts the player for permission to begin

To begin the game, the player must type y and press Enter. Alternatively, the player can type n to instruct the game to terminate. Any input other than y or n is ignored. If the player elects not to play, the message shown in Figure 6-3 is displayed.

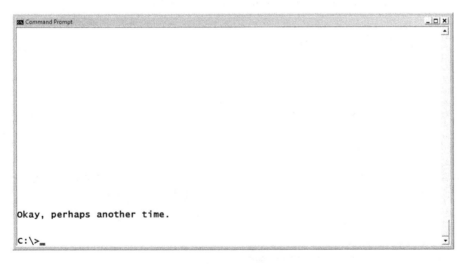

Figure 6-3 The player is encouraged to play another time

If the player decides to play the game, the instructions shown in Figure 6-4 are displayed.

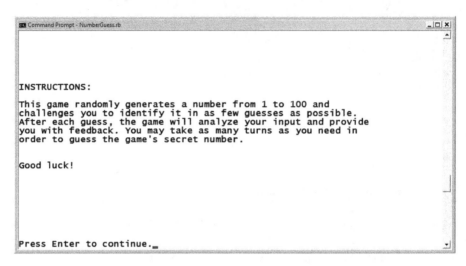

Figure 6-4   The game provides the player with instructions on how to play

Once the player has read the instructions and pressed Enter, she is prompted to make an initial guess, as shown in Figure 6-5.

Figure 6-5   The player is prompted to enter a guess

After each guess, the game gives the player a hint to help her hone in on the number. Figure 6-6 shows the message that is displayed when the guess is too high.

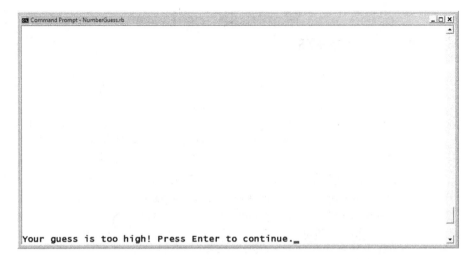

Command Prompt - NumberGuess.rb

Your guess is too high! Press Enter to continue.

Figure 6-6   The game notifies the player that the guess is too high

The player may take as many tries as necessary to correctly guess the number. At that time, the message shown in Figure 6-7 is displayed.

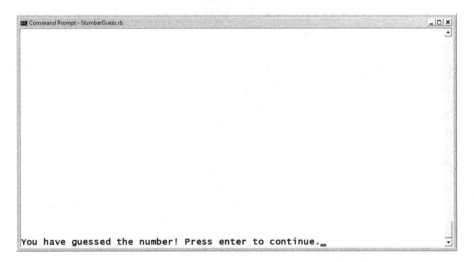

Command Prompt - NumberGuess.rb

You have guessed the number! Press enter to continue.

Figure 6-7   The player has won the game by guessing the number

After pressing Enter, the player is prompted for permission to play the game again, allowing her to play as many times as she wants.

Storing and Manipulating Lists Using Arrays

So far, all the examples in this book have involved the storage, manipulation, and retrieval of small amounts of data. Variables have been used as the primary means of managing that data. As your scripts grow longer and more complex, however, the amount of data becomes too large to be effectively managed using variables. For these projects, as long as the data is related, you can manage it using a list.

A **list** is a collection of data, like a set of names or account numbers. Within Ruby programs, items in a list are separated by commas. In Ruby, lists can be used to populate arrays. An **array** is an indexed list of items. In Ruby, array indexes begin at 0 and are incremented by 1 each time a new item is added. Index numbers can only be whole numbers (nonnegative integers). In Ruby, arrays are viewed as objects.

Ruby arrays have an initial item, a final item, and any number of items in between. Once added to an array, an item is referred to by specifying the array name and its index position within the array. The following syntax is used when creating an array:

```
VariableName = [Elements]
```

Here, *VariableName* represents the name of the array, and *Elements* represents the contents of the array. The array itself is stored as a list enclosed within square brackets, the individual items separated by commas. As an example, the following statement defines an array named x and stores five numbers in it:

```
x = [2, 4, 6, 8, 10]
```

Most of Ruby's object classes support the method called inspect. It is used here to display a list of the items stored in the array.

You can experiment with arrays using IRB. Start an IRB session, type the preceding statement, and then press Enter to execute it. The x array is defined and is now ready for you to do something with it. Use the inspect method to view the array's contents, as shown here:

```
irb(main):002:0> puts x.inspect
[2, 4, 6, 8, 10]
```

You can use arrays to store any types of objects Ruby supports. For example, the following statement defines an array called children and stores three text strings in it:

```
children = ["Alexander", "William", "Molly"]
```

Managing Data Using Arrays

Ruby does not require you to define an array before using it. All you have to do is reference it, and Ruby defines the array. Ruby also does not require you to specify in advance how big an array will be.

Instead, you can expand the array as you go along, adding as many items as you want.

Creating Arrays

One way to create an array is to define it and assign a list to it in the same step, as shown here:

```
children = ["Alexander", "William", "Molly"]
```

You can do the same thing by using the %w(and) characters, as shown here:

```
children = %w(Alexander William Molly)
```

Here, an array named children is defined and assigned three strings. The array is created by retrieving string items separated by spaces. The advantage of creating a string array this way is that you do not have to provide quote marks or commas.

Another Way of Creating Arrays

Another way to create an array is with an object-oriented approach using the Array object's new method, as shown here:

```
x = Array.new
```

Here, an empty array named x is created. You might use the new method, for example, to create an array at the beginning of a program, knowing that the data that the array will store will not be generated until later, when the program executes. Another way of creating an empty array is shown here:

```
x = []
```

Here, an array named x is created but isn't assigned a list.

Using the Content of One Array to Create Another Array

You can also create an array by assigning the contents of one array to another array, as shown here:

```
x = [1, 2, 3]
y = x
```

Here, an array named x, which contains three numbers, is assigned to a variable named y. As a result of the assignment, y is set up as an array containing a list of three numbers. To prove that the y array was created, you can use the inspect method, as shown here:

```
puts y.inspect
```

When it is executed, this statement displays the following result:

```
[1, 2, 3]
```

Creating an Array from Two Existing Arrays

You can also create an array by adding two arrays together using the + operator, as shown here:

```
x = [1, 2, 3]
y = [4, 5, 6]
z = x + y
puts z.inspect
```

When used to add two arrays together, the + operator places the array items together consecutively, with the array items in the second array following the array items in the first array. When executed, this example displays the following output:

```
[1, 2, 3, 4, 5, 6]
```

Using the Subtraction Operator to Create an Array

You can also create an array using the subtraction operator, which is represented by a minus sign. Array subtraction consists of taking two arrays and removing any items from the first array that are also in the second array, which results in a new array, as shown here:

```
family = %w(Alexander William Molly Daddy Mommy)
parents = %w(Daddy Mommy)
children = family - parents
puts children.inspect
```

Here, two arrays are defined, one named family that has five items and one named parents that has two items. A new array named children is created by subtracting parents from family. When executed, this example displays the following output:

```
["Alexander", "William", "Molly"]
```

As you can see, the items found in both the family and parents arrays are not part of the children array.

Replacing and Adding Array Items

Ruby allows you to replace or add items to an array. Using the methods outlined in the sections that follow, you will learn how to replace individual array items. In addition, you will learn a number of ways to add items to the end of arrays.

Adding or Replacing Array Items Based on Index Position

One way of adding or replacing array items is to specify the array name and index position of the item to be added or replaced using the syntax shown here:

arrayname[*indexNo*]

Here, *arrayname* is the name of the array, and *indexNo* is the index position of the array item that is to be added or replaced.

Replacing an Array Item

To get a feel for how to modify an array item, look at the following example, which replaces one of the items stored in an array:

```
children = ["Alexander", "William", "Molly"]
children [2] = "Mighty One"
puts children.inspect
```

Here, an array named `children` is defined and assigned three items. Next, the item stored at index position 2 is replaced with a value of "`Mighty One`". When executed, this example displays the following output:

```
["Alexander", "William", "Mighty One"]
```

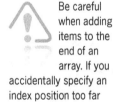

The index positions in a Ruby array start with 0, so the first item has an index position of 0, and the second item has an index position of 1.

Adding an Item to an Array

You add an item to an array by using the index position that is one greater than the index position of the last item stored in the array, as shown here:

```
children = ["Alexander", "William", "Molly"]
children[3] = "Dolly"
puts children.inspect
```

The first statement defines an array named `children`, assigning it three string items. The second statement adds a fourth item to the end of the array by specifying index position 3. The last method uses the inspect method to display the array's contents, as shown here:

```
["Alexander", "William", "Molly", "Dolly"]
```

Be careful when adding items to the end of an array. If you accidentally specify an index position too far beyond what was previously the last index position, you will end up with a range of undefined items.

Working with the << Method

In Ruby, an array is an object, so you can call on any of the methods associated with Ruby's `Array` class. Using the << method, for instance, you can add items to an array by appending them to the end of the array, as shown here:

```
Names = []
Names << "Alexander"
Names << "William"
Names << "Molly"
puts Names.inspect
```

When executed, the `Names` array contains the following list of items:

```
["Alexander", "William", "Molly"]
```

Working with the *push* Method

You can also use the push method to add items to an array by pushing them onto the end of the array, as shown here:

```
Names = []
Names.push("Alexander")
Names.push("William")
Names.push("Molly")
puts Names.inspect
```

When executed, the Names array contains the following list of items:

```
["Alexander", "William", "Molly"]
```

Determining if an Array Is Empty

Before working with an array, you may want to see if it contains any items. One way to do this is by using the Array class's length or size method to see if it returns a value equal to zero. An easier way to do it is to use the empty? method, which returns a value of **true** if the array is empty and a value of **false** if it contains at least one item.

For an example of how to work with the empty? method, look at the following:

```
children = ["Alexander", "William", "Molly"]
if children.empty? == false then
  children.each {|child| puts child}
else
  puts "The children array is empty"
end
```

Here, an array is defined that contains three strings. An if statement is then set up that uses the empty? method to determine if the children array has any items in it. If it does, the each method displays the names of each item in the list. If the array is empty, a text message is displayed instead.

Retrieving Items from an Array

There are many ways to retrieve the data stored in an array. You can retrieve items based on actual or relative positions or you can retrieve whole ranges of items.

Retrieving Individual Array Items Based on Index Position

To retrieve an item in an array, specify the name of the array followed by the item's index position, as shown here:

```
children = ["Alexander", "William", "Molly"]
middleChild = children[1]
```

Here, the first statement defines an array named `children` and assigns three items to it. The second statement assigns the value of the second item in the array (`"William"`) to a variable named `middleChild`.

Retrieving Individual Array Items Using the *at* Method

You can also use the `Array` class's `at` method to retrieve an individual array item. The method uses an integer value (corresponding to the index position) passed to it as an argument, as shown here:

```
children = %w(Alexander William Molly)
puts children.at(1)
```

Here, an array named `children` is defined, then the `at` method is used to retrieve a value of `"William"` from the `children` array.

Retrieving a *slice*

You can retrieve a range of items, referred to as a `slice`, by using the `Array` class's `slice` method. Simply enclose a list or range of index positions within a pair of parentheses, as shown here:

```
children = %w(Alexander William Molly)
boys = children.slice(0..1)
```

When executed, the `slice` method retrieves the first and second items stored in the `children` array and assigns them to the `boys` array.

Retrieving the First and Last Items

You can retrieve the first item of an array by using the `Array` class's `first` method, as shown here:

```
children = %w(Alexander William Molly)
puts children.first
```

When executed, these statements display the following output:

```
Alexander
```

You can retrieve the last item from an array by using the `Array` class's `last` method, as shown here:

```
children = %w(Alexander William Molly)
puts children.last
```

When executed, these statements display the following output:

```
Molly
```

Ruby also lets you retrieve the contents of an array by using negative index positions. The index position –1 refers to the last item in the array, –2 refers to the second-to-last item, and so on.

Using a Loop to Iterate Through the Contents of an Array

As was shown in Chapter 5, loops allow you to process the contents of an array using a minimal number of script statements. You can use the `while` and `until` loops to process the contents of an array, of course, but the `Array` class's `each` method is tailor-made to process arrays.

The following statements show how to set up a loop that displays each item in an array named `children`:

```
children = %w(Alexander William Molly)
children.each do |child|
  puts child
end
```

Here, an array named `children` is defined. The `each` method is used to automatically repeat once for each item stored in the specified array. Each time the loop iterates, the value of the current array item is assigned to the `child` variable, which is then displayed, resulting in the following output:

```
Alexander
William
Molly
```

Deleting Items from an Array

Ruby provides a number of object methods for deleting array items. You can delete all the items in an array, or you can delete particular items based on their positions within the array. You can also delete items based on their values.

Deleting All the Items

You can delete all the items stored in an array by using the `Array` class's `clear` method, as shown here:

```
children = %w(Alexander William Molly)
children.clear
```

Here, an array named `children` is defined, and the `clear` method is used to delete all the items stored in an array named `children`, resulting in an empty array.

Deleting the First Item

You can delete the first item in an array by using the Array class's shift method (which shifts the index positions of all the remaining items down by one), as shown here:

```
children = %w(Alexander William Molly)
x = children.shift
puts children.inspect
```

Here, an array named children is defined, and the shift method is used to retrieve the value of the first item stored in the array, which is assigned to the x variable. The shift method also deletes the first item from the array, which results in an array named children that contains the following list of items:

```
["William", "Molly"]
```

Deleting the Last Item

You can delete the last item in an array by using the Array class's pop method, as shown here:

```
family = %w(Alexander William Molly Daddy Mommy)
family.pop
family.pop
puts family.inspect
```

Here, an array named family is assigned five items. Next, the pop method is used twice, removing the last two items from the array. As a result, the family array is left with the following list of items:

```
["Alexander", "William", "Molly"]
```

Deleting Items Based on Their Values

Instead of deleting array items based on their positions, you can delete them based on their values. To do this, pass an argument to the Array class's delete method that identifies the value used to identify the items to be deleted, as shown here:

```
fruit = %w(Apples Oranges Bananas Oranges Grapes)
fruit.delete("Oranges")
```

Here, an array named fruit is defined and assigned five items. Next, the Array class's delete method is executed and passed a value of "Oranges". Based on this input, the delete method removes two items from the fruit array, leaving the array with the following list of items:

```
["Apples", "Bananas", "Grapes"]
```

Deleting Items Based on Their Index Positions

You can delete an item based on its index position by using the Array class's delete_at method, as shown here:

```
fruit = %w(Apples Pears Bananas Oranges Grapes)
fruit.delete_at(3)
```

Here an array named fruit is defined and assigned five items. Next, the Array class's delete_at method is executed and passed an argument of 3. The method removes the item from the array stored in index position 3 (i.e., its fourth item). As a result, the fruit array ends up containing the following list of items:

```
["Apples", "Pears", "Bananas", "Grapes"]
```

When an item is deleted using the delete_at method, all the items that follow it in the array are automatically shifted to the left one position.

194

The Array class's insert_at method is the opposite of the delete_at method. It adds an item to an array at the specified index position. To make room for the new item, all the items after it are shifted to the right one position.

Sorting the Contents of an Array Alphabetically

By default, array items are stored in the order they were added to the array. This may not be the order you want them to be in, however. To sort the contents of an array alphabetically, use the Array class's sort method, as shown here:

```
fruit = %w(Apples Oranges Bananas Grapes)
puts fruit.sort.inspect
```

Here, an array named fruit is created and assigned four items. The contents of the array are then sorted and displayed, as shown here. Notice that, in this example, the contents of the array itself remain unaltered.

```
["Apples", "Bananas", "Grapes", "Oranges"]
```

In the fruit-sorting example, the output of the sort method is input for the inspect method. The two methods are said to be chained together.

Sorting Array Contents in Reverse Alphabetical Order

The Array class's reverse method reverses the order of array items after they have been sorted, as shown here:

```
fruit = %w(Apples Oranges Bananas Grapes)
puts fruit.sort.reverse.inspect
```

Here, the items stored in the fruit array are first sorted alphabetically. Next, the order of the sorted items is reversed. Finally, the inspect method displays the resulting list:

```
["Oranges", "Grapes", "Bananas", "Apples"]
```

Searching an Array

You can find something stored in an array by setting up a loop, but if the array contains thousands of items, processing its contents takes a lot of time. Before you perform such a resource-intensive operation, use the Array class's `include?` method to see if the array contains the item or items you are looking for, as shown here:

```
children = %w(Alexander William Molly)
puts "I found him!" if children.include?("William")
```

Here, an array named `children` is created, and the `include?` method is used to search the `children` array to see if it contains a value of `"William"`. If it does, the string `I found him!` is displayed. Once you determine that an array contains the item or items you are looking for, you can decide whether to loop through the array and process the items in some way.

Short Quiz

1. (True/False) You can retrieve an item stored in an array by specifying the name of the array followed by its index position.

2. Which of the following statements is true of an array?

   a. An array is an indexed list of items.

   b. An array's index positions begin with 0 and are incremented by 1 for each additional item.

   c. An array's index positions can only be integers.

   d. All of the above

3. Which of the following are valid options for determining if an array has any items stored in it?

   a. Using the Array class's `length` method to see if it returns a value of 0

   b. Using the Array class's `empty?` method to see if it returns a value of `true`

   c. Using the Array class's `size` method to see if it returns a value of 0

   d. All of the above

4. Which of the following statements about the creation of arrays is true?

   a. Ruby allows you to create an array without formally declaring it.

   b. Ruby does not require you to specify an array's size when you create it.

   c. Ruby allows you to expand an array as you go along.

   d. All of the above

5. (True/False) Arrays begin with an index position of 1, so the first item stored in an array has an index position of 1, and the second item has an index position of 2.

Storing and Manipulating Lists Using Hashes

You can also store and retrieve data using hashes. A **hash,** which other programming languages sometimes refer to as an **associative array** or a **dictionary,** is a list of data stored in key-value pairings. Each piece of data in the hash is stored as a value and is assigned a key that uniquely identifies it. Instead of referencing items using index positions, you reference values by specifying their keys.

Like arrays, hashes are objects, and Ruby provides you with a number of methods to create and interact with them. Also like arrays, hashes can store any type of object that Ruby supports, including numbers and strings. To retrieve a particular value, you need its associated key.

Access to data stored in a hash is relatively fast and does not significantly diminish as additional key-value pairs are added. Hash keys and values can be of any length. Unlike arrays, which store items in the order they are added, hashes do not store their contents in any particular order.

Creating a Hash

Ruby provides a number of ways to create a hash. You can also create and populate a hash at the same time. And you can spread out the hash's definitions over multiple lines. Or you can use the Hash class's new method to create empty hashes.

Defining a Hash

The syntax for creating a hash and populating it with a set of key-value pairs is outlined here:

variableName = {key => value, ... key => value}

Here, *variableName* represents the name of a variable to which the hash is assigned, *key* represents a key name associated with a particular value, and *value* is a piece of data stored in the hash. Notice that the key-value pairs are enclosed within braces, not square brackets.

Creating a hash is pretty straightforward, as the following example shows:

```
kids = {"first" => "Alexander", "second" => "William",
   "third" => "Molly"}
```

Here, a hash named `kids` is defined and populated with three key-value pairs. The first key is named `"first"`, for example, and its associated value is `"Alexander"`. A key and its associated value are separated by the `=>` character, and successive key-value pairs are separated by commas.

If you prefer, you can replace the `=>` character with the `,` character when defining a hash, as shown here:

```
kids = {"first", "Alexander", "second", "William",
   "third", "Molly"}
```

Once it is defined, you can view a hash using the following statement:

```
puts kids.inspect
```

When executed, this statement displays the following output, showing the structure of the hash that has been defined:

```
{"third"=>"Molly", "second"=>"William",
 "first"=>"Alexander"}
```

Spreading a Hash Definition over Multiple Lines

To make it easier to understand and easier to read, you can spread out a hash's definition across multiple lines, as shown here:

```
kids = {"first" => "Alexander",
  "second" => "William",
  "third" => "Molly"
}
```

Using the *Hash* Class's *new* Method

You create an empty hash using the Hash class's new method, as shown here:

```
kids = Hash.new
```

When executed, this statement creates an empty hash that you can add as many key-value pairs to as you want.

Adding a Hash's Key-Value Pairs

You add key-value pairs to a hash using the following syntax:

```
hashVariable[key] = value
```

Here, *hashVariable* represents the name of the variable to which the hash is assigned, *key* represents the name of the key assigned to the key-value pair, and *value* represents the data that is stored. As an example, the following statement creates a hash and assigns three key-value pairs to it:

```
kids = {"first" => "Alexander", "second" => "William",
   "third" => "Molly"}
```

You can add additional key-value pairs to the hash, as shown here:

```
kids["fourth"] = "Dolly"
kids["fifth"] = "Regis"
```

Here, two key-value pairs have been added to the kids hash. The hash now contains five key-value pairs, as shown here:

```
{"third" => "Molly", "fifth" => "Regis",
  "second" => "William", "first" => "Alexander",
  "fourth" => "Dolly"}
```

As you can see, the contents of the hash are not stored in a specified order.

Using One Hash to Populate Another Hash

Another way of adding key-value pairs to a hash is to copy the contents of one hash into a new hash, as shown here:

```
kids = {"first" => "Alexander", "second" => "William",
   "third" => "Molly"}
family = kids
```

Here, a hash named kids is defined and assigned three key-value pairs. A second hash is then defined and assigned an exact copy of the key-value pairs stored in the kids hash.

Using the *Hash* Class's *merge* Method

Another way of creating and adding key-value pairs to a hash is to combine the contents of two existing hashes. To do this, you need to use the Hash class's merge method, as shown here:

```
kids = {"first" => "Alexander", "second" => "William",
   "third" => "Molly"}
parents = {"daddy" => "Jerry", "mommy" => "Mary"}
family = kids.merge(parents)
```

Here, a hash named kids is defined. Next, a hash named parents is defined. The merge method is then used to create a hash named family that contains the key-value pairs from both hashes.

Every key in a hash must be unique. If you accidentally assign a value to a hash with a key that is already in the hash, Ruby will perform a replacement operation instead of adding the new item to the hash.

199

Deleting a Hash's Key-Value Pairs

Ruby provides several ways of deleting key-value pairs from hashes. Using different methods, you can delete all key-value pairs or just specific key-value pairs. You can even conditionally delete key-value pairs.

Deleting All Key-Value Pairs

You can use the Hash class's clear method to delete all the key-value pairs from a hash, as shown here:

```
kids = {"first" => "Alexander", "second" => "William",
   "third" => "Molly"}
kids.clear
```

When executed, the first statement creates a hash and populates it with three key-value pairs. The second statement then executes the Hash class's clear method, deleting all the key-value pairs from the hash, leaving it empty.

You can also delete the contents of a hash by assigning an empty list to a hash, as shown here:

```
kids = {"first" => "Alexander", "second" => "William",
   "third" => "Molly"}
kids = {}
```

Deleting Specific Key-Value Pairs

You use the Hash class's delete method to remove a key-value pair by passing the name of the key to the method, as shown here:

```
kids = {"first" => "Alexander", "second" => "William",
   "third" => "Molly"}
kids.delete("second")
```

When executed, the first statement creates a hash and populates it with three key-value pairs. The second statement then deletes the key-value pair with the key named "second".

Conditionally Deleting Key-Value Pairs

You can also delete key-value pairs from a hash using the Hash class's delete_if method. This method takes an expression as an argument. If the expression evaluates as true for a key-value pair, that key-value pair is deleted from the hash. The following example demonstrates how to use this method:

```
kids = {"first" => "Alexander", "second" => "William",
   "third" => "Molly"}
kids.delete_if {|key, value| key >= "third"}
```

When executed, the first statement creates a hash and populates it with three key-value pairs. The second statement deletes the last key-value pair in the hash, since its key name matches the specified condition passed to the delete_if method.

Determining the Number of Key-Value Pairs in a Hash

You can use the empty? method to determine if a hash contains any key-value pairs. It returns a value of true if the hash contains no key-value pairs.

For a better understanding of how the empty? method works, look at the following example:

```
kids = {"first" => "Alexander", "second" => "William",
   "third" => "Molly"}

if kids.empty? == false then
   puts kids.inspect
else
   puts "The kids hash is empty"
end
```

Here, a hash named kids is defined and assigned three key-value pairs. Next, the Hash class's empty? method determines if the hash is empty. Since the hash is not empty, the inspect method is executed, displaying the hash's contents. Had the hash been empty, however, the statement following the else keyword would have been executed.

You can determine the number of key-value pairs stored in a hash using the Hash class's `length` or `size` methods, as shown here:

```
kids = {"first" => "Alexander", "second" => "William",
    "third" => "Molly"}
puts kids.size
```

When executed, this example displays the following output:

```
3
```

Retrieving Data Stored in Hashes

Data stored in key-value pairs can be retrieved in a number of ways. Items can be retrieved one at a time, or they can be retrieved and processed using loops. When loops are used, items can be retrieved using either hash keys or hash values.

Retrieving Individual Hash Items

Data is retrieved from a hash in much the same way data is retrieved from an array, except you specify a key instead of an index position. Take a look at the following statement:

```
kids = {"first" => "Alexander", "second" => "William",
    "third" => "Molly"}
x = kids["third"]
```

Here, a hash named `kids` is created and assigned three key-value pairs. Next, the value associated with the "third" key is retrieved and assigned to a variable named x.

Looping Through a Hash's Keys

Hashes are not indexed. They have no beginning or ending positions. Therefore, you cannot set up a loop to process their contents from beginning to end. However, Ruby gives you a way around this limitation with the keys method, which creates a list of all the keys stored within a specified hash. Using this list, you can set up a loop to process the hash's keys, as shown here:

```
kids = {"first" => "Alexander", "second" => "William",
    "third" => "Molly"}

puts "\n\nKeys belonging to the kids hash:\n\n"
kids.keys.each do |child|
  puts child
end
```

Here, a hash named `kids` is defined and assigned three key-value pairs. Next, the `puts` method displays a string. Then, using chaining, the output of the **keys** method is passed to the **each** method, which displays each key name as it iterates through the list. The output displayed when these statements are executed is shown here:

```
Keys belonging to the kids hash:

third
second
first
```

Looping Through a Hash's Values

Now that you know how to iterate through a list of the keys stored in a hash, you are one step away from being able to retrieve and process the keys' associated values. All you have to do is precede the reference to the keys, enclosed within square brackets, with the name of the hash, as shown in the following:

```
kids = {"first" => "Alexander", "second" => "William",
    "third" => "Molly"}
puts "\n\nValues belonging to the kids hash:\n\n"
kids.keys.each do |child|
  puts kids[child]
end
```

Here, a hash named **kids** is defined, and an **each** loop is used to retrieve and process hash values. The output displayed when these statements are executed is shown here:

```
Values belonging to the kids hash:

Molly
William
Alexander
```

You can also use the **Hash** class's **values** method to generate a list of all the values stored in a hash, as shown here:

```
kids = {"first" => "Alexander", "second" => "William",
    "third" => "Molly"}
x = kids.values
puts x.inspect
```

When executed, this example assigns the following list to the x array:

```
["Molly", "William", "Alexander"]
```

Sorting Hash Keys

Hashes do not store their key-value pairs in any particular order. If you want the keys that are retrieved with the **keys** method to be in a particular order, however, pass the **keys** method's output to the **sort** method prior to looping through the hash's keys, as shown here:

```
kids = {"first" => "Alexander", "second" => "William",
  "third" => "Molly"}
kids.keys.sort.each do |child|
  puts child
end
```

When executed, this example generates the following output, sorted by key name:

```
first
second
third
```

Ruby's **Hash** class also supports the **reverse** method, which allows you to reverse the order of a sort, as shown here:

```
kids = {"first" => "Alexander", "second" => "William",
  "third" => "Molly"}
kids.keys.sort.reverse.each do |child|
  puts child
end
```

When executed, this example generates the following output:

```
third
second
first
```

Short Quiz

1. (True/False) To retrieve a value from a hash, you must specify its index position.

2. (True/False) The **Hash** class's **empty?** method can be used to determine if a hash contains any key-value pairs.

3. When the output of one method is used as input for another method, the methods are said to be:

   a. Chained

   b. Linked

   c. Bonded

   d. None of the above

4. Every key in a hash must be unique. If a value is added to a hash using a key that is already in the hash, what happens to the preexisting value?

   a. It is replaced by the new value.

   b. The new value is rejected.

   c. The new value is added to the hash with a modified key name.

   d. None of the above

5. Which of the following statements regarding Ruby's support for hashes is true?

   a. A hash is a list of data stored in key-value pairs.

   b. Each piece of data is stored as a value and has an assigned key.

   c. Each piece of data stored in a hash can be retrieved using its assigned key.

   d. All of the above

Back to the Ruby Number Guessing Game

It is time to develop this chapter's game project, the Ruby Number Guessing game. Make sure you follow each step carefully to avoid any time-consuming mistakes.

Designing the Game

The development of the Ruby Number Guessing game is completed in 12 steps, as outlined here:

1. Open your text or script editor, and create a new file.

2. Add comment statements to the beginning of the script file to document the script and its purpose.

3. Define a Screen class representing the terminal window.

4. Define a Game class representing the Ruby Number Guessing game.

5. Add a display_greeting method to the Game class.

6. Add a display_instructions method to the Game class.

7. Add a `generate_number` method to the Game class.

8. Add a `play_game` method to the Game class.

9. Add a `display_credits` method to the Game class.

10. Instantiate script objects.

11. Prompt the player for permission to begin the game.

12. Administer game play.

Step 1: Create a New Ruby File

Open your favorite text or script editor, and create a new Ruby script file. Save the file with the name NumberGuess.rb.

Step 2: Document the Script and Its Purpose

Add the following comment statements to the new script file. These comments provide a description of the script and its purpose.

```
#-----------------------------------------------------------
#
# Script Name: NumberGuess.rb
# Version:     1.0
# Author:      Jerry Lee Ford, Jr.
# Date:        March 2010
#
# Description: This Ruby script is a number guessing game
#              that challenges the player to guess a
#              randomly generated number in as few
#              guesses as possible.
#
#-----------------------------------------------------------
```

Step 3: Define the *Screen* Class

The Ruby Number Guessing game uses two custom classes, Screen and Game, each of which contains numerous methods for controlling the interaction with the user and executing the game.

Define a class named Screen by adding the following statements to the end of the script file:

```
# Define custom classes ------------------------------------

#Define a class representing the console window
class Screen

  def cls #Define a method that clears the display area
    puts ("\n" * 25) #Scroll the screen 25 times
```

```
      puts "\a"  #Make a little noise to get the player's
                 #attention
   end

   def pause    #Define a method that pauses the display
                #area
      STDIN.gets #Execute the STDIN class's gets method to
                 #pause script execution until the player
                 #presses the Enter key
   end

end
```

The first method defined in the Screen class is the cls method. It contains two statements. The first statement writes 25 blank lines to the terminal window to clear the screen. The second statement processes a string containing the \a escape character, which makes a beep sound, thus notifying the player that the terminal screen has been cleared.

The Screen class's second method, pause, executes the STDIN class's gets method so that the script's execution is paused until the player presses Enter.

Step 4: Define the Game Class

The Game class contains five methods used to control the execution of the game. To define the Game class, add the following statements to the end of the script file:

```
#Define a class representing the Ruby Number Guessing Game
class Game

end
```

Step 5: Define the display_greeting Method

Define the first of five methods belonging to the Game class by inserting the following statements between the class's opening and closing statements. These statements define the display_greeting method, which is responsible for displaying the game's welcome message.

```
#This method displays the game's opening screen
def display_greeting

   Console_Screen.cls #Clear the display area

   #Display welcome message
   print "\t\t Welcome to the Ruby Number Guessing Game!" +
      "\n\n\n\n\n\n\n\n\n\n\n\n\n\nPress Enter to " +
      "continue."

   Console_Screen.pause        #Pause the game

end
```

Step 6: Define the *display_instructions* Method

Define the second of five methods belonging to the Game class by adding the following statements at the end of the class definition, immediately after the display_greeting method. These statements define the display_instructions method, which is responsible for displaying the game's instructions.

```
#Define a method to be used to present game instructions
def display_instructions

  Console_Screen.cls        #Clear the display area
  puts "INSTRUCTIONS:\n\n"  #Display a heading

  #Display the game's instructions
  puts "This game randomly generates a number from 1 to 100 " +
      "and"
  puts "challenges you to identify it in as few guesses " +
      "as possible."
  puts "After each guess, the game will analyze your " +
      "input and provide"
  puts "you with feedback. You may take as many turns as " +
      "you need in"
  puts "order to guess the game's secret number.\n\n\n"
  puts "Good luck!\n\n\n\n\n\n\n\n\n"
  print "Press Enter to continue."

  Console_Screen.pause      #Pause the game

end
```

This method, named display_instructions, displays a series of text strings that contain instructions for playing the game.

Step 7: Define the *generate_number* Method

Define the third of five methods belonging to the Game class by adding the following statements at the end of the class definition, immediately after the display_instructions method:

```
#Define a method that generates the game's number
def generate_number

  #Generate and return a random number from 1 to 100
  return randomNo = 1 + rand(100)

end
```

This method generates a random number from 1 to 100. First, the rand method is executed and passed a value of 100. This results in an integer value between 0 and 99. A value of 1 is then added to the returned value to wind up with a number in the target range. This integer value is then returned to the statement that calls upon the generate_number method using the return command.

Step 8: Define the *play_game* Method

Define the fourth of five methods belonging to the Game class by adding the following statements at the end of the class definition, immediately after the generate_number method:

```ruby
#Define a method to be used to control game play
def play_game

    #Call on the generate_number method to get a random
    #number
    number = generate_number

    #Loop until the player inputs a valid answer
    loop do

        Console_Screen.cls        #Clear the display area

        #Prompt the player to make a guess
        print "\nEnter your guess and press the Enter key: "

        reply = STDIN.gets  #Collect the player's answer
        reply.chop!         #Remove the end of line character
        reply = reply.to_i  #Convert the player's guess to an
                            #integer

        #Validate the player's input only allowing guesses
        #from 1 to 100
        if reply < 1 or reply > 100 then
            redo  #Redo the current iteration of the loop
        end

        #Analyze the player's guess to determine if it is
        #correct
        if reply == number then     #The player's guess was
                                    #correct
            Console_Screen.cls          #Clear the display area
            print "You have guessed the number! Press Enter" +
                "to continue."
            Console_Screen.pause        #Pause the game
            Break                       #Exit loop
        elsif reply < number then   #The player's guess was
                                    #too low
            Console_Screen.cls          #Clear the display area
            print "Your guess is too low! Press Enter to" +
                "continue."
            Console_Screen.pause        #Pause the game
        elsif reply > number then   #The player's guess was
                                    #too high
            Console_Screen.cls          #Clear the display area
```

```
      print "Your guess is too high! Press Enter to" +
        "continue."
      Console_Screen.pause       #Pause the game
    end

  end

end
```

The `play_game` method begins by calling upon the `Game` class's `generate_number` method, which generates a random number from 1 to 100. This value is then assigned to a variable named `number`. The rest of the statements that make up the `play_game` method are enclosed within a loop that is set up to execute forever, allowing the player to make as many guesses as needed.

Within the loop, the screen is cleared, then the player is prompted to guess the game's number. The guess is stored in a variable named `reply`. The value stored in `reply` is then converted to an integer using the `to_i` method. Next, the value assigned to `reply` is analyzed to see if it is less than 1 or greater than 100. If it is, the `redo` command is executed, restarting the loop's current iteration to prompt the player to guess again.

If a valid guess was entered, the value of `reply` is analyzed to see if it is equal to the game's number, lower than the number, or higher than the number. If the player has guessed the game's number, a message is displayed notifying the player that the number has been guessed, then the `break` command is executed, terminating the execution of the `play_game` method's loop. If the player's guess is too low or too high, however, the player is given a hint toward the next guess, and the `play_game` method's loop is repeated, giving the player the chance to make another guess.

Step 9: Define the `display_credits` Method

The `display_credits` method displays information about the game and its developer, including the developer's URL. Define this fifth of five methods belonging to the `Game` class by adding the following statements to the end of the class definition:

```
#This method displays the information about the Ruby
#Number Guessing game
def display_credits

  Console_Screen.cls #Clear the display area

  #Thank the player and display game information
  puts "\t\tThank you for playing the Ruby Number Guessing↵
    Game.\n\n\n\n"
```

```
puts "\n\t\t\t Developed by Jerry Lee Ford, Jr.\n\n"
puts "\t\t\t\t Copyright 2010\n\n"
puts "\t\t\tURL: http://www.tech-publishing.com\n\n\n\n↵
   \n\n\n\n\n\n"
```

end

Step 10: Instantiate Script Objects

Instantiate an instance of the Screen and Game classes by adding the
following statements to the end of the script file:

```
# Main Script Logic ------------------------------------

Console_Screen = Screen.new #Instantiate a new Screen object
SQ = Game.new             #Instantiate a new Game object

#Execute the Game class's display_greeting method
SQ.display_greeting

answer = ""
```

In addition to instantiating the Console_Screen and SQ objects,
these statements define a global variable named answer, which is
used to control the execution of the loop that prompts the player for
permission to begin a round of play.

Step 11: Get Permission to Start the Game

Set up the prompt for getting the player's permission to play the game
by adding the following statements to the end of the script file:

```
#Loop until the player enters y or n and do not accept any
#other input
loop do

   Console_Screen.cls #Clear the display area

   #Prompt the player for permission to start the game
   print "Are you ready to play the Ruby Number Guessing
      Game? (y/n): "

   answer = STDIN.gets #Collect the player's response
   answer.chop! #Remove any extra characters appended to
                #the string

   #Terminate the loop if valid input was provided
   break if answer == "y" || answer == "n"

end
```

Here, a loop is set up to run forever. Upon each iteration of the
loop, the player is prompted to enter a value of y or n to indicate
whether a new round of play should be initiated or the game should

be terminated. Any input other than a y or n is ignored. Once a valid response is entered, the break command is executed, terminating the loop and allowing the rest of the script to run.

Step 12: Administering Game Play

The remainder of the script file consists of statements responsible for controlling the overall execution of the game. The execution of these statements depends on whether the player decided to terminate the game or play another round. Add the following statements to the end of the script file:

```ruby
#Analyze the player's input
if answer == "n"   #See if the player elected not to take
                   #the game

  Console_Screen.cls  #Clear the display area

  #Invite the player to return and play the game some other
  #time
  puts "Okay, perhaps another time.\n\n"

else #The player wants to play the game

  #Execute the Game class's display_instructions method
  SQ.display_instructions

  loop do

    #Execute the Game class's play_game method
    SQ.play_game

    Console_Screen.cls  #Clear the display area

    #Prompt the player for permission to start a new round
    #of play
    print "Would you like to play again? (y/n): "

    playAgain = STDIN.gets  #Collect the player's response
    playAgain.chop! #Remove any extra characters appended
                    #to the string

    break if playAgain == "n"  #Exit loop

end

  #Call upon the Game class's determine_credits method to
  #thank the player for playing the game and to display
  #game information
  SQ.display_credits

end
```

If the player decides to stop playing the game, the first statement in the if code block is executed, clearing the screen and inviting the player to play another time. If the player decides to play another round, however, the statements that follow the else keyword are processed, and the Game class's display_instructions method is called.

Next, a loop is set up to facilitate the execution of as many rounds of play as the player wants. Each time the loop repeats, it calls on the play_game method, which manages the playing of the game. Once the play_game method has finished executing, the screen is cleared, and the player is asked if she would like to play another game. If the player enters an n and presses Enter, the break command is executed, terminating the loop and causing the display_credits method to be called, after which the script terminates. If the player enters a value of y and presses Enter, the loop iterates, and a new round of play is initiated.

Running Your New Ruby Script Game

Save your Ruby script. If you typed the code statements correctly, the program should work as expected. If you run into any errors, read the error messages carefully to ascertain what went wrong. If necessary, review the script, and look for mistyped or missing statements.

Summing Up

- Variables are not an efficient means of managing large collections of related data, such as a personal address book or a small database. Storing and managing this type of data is best done using arrays and hashes.

- A list is a collection of data. Lists are created as comma-separated items. In Ruby, lists can be used as the basis for populating arrays.

- An array is an indexed list of items. In Ruby, array indexes begin at 0 and are incremented by 1 each time a new item is added. Index positions can only be whole numbers (integers).

- You use the inspect method to view an array or hash's contents.

- One way to create an array is to assign a list to it. Another way is to use the %w(and) characters. Arrays can be created using the Array object's new method. They can also be created by assigning the contents of one array to another array or by combining two arrays.

- Ruby allows you to modify arrays by specifying the index position of the item to be replaced or added.

- Using the << or push methods, you can add items to an array by pushing them to the end of the array.

- To determine whether an array has any items in it, you can use the length or size methods. Alternatively, you can use the empty? method.

- You can retrieve items from an array by specifying the name of the array followed by the index positions that mark where the items are stored. You can also retrieve items using the at method and the items' index positions.

- You can retrieve a range of items from an array by passing a list or range of index positions within a pair of parentheses to the slice method.

- The first method retrieves the first item from a specified array. The last method retrieves the last item from a specified array.

- The while and until loops can be used to process the contents of an array. However, the each method is tailor-made for processing arrays.

- You can remove all the items stored in an array using the clear method.

- The shift method deletes the first item stored in an array, shifting the index positions of the remaining items down by one. The pop method deletes the last item stored in an array. You can also use the delete method to delete array items based on their values. And you can use the delete_at method to conditionally delete items from arrays.

- You can use the sort method to sort the contents of an array alphabetically.

- The include? method allows you to determine if an array contains any instances of a specified item.

- A hash, also referred to as an associative array, is a list of data stored in key-value pairs. Each piece of data is stored as a value and assigned a key, which uniquely identifies it. Instead of referencing data using index positions, you reference values by specifying their keys.

- You can use the new method to create an empty hash. Alternatively, you can create a hash by assigning a collection of key-value pairs.

- You can use one hash to populate another hash, or you can use the merge method to combine the contents of two existing hashes.

- You can use the clear method to remove all key-value pairs from a hash.

- You can use the `delete` method to remove key-value pairs based on a specified key and the `delete_if` method to conditionally delete key-value pairs.

- You can use the `empty?` method to determine if a hash contains any key-value pairs or not.

- Data is extracted from a hash in much the same way it is extracted from an array, except you specify a key instead of an index position.

- Hashes are not indexed. Therefore, you cannot set up a loop to process them. Ruby provides a way around this limitation via the Hash class's `keys` method, which creates a list of all the keys stored within a specified hash. This list can be used to set up a loop that iterates through and processes the hash's values. Conversely, you can use the Hash class's `hash` method to generate a list of hash values.

- Hashes do not store their key-value pairs in any particular order, so the order in which keys are retrieved when working with the `keys` method may not always be optimal. If you want the keys that are retrieved with the `keys` method to be in a particular order, however, you can pass the `keys` method's output to the `sort` method prior to looking through a hash's keys.

Comprehension Check

1. In Ruby, a list is managed and stored using which of the following structures?

   a. Arrays

   b. Hashes

   c. Variables

   d. a and b, but not c

2. (True/False) Once added to an array, an item can be referred to by specifying its index position within the array.

3. Which of the following methods can be used to display a text view of an array's contents?

   a. `view`

   b. `display`

   c. `show`

   d. `inspect`

4. Which of the following is a way to create an array?

    a. Using the %w(and) characters

    b. Using the %W(and) characters

    c. Using the `Array` object's new method

    d. All of the above

5. Instead of deleting array items using their index positions, you can delete them (based on their values) using the `Array` class's _____ method.

6. Which of the following methods can be used to delete the first item stored in an array?

    a. `shift`

    b. `clear`

    c. `pop`

    d. None of the above

7. (True/False) As arrays get larger, it becomes more difficult to keep track of the items' index positions.

8. (True/False) The advantage of using the %w(and) characters to define a new array is that it eliminates the need to enclose the text string within single or double quotes.

9. Which of the following methods can be used to remove an item from the end of an array?

    a. `shift`

    b. `clear`

    c. `pop`

    d. None of the above

10. You can use the `Array` class's _____ method to retrieve a series of array items.

11. (True/False) Ruby allows arrays to be retrieved by specifying a negative index position, in which case retrieval occurs relative to the end of the array.

12. Which of the following statements is true regarding hashes?

   a. A Ruby hash can store any type of object that Ruby supports.

   b. To retrieve a value stored in a hash, you can use its key.

   c. The time it takes to retrieve a value stored in a hash does not change as the hash grows in size.

   d. All of the above

13. One option for creating a hash is to take two existing hashes and combine their contents. This is done using the Hash class's _____ method.

14. Which of the following methods can be used to remove all the key-value pairs at once from a hash?

   a. delete

   b. clear

   c. remove

   d. All of the above

15. Using the Hash class's _____ method, you can conditionally delete key-value pairs.

16. Which of the following methods can be used to remove all the items stored in an array at one time?

   a. shift

   b. clear

   c. pop

   d. None of the above

17. (True/False) You cannot set up a loop to process a hash's contents from beginning to end.

18. Which of the following methods generates a list of all the keys stored within a hash?

   a. keys

   b. hash

   c. index

   d. None of the above

19. (True/False) A hash is an indexed list of items stored in key-value pairs.

20. Which of the following options can be used to iterate through the contents of a loop?

    a. The while loop

    b. The each loop

    c. The until loop

    d. All of the above

Reinforcement Exercises

The following exercises are designed to further your understanding of Ruby programming by challenging you to make improvements to the chapter's game project, the Ruby Number Guessing game.

1. Currently, the game allows players to play as many times as they wish. It does not provide any feedback on how the players are doing, however. Modify the game so that it keeps track of the number of games played as well as the average number of guesses made per game.

   To implement this change, add the following list of global variables to the beginning of the script's Main Script Logic section. Assign each variable an initial value of zero.

   - $gameCount

   - $noOfGuesses

   - $totalNoOfGuesses

   - $avgNoOfGuesses

   Next, modify the Game class's play_game method by adding a statement that automatically increments the value assigned to $noOfGuesses. Finally, modify the programming logic (located in the loop at the end of the Main Script Logic section) that is responsible for prompting players to play again. The required modifications are outlined here:

   - Increment $gameCount

   - Calculate $totalNoOfGuesses

   - Calculate $avgNoOfGuesses

   - Display two text strings showing the number of games played and the average number of guesses per game

2. The game challenges the player to guess a randomly generated number from 1 to 100 in as few guesses as possible. Make the game more challenging by increasing the range of numbers to 1 and 1000.

   To implement this change, modify the Game class's generate_number method to support the expanded range. Also modify the play_game method's validation check so that it accepts numbers in the range of 1 to 1000. Finally, update the instructions displayed at the beginning of the game so that they indicate the game's expanded number range.

3. The game lets players know whether their guesses are too high or too low. It also rejects any guesses outside of its supported range of numbers, such as negative numbers, numbers greater than 1000, or alphabetic or special characters. Modify the game so that it notifies players when invalid guesses have been made and reminds players of what constitutes valid input.

   To implement this change, modify the Game class's play_game method so that it clears the screen, displays an error message, and then pauses the game to ensure that players see the message before continuing.

4. Currently, the game allows players to make an unlimited number of guesses. Therefore, players cannot lose the game. Modify it so that players are allowed a maximum of 10 guesses, after which the game is declared lost.

   To implement this change, modify the Game class's play_game method by adding programming logic that terminates the method's execution if the player does not guess the number within 10 guesses. In addition, modify the display_instructions method so that it informs players of the maximum number of guesses.

5. You should thoroughly test all your Ruby scripts to make sure they are running as expected. With the Number Guessing game, that means playing the game repeatedly. To make this easier on you, add a hidden "cheat" to the game that allows you to display the game's number.

   To implement this change, modify the game so that, in addition to accepting a reply of y or n when prompting the player for permission to begin the game, it accepts a reply of c (for cheat). Next, modify the Game class's play_game method so that it displays the game's number when it's run in cheat mode.

Discovery Projects

 Discovery Project 6-1

Variables are well suited to storing individual values, but arrays and hashes are required if you're storing and managing large collections of data. You need to understand all three. Write a one-page paper comparing and contrasting variables, arrays, and hashes. Identify the strengths and weaknesses of each, and provide examples of situations for which each structure is best suited.

 Discovery Project 6-2

The Ruby Array class supports almost 80 methods, which is many more than could be covered in this chapter. To round out your understanding of arrays, visit *http://ruby-doc.org/core/classes/Array.html,* and view the documentation for the various methods. Then complete the following exercises using IRB:

1. Create an array named Animals, and add the following items to it: Fox, Bear, Cow, Horse, and Wolf.

2. Using the Array class's difference method, compare the contents of the Animals array with the list that follows and report any items in the Animals array that are not in the list: ["Bear", "Cat", "Horse"].

3. Using the concat method, add the following list of items to the end of the Animals array, and display the contents of the array: ["Cat", "Duck"].

4. Insert a new item into the Animals array at index position 3, and display the contents of the array.

5. Use the Array class's length method to display the number of items stored in the Animals array.

6. Use the Array class's clear method to remove all the items from the Animal array, and then display the contents of the array.

7. Use the Array class's inspect method to verify that the array is now empty.

Discovery Project 6-3

The Hash class supports 50 methods, which is many more than can be covered in this chapter. To round out your understanding of hashes, visit *http://ruby-doc.org/core/classes/Hash.html*, and view the documentation for the various methods. Then complete the following exercises using IRB:

1. Create a hash named Accounts, and add the following items to it:

   10001, AFord
   20001, JAlex
   30001, AJolie

2. Use the Hash class's delete method to remove the key-value pair with a key of 30001 from the Accounts hash.

3. Use the Hash class's inspect method to verify the contents of the hash.

4. Use the Hash class's invert method to convert the Accounts hash's keys to values and convert its values to keys.

5. Use the Hash class's has_key? method to determine if any of the following keys are stored in the Accounts hash: JAlex, 10001.

6. Use the Hash class's size method to display a count of the number of key-value pairs stored in the Accounts hash.

7. Use the Hash class's clear method to remove all items from the Accounts hash, and then display the contents of the hash.

8. Use the Hash class's inspect method to verify that the array is now empty.

Working with Regular Expressions

In previous chapters, you have created a number of computer games. For most of these games, you had to accept whatever input the player provided, with little or no validation. In this chapter, you learn how to use regular expressions, which allow you to perform a detailed analysis of user input to determine if it meets criteria you have specified. Regular expressions also allow you to dissect and process data, regardless of its source, for example. In this chapter, you also learn how to perform text-substitution operations and how to deal with differences in case.

Project Preview: The Ruby Word Guessing Game

In this chapter, you create a computer game called the Ruby Word Guessing game, which challenges the player to guess a randomly selected secret word in three guesses or less. Before making any guesses, the player specifies five consonants and one vowel, which, if present in the secret word, are revealed, giving the player a clue to what the word might be.

The game begins by displaying the welcome screen shown in Figure 7-1.

Figure 7-1 The welcome screen for the Ruby Word Guessing game

Next, the game prompts the player for permission to begin the game, as shown in Figure 7-2. The player is instructed to respond with a y or an n.

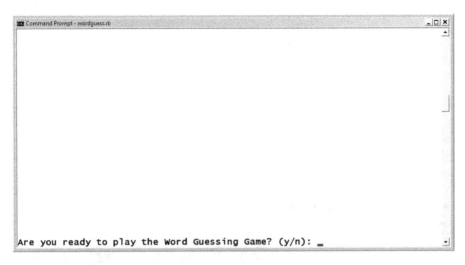

Figure 7-2 The player is prompted for permission to begin the game

Before the first round begins, the player is told how to play the game, as shown in Figure 7-3.

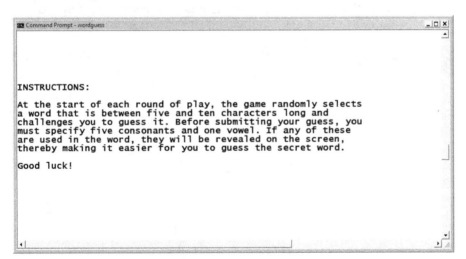

Figure 7-3 The player is told how to play the game

Next, the player is told to specify five consonants, as shown in Figure 7-4.

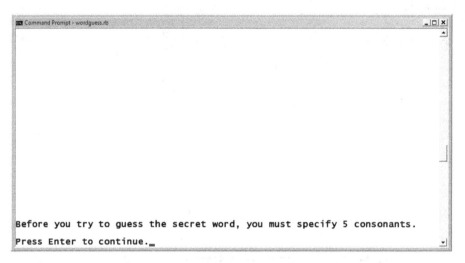

Figure 7-4   The player is told to specify five consonants before trying to guess the secret word

Consonants are specified one at a time, as shown in Figure 7-5. If the player attempts to enter a vowel, a number, a special character, or more than one character, the input is rejected, and the player is prompted to try again.

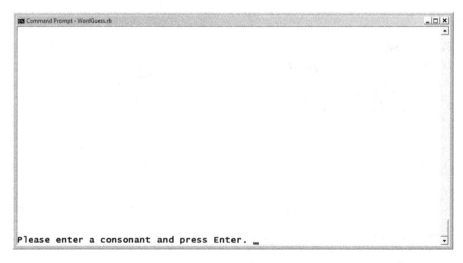

Figure 7-5   The player is told to enter a consonant

Once all five consonants have been specified, the player is prompted to specify a vowel. The game then displays a clue to the secret word, with blank spaces for each letter except for the ones that have been correctly guessed, which appear where they normally would appear in the word. The player is asked to guess the secret word, as shown in Figure 7-6.

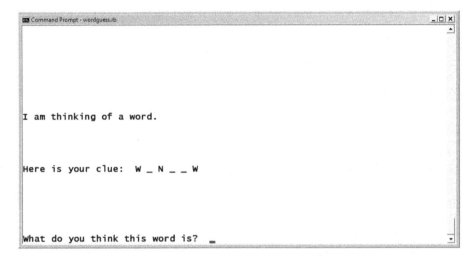

Figure 7-6   The player is given a clue and asked to guess the secret word

If the player guesses the secret word, the message shown in Figure 7-7 appears.

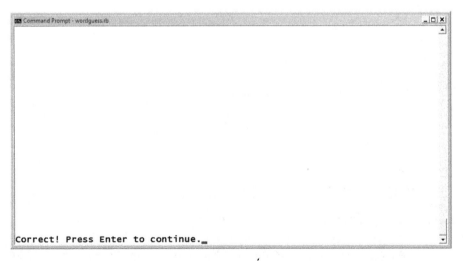

Figure 7-7   The player has won the game by correctly guessing the secret word

The player gets three tries to guess the secret word. Figure 7-8 shows the message that is displayed before the player makes a final guess.

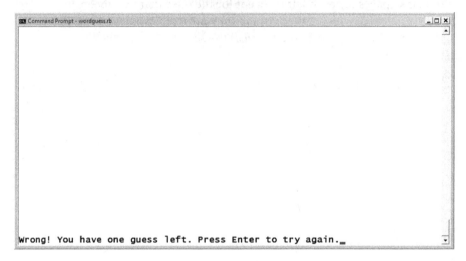

```
Command Prompt - wordguess.rb                                              _□×




Wrong! You have one guess left. Press Enter to try again._
```

Figure 7-8   The game gives the player one last guess

If the player is unable to guess the secret word in three tries, the game has been lost, and the correct answer is displayed, as shown in Figure 7-9.

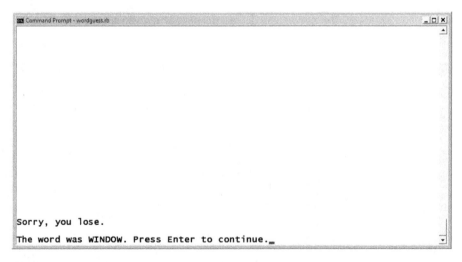

```
Command Prompt - wordguess.rb                                              _□×




Sorry, you lose.
The word was WINDOW. Press Enter to continue._
```

Figure 7-9   The player has failed to guess the secret word

At the end of each round of play, the game prompts the player for permission to start another round. Depending on the player's response, the game is either terminated or a new secret word is selected, and play begins again.

Using Regular Expressions for Data Validation

The data processed by computer scripts can come from many sources, including databases, files, users, and input from other scripts and programs. Although you may trust an individual source to provide you with valid data, you will often do so at your own peril. Instead, you should build data validation logic into your scripts, rejecting data that is not in the proper format.

You can perform a certain amount of data validation using conditional logic and methods belonging to Ruby classes. To create data validation routines, however, you need to use regular expressions. A **regular expression** is a pattern used to identify matching character data.

In previous chapter projects, you have performed limited amounts of data validation. In those scripts, you were able to simplify data validation by restricting valid data to specific sets of characters and rejecting any data that did not match the script's precise requirements. For example, in the Superman Movie Trivia Quiz, you rejected as invalid any player input that was not an a, b, c, or d, as shown here:

```
#Analyze the play to determine if it was valid
if reply == "a" or reply == "b" or reply == "c"
   or reply == "d" then
   break  #Terminate the execution of the loop
end
```

Using specified text patterns, regular expressions search for matches within strings. As such, they can extract information or provide data validation, among other things. There are various ways to work with regular expressions. You can, for example, search throughout a string for a match, search for a match from the beginning of a string, or search for a match starting at the end of a string and working backwards. You can define patterns that match one or fewer times, or zero or more times. You can even define patterns that match ranges of characters, such as just vowels or just consonants. The following statements demonstrate the use of a regular expression when analyzing input:

```
#Analyze the player input to determine if it was valid
if reply =~ /a|b|c|d|/ then
   break  #Terminate the execution of the loop
end
```

Here, the string stored in reply is searched to see if it consists of an a, b, c, or d character.

Matching Basic Patterns

When using a regular expression, you define a pattern that specifies the criteria for a match within a string. In most cases, the pattern is processed from left to right. A match occurs when the specified pattern is found somewhere within the source string. By default, matches are case sensitive, which means that, say, a capital "A" will not match a lowercase "a." (You can override case sensitivity, however.) Also, characters within a pattern are taken literally—i.e., represent only those characters—unless they are metacharacters, which are discussed later in this chapter.

Matching Specific Patterns

The most basic type of regular expression is one that is used to find a specific set of characters. This type of pattern is set up using the /.../ operator, which has the following syntax:

/pattern/

For example, take a look at the following pattern:

/USA/

This pattern matches the characters USA. If they are found anywhere in the string, a value of true is returned. Otherwise, a value of false is returned. To see how this pattern might be used, look at the following set of statements:

```
if "Welcome to New York Harbor, USA." =~ /USA/ then
  puts "Welcome to America!"
end
```

Here, the source string "Welcome to New York Harbor, USA." is searched using the pattern USA. Since the string contains the words USA, a match occurs, and the following output is displayed when the statements are executed:

"Welcome to America!"

Notice the use of the =~ operator—i.e., the regular-expression equals operator. In addition to this operator, you should be familiar with the !~ operator—i.e., the regular-expression not equals operator.

Matching Multiple Patterns

You can also set up regular-expression patterns to find any of a set of specified matches. To do so, you use the | character, known as a pipe, to separate each possible match, as shown here:

```
if "Welcome the USA!." =~ /USA|America/ then
  puts "We have a match!"
end
```

Here, a search pattern looks for the string USA or the string America. If either string is found in the source string, the match is successful.

Using this approach, you can set up a pattern that searches for as many sets of characters as you want, as shown here:

```
if "Remember to call your mother." =~
    /tall|call|wall|ball|fall|mall/ then
  puts "We have a match!"
end
```

Here, a check is performed to determine if the string Remember to call your mother matches tall, call, wall, ball, fall, or mall.

Multiple pattern matches are very convenient, but they can also be unwieldy. To make things easier, use parentheses to separate the unique parts of the search pattern from the common parts, as shown here:

```
if "Remember to call your mother." =~ /(t|c|w|b|f|m)all/ then
  puts "We have a match!"
end
```

Here, /(t|c|w|b|f|m)all/ is just a shorthand way of writing /tall|call|wall|ball|fall|mall/.

Short Quiz

1. (True/False) A regular expression is a pattern used to identify matching character data.

2. Which of the following statements about regular expressions is true?

   a. They allow you to search for pattern matches within strings.

   b. They support the use of metacharacters.

   c. They are case sensitive by default.

   d. All of the above

3. Which of the following is the regular-expression equals operator?

   a. ==

   b. =~

   c. =

   d. !~

4. Which of the following represents a valid source of input for a computer program?

    a. File

    b. User input

    c. Database

    d. All of the above

5. (True/False) The !> operator is the regular-expression not equals operator.

Working with Metacharacters

Normally, a character included in a regular-expression pattern will form a match with the same character if it is found in the source string. However, there are many non-alphanumeric characters that have special meanings when used in regular expressions. These are referred to as metacharacters. As an example, the | metacharacter is used to separate items within a regular expression. Table 7-1 lists a number of additional metacharacters that you should become familiar with.

Character	Description
.	Matches any one character
+	Matches one or more instances of a character
*	Matches zero or more instances of a character
?	Matches one or zero instances of a character
^	Looks for a match at the beginning of a source string
$	Looks for a match at the end of a source string
\A	Looks for a match at the beginning of a source string
\Z	Looks for a match at the end of a source string
\d	Matches any numeric character
\w	Matches any alphabetic, numeric, or underscore character
\D	Matches any non-numeric character
\W	Matches any non-alphabetic, non-numeric, or non-underscore character
\s	Matches blank space
\S	Matches non-blank space

Table 7-1   Regular-Expression Metacharacters

Escaping Metacharacters

You can escape (disable) a metacharacter's special function by preceding it with the \ character. For example, if you precede the . metacharacter with the \ character, it gets treated like a period. For an example of how to escape a metacharacter in a regular expression, look at the following statements:

```
if "Type your name (and press Enter):" =~ /press Enter\) / then
  print "We have a match!"
end
```

Here, the source string is searched using the regular-expression pattern press Enter). When Ruby sees the) metacharacter in the first statement's search pattern, an error is generated because, syntactically, Ruby expects there to have been a preceding (character. (Parentheses have a special meaning in Ruby.) To force the) to be interpreted literally, the) metacharacter must be escaped, which is accomplished using the \ character. The result is a match.

Matching Individual Characters

You can use the . metacharacter as part of a pattern to match any individual character (except the new-line character). You can also use the . metacharacter multiple times in the same pattern, as shown here:

```
if "My name is Jerry. My father's name is Mr. Ford." =~
    /f...er/ then
  print "We have a match!"
end
```

Here, a pattern has been set up to match the lowercase character f followed by any three characters followed by the characters er.

Matching a Pattern at the Beginning of a String

By default, a regular expression looks anywhere within a string for a match. Using the ^ metacharacter, however, you can create regular-expression patterns that look for a match only at the beginning of a source string. For example, the pattern /^My name/ results in a match only if it is found at the beginning of the source, as shown in the following example:

```
if "My name is Jerry. My father's name is Mr. Ford." =~
    /^My name/ then
  print "We have a match!"
end
```

You can combine the ^ and $ metacharacters to search for any one character that appears both at the beginning and at the end of a source string. You can even combine them with the . metacharacter to create a pattern that matches only if the source string is made up of a single character, as shown here:

`/^.$/`

Matching a Pattern at the End of a String

The $ metacharacter results in a match only if the pattern is found at the end of a source string, as it does in the following example:

```
if "My name is Jerry. My father's name is Mr. Ford." =~
   /Ford\.$/ then
   print "We have a match!"
end
```

Matching Once or Not at All

There may be situations when you need to look for a character (or a group of characters) that occurs once or not at all, either possibility resulting in a match. You do this using the ? metacharacter modifier, as shown here:

```
if "My name is Jerry. My father's name is Mr. Ford." =~ /Mrs?/ then
   print "We have a match!"
end
```

Here, the pattern /Mrs?/ has been specified. It will match a Mrs string, but it will also match a Mr string. In this particular example, it is the Mr string that results in a match.

You can also use the ? metacharacter modifier on groups of characters. To do so, use parentheses to enclose the group of characters, as shown here:

```
if "My father's name is Mr. Ford." =~ /father('s name)?/ then
   print "We have a match!"
end
```

Here, a match occurs if either father or father's name is found in the source string. In this particular example, both patterns match.

Matching Zero or More Times

The * metacharacter is similar to the . metacharacter, except the * metacharacter matches zero or more instances of the preceding character. As an example of how to work with this metacharacter, consider the following statements:

```
if "I gave your paper a grade of A+" =~ /A\+*/ then
   print "We have a match!"
end
```

Here, the specified pattern matches the A character followed by zero or more instances of the + character. Because the + character is a metacharacter, is had to be escaped in the pattern.

As written, the pattern /A\+*/ would match any of the following set of characters that might be found in a source string:

- A

- A+

- A++

- A+++++++++++++

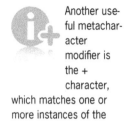

Another useful metacharacter modifier is the + character, which matches one or more instances of the preceding character.

Matching Any of a Collection of Characters

You may need to search for anything that is included within a range of characters. To do so, use **character classes**, placing the range of characters inside a pair of square brackets. Ruby supports the character-class patterns shown in Table 7-2.

Pattern	Description
/[abc]/	Matches any of the specified lowercase letters (a, b, c)
/[abcdefghijklmnopqrstuvwxyz]/	Matches any lowercase letter
/[0123456789]/	Matches any number from 0 to 9
/[0-9]/	Shorthand option for matching any number from 0 to 9
/[a-z]/	Shorthand option for matching any lowercase letter
/[A-Z]/	Shorthand option for matching any uppercase letter

Table 7-2   Character-Class Patterns

Here's an example of how to work with character-class patterns:

```
print "Please enter a vowel and press Enter. "
input = STDIN.gets
input.chop!

if input =~ /[aeiou]/ then
  puts "A vowel has been submitted."
end
```

Here, the user is prompted to enter a vowel. Data validation is then performed using the regular expression /[aeiou]/. A match results if the user has entered a response that includes a lowercase vowel.

Other Uses for Regular Expressions

Ruby's support for regular expressions is quite extensive. As a result, there are many things you can do with them. For example, you can perform pattern searches that ignore case. You can also perform string substitutions, where one or more search patterns are used to replace characters in a source string.

Overcoming Differences in Case

Thus far, the regular-expression patterns used in this chapter have been case sensitive. They resulted in matches because the case used in the pattern matched the case used in the source string. You don't have to use case-sensitive patterns, however. To turn off case sensitivity, use the i modifier. This allows a pattern to match both lowercase and uppercase characters, as shown here:

```
if "Welcome to New York Harbor, USA." =~ /usa/i then
    puts "Welcome to America!"
end
```

Here, the result is a match, even though lowercase characters have been specified in the pattern and the matching characters in the source string are uppercase. If there were no i modifier in this example, the result would be no match.

String Substitution

You can use regular expressions to modify strings through character substitution using the String class's sub method. This method accepts as arguments a search pattern and a replacement pattern. The sub method has the following syntax:

```
string.sub(search, replace)
```

Here, *search* represents the search pattern, and *replace* represents the replacement pattern. The method searches the string and substitutes the first instance of the search pattern that it finds with the replacement pattern.

To see how this method works in practice, consider the following example:

```
x = "Once upon a time there was a small boy who climbed
    a small tree."
puts x.sub("small", "big")
```

Here, a string is assigned to a variable named x. Next, the sub method is called and passed small as the search pattern and big as the replacement pattern. The following output is displayed when these statements are executed:

```
Once upon a time there was a big boy who climbed a small tree.
```

In this example, the first instance of the string small was replaced with the word big. Notice, however, that the source string contained two instances of the string small and that the second instance was not replaced. The sub method only replaces the first instance of a search pattern.

If you want to replace all the instances of a search pattern, you need to use the String class's gsub method. This method has the following syntax:

```
string.gsub(search, replace)
```

Here, *search* represents a search pattern, and *replace* represents the replacement pattern. Like the sub method, the gsub method accepts as an argument a search pattern, which can be any regular-expression pattern or string, and a replacement pattern. Using gsub, you can rewrite the previous example, as shown here:

```
x = "Once upon a time, there was a small boy who" +
  "climbed a small tree."
puts x.gsub("small", "big")
```

When executed, this example displays the following output:

```
Once upon a time, there was a big boy who climbed a big tree.
```

Short Quiz

1. (True/False) By default, any character that is included in a regular expression results in a match if that same character is found in a source string.

2. _____ are enclosed within matching square brackets and are used to set up a search for a range of characters within a source string.

3. You can escape a metacharacter by preceding it with which of the following characters?

   a. \

   b. -

   c. @

   d. None of the above

4. Which of the following regular-expression metacharacters can be used to match any numeric character?

   a. ^

   b. \s

   c. \d

   d. \W

5. In Ruby, you can disable case sensitivity using which of the following modifiers?

    a. a

    b. e

    c. i

    d. o

Back to the Ruby Word Guessing Game

It is time to develop this chapter's game project, the Ruby Word Guessing game. As you create this script, watch for typos, and do not omit any steps.

Designing the Game

The development of the Word Guessing game is completed in 15 steps, as outlined here:

1. Open your text or script editor, and create a new file.

2. Add comment statements to the beginning of the script file to document the script and its purpose.

3. Define a `Screen` class representing the terminal window.

4. Define a `Game` class representing the Word Guessing game.

5. Add a `display_greeting` method to the `Game` class.

6. Add a `display_instructions` method to the `Game` class.

7. Add a `select_word` method to the `Game` class.

8. Add a `get_consonants` method to the `Game` class.

9. Add a `get_vowel` method to the `Game` class.

10. Add a `prompt_for_guess` method to the `Game` class.

11. Add a `play_game` method to the `Game` class.

12. Add a `display_credits` method to the `Game` class.

13. Instantiate script objects.

14. Prompt the player for permission to begin the game.

15. Set up the game's controlling logic.

Step 1: Create a New Ruby File

Open your text or script editor, and create a new Ruby script file. Save the file with the name WordGuess.rb, and store it in the folder with your other Ruby scripts.

Step 2: Document the Script and Its Purpose

Add the following comment statements to the new script file. These comments provide a description of the script and its purpose.

```
#---------------------------------------------------------
#
# Script Name: WordGuess.rb
# Version:     1.0
# Author:      Jerry Lee Ford, Jr.
# Date:        April 2010
#
# Description: This Ruby script demonstrates how to work
#              with regular expressions through the
#              development of a computer game that
#              challenges the player to guess a
#              mystery word after being first
#              allowed to guess 5 consonants and
#              1 vowel.
#
#---------------------------------------------------------
```

Step 3: Define the *Screen* Class

Define a class named Screen by adding the following statements to the end of the script file:

```
# Define custom classes -----------------------------------

#Define a class representing the console window
class Screen

  def cls  #Define a method that clears the display area
    puts ("\n" * 25)  #Scroll the screen 25 times
    puts "\a"    #Make a little noise to get the player's attention
  end

  def pause     #Define a method that pauses the display area
    STDIN.gets  #Execute the STDIN class's gets method to
                #pause script execution until the player
                #presses the Enter key
  end

end
```

The first method defined in the class is the `cls` method. It contains two statements. The first statement writes 25 blank lines to the terminal window to clear the screen. The second statement processes a string containing the \a escape character, which makes a beep sound, thus notifying the player each time the terminal screen is cleared.

Step 4: Define the *Game* Class

Define a class named Game by adding the following statements to the end of the script file:

```
#Define a class representing the Word Guessing Game
class Game

end
```

This class contains eight methods that control the game's execution.

Step 5: Define the *display_greeting* Method

Define the first of eight methods belonging to the Game class by inserting the following statements between the class's opening and closing statements:

```
#This method displays the game's opening message
def display_greeting

   Console_Screen.cls  #Clear the display area

   #Display welcome message
   print "\t\t\tWelcome to the Word Guessing Game!" +
     "\n\n\n\n\n\n\n\n\n\n\n\n\n\nPress Enter to " +
     "continue."

   Console_Screen.pause        #Pause the game
End
```

This method, named display_greeting, displays the game's welcome screen.

Step 6: Define the *display_instructions* Method

Define the second of eight methods belonging to the Game class by adding the following statements at the end of the class definition, immediately after the display_greeting method:

```
#Define a method to be used to present game instructions
def display_instructions

   Console_Screen.cls       #Clear the display area
   puts "INSTRUCTIONS:\n\n"  #Display a heading
```

```
#Display the game's instructions
puts "At the start of each round of play, the game ↵
    randomly selects"
puts "a word that is between five and ten characters long and" ↵
puts "challenges you to guess it. Before submitting your
    guess, you"
puts "must specify five consonants and one vowel. If any ↵
    of these"
puts "are used in the word, they will be revealed on ↵
    the screen,"
puts "thereby making it easier for you to guess the ↵
    secret word\n\n"
puts "Good luck!\n\n\n\n\n\n\n\n\n"
print "Press Enter to continue."

Console_Screen.pause        #Pause the game

end
```

This method, named display_instructions, displays a text string containing instructions for playing the game.

Step 7: Define the select_word Method

Define the third of eight methods belonging to the Game class by adding the following statements at the end of the class definition, immediately after the display_instructions method:

```
#Define a method that generates the secret word
def select_word

    #Define an array of 20 words from which the game will
    #randomly select
    words = ["W I N D O W", "S T A T I O N", "H A M B U R G E R",
            "E X P R E S S I O N", "W A L L E T", "C A M E R A",
            "A I R P L A N E", "C A N D L E", "C O M P U T E R",
            "P I C T U R E", "F R A M E", "S H E L F",
            "B O W L I N G", "P O L I T E", "S T A T E M E N T",
            "P O L I T E", "S T A T E M E N T", "N E G A T I V E",
            "N E G A T I V E", "M E T H O D", "F I S H I N G",
            "C O M P E N S A T E", "H A P P Y"]

    #Generate and return a random number between 0 and 19
    randomNo = rand(19)

    #Return a randomly selected word to the calling statement
    return words[randomNo]

end
```

The select_word method defines an array named words and populates the array with 20 uppercase text strings representing the game's words. Spaces are added between each letter in each word to facilitate the splitting up of the characters that make up each word into an array.

Next, a random number from 0 to 19 is generated. Finally, the method returns a word extracted from the words array to the statement that called on the method to execute.

Step 8: Define the get_consonants Method

Define the fourth of eight methods that make up the Game class by adding the following statements at the end of the class definition, immediately after the select_word method:

```
#Define a method that collects the player's consonant guesses
def get_consonants

    list = Array.new  #define an array in which to store
                      #the consonants

    #Give the player an idea of what is coming
    puts "Before you try to guess the secret word, you" +
     "must specify 5 consonants. \n\n"
    print "Press Enter to continue."

    Console_Screen.pause      #Pause the game

    5.times do  #Iterate 5 times

      Console_Screen.cls        #Clear the display area

      #Prompt the player to enter a consonant
      print "\nPlease enter a consonant and press Enter. "

      input = STDIN.gets #Collect the player's input
      input.chop!        #Remove the end of line marker

      #Only accept consonant characters
      if input !~ /[bcdfghjklmnpqrstvwxyz]/i then
        Console_Screen.cls        #Clear the display area
        print "Error: " + input + " is not a consonant." +
        #Press Enter to continue."
        Console_Screen.pause      #Pause the game
        redo #Repeat the current iteration of the loop
      end

      #Only accept one character of input per guess
      if input.length > 1 then
        Console_Screen.cls        #Clear the display area
        print "Error: You may only enter one" +
        #character at a time. Press Enter to" +
        "continue."
        Console_Screen.pause      #Pause the game
        redo #Repeat the current iteration of the loop
      end
```

```
#Do not allow the player to submit the same guess twice
if list.include?(input.upcase) == true then
  Console_Screen.cls       #Clear the display area
  print "Error: You have already guessed" + input +
   #Press Enter to Continue."
  "Enter to continue."
  Console_Screen.pause      #Pause the game
  redo  #Repeat the current iteration of the loop
else
  list.push(input.upcase)   #Convert the consonant to
                            #uppercase and add it to
                            #the list of consonants
end

  return list  #Return the list of consonants to the
    calling statement
end
```

The get_consonants method prompts the player to provide five consonants, which the game uses to disclose matching letters in its secret word prior to prompting the player to try to guess the word.

This method defines an array named list, which is used to store a list of consonants supplied by the player. Next, a message is displayed informing the player that it's time to provide the game with five consonants. A loop is then set up that executes five times (once for each collected consonant).

Within the loop, the player is prompted to enter a consonant. The player's input is then validated in a series of three conditional checks. The first conditional check sets up a regular expression that performs a comparison (ignoring case) of the player's input against a list of all the consonants in the alphabet. The player's input is rejected if it does not match one of the consonants listed in the regular expression.

The second conditional check uses the String class's length method to determine if the player has entered more than one character, rejecting it if so. The third conditional check uses the String class's include? method to determine if the player's input (converted to uppercase) has already been submitted (i.e., has been added to the list array), rejecting it if so. If the player's input is valid after the third conditional check, it is added to the end of the list array using the push method (after being converted to all uppercase).

The game's words are stored as all-uppercase letters in an array named words. By converting player input to uppercase, you can simplify the comparisons between the player's input and the game words.

The final statement in the get_consonants method returns a list of consonants back to the statement that called upon the method.

 Any time a conditional check rejects the player's input, the redo command causes the loop to execute again, preventing the loop from iterating. Only valid input that has been converted to uppercase is added to the list array.

Step 9: Define the get_vowel Method

Define the fifth of the eight methods that make up the Game class by adding the following statements at the end of the class definition, immediately after the get_consonants method:

```
#Define a method that collects the player's vowel guess
def get_vowel

    #Give the player an idea of what is coming
    puts "Before you try to guess the secret word," +
        #you must specify 1 vowel.\n\n"

    1.times do  #Iterate 1 time

        Console_Screen.cls      #Clear the display area

        #Prompt the player to enter a vowel
        print "\nPlease enter a vowel and press Enter. "
        input = STDIN.gets  #Collect the player's input
        input.chop!         #Remove the end of line marker

        #Only accept vowel characters
        if input !~ /[aeiou]/i then
          Console_Screen.cls        #Clear the display area
          print "Error: " + input + " is not a vowel" +
          "Press Enter to continue."
          Console_Screen.pause      #Pause the game
          redo  #Repeat the current iteration of the loop
        end

        #Only accept one character of input per guess
        if input.length > 1 then
          Console_Screen.cls        #Clear the display area
          print "Error: You may only enter one character" +
          "at a time. Press Enter to continue."
          Console_Screen.pause      #Pause the game
          Redo  #Repeat the current iteration of the loop
        end

        input = input.upcase  #Convert the vowel to uppercase
        return input  #Return the vowel to the calling statement

    end

end
```

This method prompts the player to provide a vowel, which the game uses to disclose matching vowels in its secret word prior to prompting the player to try to guess the word.

The program statements in this method are very similar to those in the previous method, except only two conditional validation checks are performed on the user's input, and the input is returned to the calling statement as an individual value, not a list. Note the use of the time loop, which is necessary to support data validation and to ensure that the game does not progress until a vowel is entered.

Step 10: Define the *prompt_for_guess* Method

Define the sixth of the eight methods that make up the Game class by adding the following statements at the end of the class definition, immediately after the get_vowel method:

```ruby
#Define a method that collects player guesses
def prompt_for_guess(shortWord, word, consonants, vowel)

  Console_Screen.cls        #Clear the display area

  consonants.push(vowel)  #To make things easy, add the
                          #vowel to the list of consonants

  wordArray = word.split(" ") #Split the secret word into
                              #an array

  i = 0  #Initialize index variable to zero

  #Loop once for each letter in the word (stored in an array)
  wordArray.each do |letter|

    match = false  #Initial the variable with a starting
                   #value of false

    #Loop once for each consonant stored in the consonants array
    consonants.each do |character|

      #Compare the current character from the consonants
      #array to the current letter in the wordArray array
      if character == letter then
        match = true  #Set variable value to indicate a match
        break  #Terminate loop execution when a match occurs
      end

    end

    #If there is no matching character in the consonants
    #array for the current letter in the wordArray
    #array, replace that letter in the wordArray with
    #an underscore character
    if match == false then
      wordArray[i] = "_"  #Replace the current character with an
    end                   #underscore
```

```ruby
    i = i + 1  #Increment the variable's value by 1

end

#Once the contents of the array have been formatted
#with underscores, convert the contents of the array
#back into a word
word = wordArray.join(" ")

#Allow the player up to three guesses
3.times do |i|  #i equals 0 on the first iteration of the loop

  Console_Screen.cls      #Clear the display area

  #Prompt the player to try to guess the secret word
  puts "I am thinking of a word.\n\n\n\n\n\n"
  print "Here is your clue:  " + word + "\n\n\n\n\n\n\n\n"
  print "What do you think this word is?  "
  reply = STDIN.gets  #Collect the player's reply
  reply.chop!         #Remove the end of line marker
  reply = reply.upcase #Convert the reply to all uppercase

  #Analyze the player's guess
  if reply == shortWord then  #The player guessed the
                              #secret word

    Console_Screen.cls       #Clear the display area
    print "Correct! Press Enter to continue."
    Console_Screen.pause        #Pause the game
    break  #Terminate the execution of the loop

  else  #The player did not guess the secret word

    Console_Screen.cls         #Clear the display area

    #Display a message based on how many turns remain
    if i == 1 then
      print "Wrong! You have one guess left. Press Enter to " +
      "try again."
    elsif i == 2
      print "Sorry, you lose.\n\n"
      print "The word was " + shortWord +
       ". Press Enter to continue."
    else
      print "Wrong! Press Enter to try again."
    end

    Console_Screen.pause         #Pause the game

  end

end

end
```

The `prompt_for_guess` method formats the display of the secret word and manages the game's interaction with the player during the guessing of the word.

This method processes four arguments. The first argument, `shortWord`, is a copy of the game's secret word, with no spaces in it. The second argument, `word`, is a copy of the game's secret word, with spaces inserted between each letter. The third argument, `consonants`, is a list of the five consonants supplied by the player. And the fourth argument, `vowel`, is a string representing the vowel specified by the player when the `get_vowel` method was executed.

The `prompt_for_guess` method begins by adding `vowel` to the `consonants` array. This groups all the player's input into a single array, making the data easy to process. Next, an array named `wordArray` is created and assigned a list of letters retrieved from `word`.

Next, a value of zero is assigned to a variable named `i`. This variable keeps track of which item (letter) is being examined in the `wordArray` array as it's being processed by a loop. Each letter is compared to each of the six letters provided by the player.

A loop is then set up that iterates through each item stored in the `wordArray` array. Within this loop, a second loop is set up that loops through each item stored in the `consonants` array. The inner loop compares the currently selected item (letter) from the `wordArray` array with each of the items (letters) in the `consonants` array. If a match is found, a value of **true** is assigned to a variable named `match`, and the inner loop is terminated using the **break** command.

Next, a conditional statement is executed, replacing the current character in the `wordArray` array with an underscore if no match was found in the `consonants` array. The underscore is used to represent the letters that make up a game word. The value of `match` is then set back to **false**, and the value of `i` is incremented by 1. Once every item in `wordArray` has been compared to every item in `consonants`, the contents of `wordArray` are converted back into a string using the Array class's `join` method.

Next, a loop is set up that gives the player three chances to guess the game's secret word. Each time the loop iterates, it displays the current version of the secret word. Any letters in the word that match the consonants and vowel that the player has specified are revealed, and all the other letters are still hidden (represented by underscore characters). The player is then prompted to guess the secret word.

The player's guess is converted to all-uppercase characters and compared with the value of `shortWord` to see if there is a match, in which case the player has successfully guessed the word. If this happens,

In order to extract each letter from the string stored in `word` and assign it as an item in the `wordArray` array, the `String` class's `split` method is used. This method splits the contents of a string into an array using a specified delimiter. A **delimiter** is a character used to separate characters within a string. In the case of the `word` variable, the delimiter is the blank space located between any two successive letters.

The `join` method takes as an argument a character that is used as a delimiter in formulating the content of a string. In the `prompt_for_guess` method, the `join` method is passed a single blank space.

Ruby treats uppercase and lower-case letters differently. So, when text strings are being compared, an uppercase letter such as "A" will not match its lower-ercase equivalent. The letters that make up the game words are stored as uppercase characters in an array. To keep things simple, the game converts all player input to uppercase, eliminating differences in case when comparing player input to game words.

the break command is executed, terminating the execution of the loop. Otherwise, the player is informed of an error and given another chance to make a guess. After the player uses up all three chances without correctly guessing the secret word, the loop terminates.

Step 11: Define the play_game Method

Define the seventh of the eight methods that make up the Game class by adding the following statements at the end of the class definition, immediately after the prompt_for_guess method:

```
#Define a method to control game play
def play_game

  word = select_word  #Call on the method that retrieves
                      #a random word

  Console_Screen.cls        #Clear the display area

  consonants = get_consonants #Call on the method that
                              #prompts the player
                              #to enter a list of consonants

  Console_Screen.cls        #Clear the display area

  #Call on the method that prompts the player to enter a vowel
  vowel = get_vowel

  #Remove blank spaces from the word to create a short
  #version of the word
  shortWord = word.gsub(" ", "")

  #Call the method that processes player guesses
  prompt_for_guess(shortWord, word, consonants, vowel)

  Console_Screen.cls        #Clear the display area

end
```

This method calls on the select_word method to retrieve a word for the player to guess. Next, the get_consonants method retrieves a list of five consonants, and the get_vowel method prompts the player to supply a vowel. Next, the String class's gsub method generates a short version of the secret word (without spaces), and the prompt_for_guess method is executed. This method is passed shortWord, word, consonants, and vowel as arguments and uses this information to prompt the player to guess the secret word.

Step 12: Define the `display_credits` Method

Define the eighth of the eight methods that make up the Game class by
adding the following statements at the end of the Game class:

```
#This method displays the information about the Word Guessing game
def display_credits

  Console_Screen.cls  #Clear the display area

  #Thank the player and display game information
  puts "\t\t      Thank you for playing the Word Guessing ↵
    Game.\n\n\n\n"
  puts "\n\t\t\t Developed by Jerry Lee Ford, Jr.\n\n"
  puts "\t\t\t\t Copyright 2010\n\n"
  puts "\t\t\tURL: http://www.tech-publishing.com\n\n\n\ ↵
    n\n\n\n\n\n\n"

end
```

This method displays the game's credits, including the author's URL.

Step 13: Instantiate Script Objects

Instantiate instances of the Screen and Game classes by adding the following statements to the end of the script file:

```
# Main Script Logic -------------------------------------

Console_Screen = Screen.new  #Instantiate a new Screen object
WordGuess = Game.new         #Instantiate a new Game object

#Execute the Game class's display_greeting method
WordGuess.display_greeting

answer = ""  #Initialize variable and assign it an empty string
```

In addition to instantiating the Console_Screen and WordGuess
objects, these statements define a variable named answer, which is
used to control the execution of the loop that prompts the player for
permission to begin a new round of play.

Step 14: Get Permission to Start the Game

Set up the prompt for getting the player's permission to play the game
by adding the following statements to the end of the script file:

```
#Loop until the player enters y, n, Y, or N and do not accept any
#other input
loop do
```

247

```
Console_Screen.cls  #Clear the display area

#Prompt the player for permission to start the game
print "Are you ready to play the Word Guessing Game? (y/n): "

answer = STDIN.gets #Collect the player's answer
answer.chop!  #Remove the new line character appended to the
              #string

#Terminate the loop if valid input was provided
break if answer =~ /y|n/i  #Accept uppercase or lowercase input
```

end

Here, a loop has been set up to run forever. Upon each iteration of
the loop, the player is prompted to enter a value of y or n to indicate
whether a new round of play should be initiated or the game should
be terminated. Any input other than a y or n is ignored. Once a valid
response has been entered, the **break** command is executed, terminating the loop and allowing the rest of the script to run.

Step 15: Control Game Play

The remainder of the script file consists of statements responsible for
controlling the overall game play. The execution of these statements
depends on whether the player decided to terminate the game or play
another round. Add the following statements to the end of the script file:

```
#Analyze the player's input
if answer == "n" or answer == "N"    #See if the player
                                     #elected not to
                                     #play the game

  Console_Screen.cls  #Clear the display area

  #Invite the player to return and play the game some
  #other time
  puts "Okay, perhaps another time.\n\n"

else  #The player wants to play the game

    #Execute the game class's display_instructions method
    WordGuess.display_instructions

  loop do  #Loop forever

    #Execute the Game class's play_game method
    WordGuess.play_game

    #Find out if the player wants to play another round
    print "Enter Q to quit or press any key to play again: "

    playAgain = STDIN.gets #Collect the player's response
    playAgain.chop!  #Remove the new line character appended
                     #to the string
```

```
    #Terminate the loop if valid input was provided
    break if playAgain =~ /Q/i

  end

  #Call upon the Game class's display_credits method
  WordGuess.display_credits

end
```

If the player decides to stop playing the game, the first statement in the if code block is executed, clearing the screen and inviting the player to play another time. If the player decides to play another round, however, the statements that follow the else keyword are processed, and the Game class's display_instructions method is called.

Next, a loop is set up to facilitate the execution of as many rounds of play as the player wants. Each time the loop repeats, it calls on the play_game method, which manages the playing of the game. Once the play_game method has finished executing, the player is asked if she would like to play another game. If the player enters a q and presses Enter, the break command is executed, terminating the loop and causing the display_credits method to be called, after which the script terminates. If the player enters anything other than a q and presses Enter, the loop iterates, and a new round of play is initiated.

Running Your New Ruby Script Game

Save your Ruby script. If you typed the code statements correctly, the program should work as expected. If you run into any errors, read the error messages carefully to ascertain what went wrong. If necessary, review the script and look for mistyped or missing statements.

Summing Up

- A regular expression is a pattern used to identify matching character data.

- Regular expressions allow you to perform a detailed analysis of user input to determine if it meets criteria you have specified.

- Regular expressions also perform string substitutions.

- Data can come from many sources, including databases, files, users, and input from other scripts and programs.

- You should build data validation logic into your scripts, rejecting data that is not in the proper format.

- By default, regular-expression patterns are processed from left to right.

- By default, pattern matches occur when a search string pattern is found anywhere within a source string.

- By default, pattern matches are case sensitive.

- Case sensitivity can be disabled using the i modifier.

- To instruct Ruby to treat metacharacters like regular characters, you must precede them with the \ character.

- The =~ operator is the equivalent of the **equals** operation in a regular expression.

- The !~ operator is the equivalent of the **not equals** operation in a regular expression.

- You can set up regular-expression patterns to find any of a set of specified matches by using the | character.

- The . metacharacter can be used as part of a pattern to match any individual character (except for the new-line character).

- The ^ metacharacter can be used as part of a pattern to look for a match at the beginning of a line.

- The $ metacharacter can be used as part of a pattern to look for a match at the end of a line.

- The ? metacharacter can be used as part of a pattern to look for a character (or a group of characters) that occurs once or not at all.

- The * metacharacter can be used as part of a pattern to look for a match within a string that occurs zero or more times.

- The + metacharacter can be used as part of a pattern to look for a match of one or more instances of the preceding character.

- Using character classes enclosed within square brackets, you can search for anything that is included within a range of characters in a string.

- The String class's sub method is used to replace the first instance of a search pattern within a target string.

- The String class's gsub method is used to replace all instances of a search pattern within a target string.

Comprehension Check

1. Which of the following actions is supported by regular expressions?

    a. Search and replace operations on strings

    b. Extracting a substring from a larger string

    c. Counting the number of instances of a pattern within a string

    d. All of the above

2. (True/False) One limitation of regular expressions is their inability to deal with differences in case when performing string substitutions.

3. Which of the following operators is the regular-expression equivalent of a not equals operator?

    a. !~

    b. !=

    c. <>

    d. None of the above

4. (True/False) In most cases, regular-expression matches are processed from right to left.

5. (True/False) By default, regular-expression matches are not case sensitive.

6. Which of the following characters is used within a regular expression to search for any of a set of possible matches?

    a. /

    b. &

    c. |

    d. =~

7. (True/False) Normally, a character included in a regular expression will form a match with the same character if it is found in the source string.

8. To instruct Ruby to treat a metacharacter like a regular character, you precede the metacharacter with which of the following characters?

    a. /

    b. &

    c. |

    d. \

9. (True/False) The regular expression /(b|c|s|f|h|p)at/ is equivalent to the following regular expression: /bat|cat|sat|fat|hat|pat/.

10. To match any individual character except the new-line character, you use the _____ character in a regular expression.

11. (True/False) Case sensitivity can be enabled or disabled within regular expressions.

12. Which of the following regular-expression metacharacters is used to look for a match at the end of a line?

    a. .

    b. ^

    c. $

    d. \Z

13. To set up a regular expression that looks for a single character or a group of characters that occur either once or not at all, you use the _____ metacharacter modifier.

14. Which of the following regular-expression metacharacters is used to set up a match for numeric data?

    a. \A

    b. \W

    c. \d

    d. \s

15. Using the _____ character, you can set up a regular expression that matches zero or more instances of a preceding character.

16. Which of the following regular-expression metacharacters is used to match non-blank space?

    a. \s

    b. \S

    c. \w

    d. \W

17. The _____ character is used to set up a regular expression that matches one or more instances of a preceding character.

18. To search for anything included within a range of characters, use _____, placing the range of characters inside a pair of square brackets.

19. Which of the following methods is used to find and replace the first instance of a search string within a larger string?

    a. gsub

    b. replace

    c. sub

    d. find

20. Which of the following can be used to set up a regular expression that matches a letter?

    a. /[abcdefghijklmnopqrstuvwxyz]/

    b. /[a-z]/

    c. /[A-Z]/

    d. All of the above

Reinforcement Exercises

The following exercises are designed to further your understanding of Ruby programming by challenging you to make improvements to the chapter's game project, the Word Guessing game.

1. The game currently draws on a pool of 20 words when selecting the secret word. Because of such a small pool, the same word may be used more than once in a single session of play. Make the game more fun by doubling the number of words that are available.

2. The text contained in the `display_instructions` method, which instructs players in how to play the game, is a bit dry and cryptic. Revise this text to provide the players with better directions. Make sure you include information about the minimum and maximum length of the game words (five to 10 characters), and make sure you explain that underscore characters are used to represent the letters that have not been guessed.

3. The game currently displays the instructions once, at the beginning. Modify the game to remove the automatic display of its instructions and instead allow players to display the instructions as a hidden cheat, accessible when the h key is pressed. Make it so the existence of this feature is revealed when the player is first prompted to play the game, as well as when the player is prompted to continue playing after a round of play.

4. The game currently prevents the player from guessing the same letter twice, acting on the assumption that the player remembers any previous guesses. To provide better feedback, modify the game so that it displays a list of all the wrong guesses each time the player enters a guess that's already been tried. Hint: Use the `inspect` method to display the contents of the `list` array. Also, use a regular expression to remove the double quotation marks that are included when array contents are displayed.

5. Whenever play ends without the player having guessed the secret word, the game displays the secret word in all-uppercase characters. Modify the game so that only the first letter of the word is uppercase. You could implement this change by retyping each of the game words stored in the list array, of course. Instead, convert all the words to lowercase, and then, using a regular expression, change the first character of the game word to uppercase.

Discovery Projects

Project 7-1

Regular expressions are an enormous topic, with entire books and websites devoted to them. To gain a deeper understanding of regular expressions, visit the following websites:

- *http://www.regular-expressions.info/*
- *http://en.wikipedia.org/wiki/Regular_expression*
- *http://regexlib.com/*

Write a one-page paper on regular expressions. Highlight the advantages they offer, and focus on their data-validation capabilities. Explain both the importance of verifying script input and data and the limitations of trying to do so with a Ruby script that does not use regular expressions.

Project 7-2

Complete each of the following exercises using IRB and regular expressions. Capture the results using screen prints, and turn them in to your instructor.

1. Enter the following statement into IRB, then use an `if` statement and a regular expression to search for the word `Lions` at the beginning of the string:

   `"Lions and tigers and bears, oh my!"`

2. Enter the following statement into IRB, then use an `if` statement and a regular expression to search for a four-letter word beginning with the letters `ti` followed by two characters, a blank space, and then a five-letter word beginning with the letters `th`:

   `"Once upon a time there were three bears."`

3. Enter the following statement into IRB, then use an `if` statement and a regular expression to search for the characters `rs.` at the end of the text string:

   `string = "Once upon a time there were three bears."`

4. Enter the following statement into IRB, then conditionally execute three different statements using regular expressions that search the string for the letter w, the letter z, and a number:

   `"Once upon a time there were three bears."`

Project 7-3

Perform each of the following string substitutions using the **sub** and **gsub** methods. Capture the results using screen prints, and turn them in to your instructor.

1. Enter the following statement into IRB, then use the **sub** method to replace the first vowel found in the string with an asterisk character:

   `"Jack and Jill went up the hill to fetch a pail of water."`

2. Enter the following statement into IRB, then use the **gsub** method to replace each vowel found in the string with an asterisk character:

   `"Jack and Jill went up the hill to fetch a pail of water."`

3. Enter the following statement into IRB, then use the **gsub** method to replace the string `may be more than` with the string `can only be`:

   `"In the end there may be more than one."`

4. Enter the following statement into IRB, then use the **gsub** method to replace the word **bob** with the word **Bob** throughout the string:

   `"Big bob told little bob to take baby bob home."`

5. Enter the following statement into IRB, then use the **gsub** method to replace each blank space in the string with a comma and a blank space:

   `"Bob Sue Sam Dick Jane Peter Paul John"`

6. Enter the following statement into IRB, then use the **sub** method to remove the pound sign and all the characters that follow it:

   `"804-991-3434 #Client phone number"`

7. Modify your solution to the above exercise to include a second regular expression that removes any blank spaces and hyphens from the string:

## CHAPTER 8

Object-Oriented Programming

In this chapter, you learn how to:

- ◎ Work with key features of object-oriented programming
- ◎ Initialize objects upon instantiation
- ◎ Develop variable scope
- ◎ Take advantage of Ruby's built-in classes
- ◎ Modify Ruby classes

In Chapter 3, "Working with Strings, Objects, and Variables," you learned about a number of elementary object-oriented programming concepts, including how to define classes and instantiate objects based on those classes. You learned how to define properties and methods within those classes and how to interact with those properties and methods once you have instantiated objects based on those classes. In subsequent chapters, you learned how to work with an assortment of predefined Ruby classes, including the string, numeric, array, and hash classes. In this chapter, you learn about some more object-oriented programming concepts, including how to initialize objects upon instantiation, how to restrict access to object variables using variable scopes, how to overwrite class methods, and how to restrict access to class methods.

Project Preview: The Rock, Paper, Scissors Game

In this chapter, you learn how to create a computer game called the Rock, Paper, Scissors game. It is a computerized version of the classic Rock, Paper, Scissors game, and it pits the player against the computer. There are three possible moves that the player and the computer can make: rock, paper, and scissors. After the computer and the player have selected their moves, the results are analyzed based on the following rules:

- Rock crushes scissors to win.

- Paper covers rock to win.

- Scissors cut paper to win.

- Both sides selecting the same move results in a tie.

The game begins by displaying the message shown in Figure 8-1.

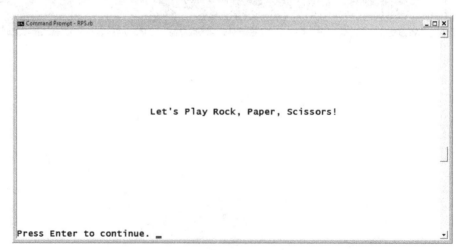

Figure 8-1   The welcome screen for the Rock, Paper, Scissors game

After pressing Enter, the player is prompted for permission to begin the game, as shown in Figure 8-2.

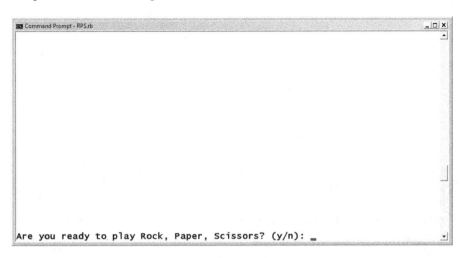

Figure 8-2 The player must decide to play before the game can begin

If the player decides to play, the instructions shown in Figure 8-3 are displayed. They provide a brief description of how the game is played.

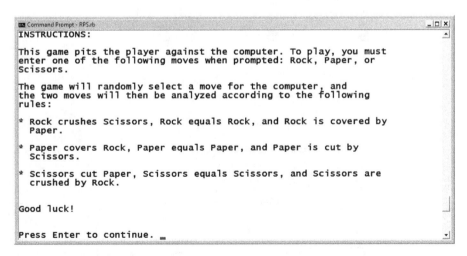

Figure 8-3 Instructions for how to play are provided

Next, the screen shown in Figure 8-4 is displayed, prompting the player to specify Rock, Paper, or Scissors.

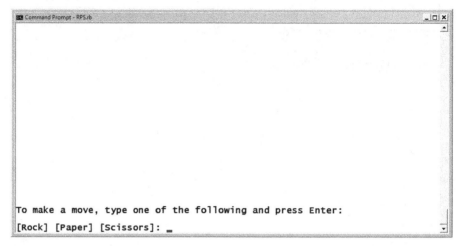

```
To make a move, type one of the following and press Enter:
[Rock] [Paper] [Scissors]: _
```

Figure 8-4 To make a move, the player must type Rock, Paper, or Scissors and press Enter

As soon as the player selects a move, the game randomly selects a move on behalf of the computer. The player's move is then compared to the computer's move to determine the result, as shown in Figure 8-5.

```
                    RESULTS:

                    ================================

                    Player's move:    ROCK

                    Computer's move:  SCISSORS

                    Result:           Player wins!

                    ================================

Press Enter to continue. _
```

Figure 8-5 The player's move beats the computer's move

At the end of each round of play, the game prompts the player for permission to play again, as shown in Figure 8-6.

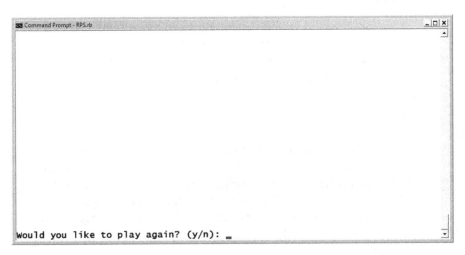

Figure 8-6 The player is prompted to play again

When the player has decided to quit playing, the screen shown in Figure 8-7 displays, and the game ends.

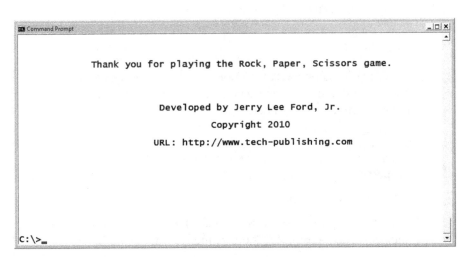

Figure 8-7 The closing message displays the developer's name and website

Key Features of Object-Oriented Programming

Thus far in this book, you have worked extensively with classes and methods, which are two key features of object-oriented programming. You will now be introduced to four other key features: abstraction, encapsulation, inheritance, and polymorphism.

Abstraction

Abstraction is the ability to make important object features available while hiding nonessential details, thereby focusing on the outside view of an object. It is implemented through classes and includes the specification of both properties and methods. Using the class as a template, you can create instances of objects. For example, you can define a class made up of a single property and one method, as shown here:

```ruby
class Automobile

  attr_accessor :color

  def drive
    puts "Vroom!!!"
  end

end
```

Here, a class named `Automobile` is defined and assigned one property and one method. Once the class is defined, you can create a new object from it, as shown here:

```ruby
myCar = Automobile.new
```

Once the object is created, you can assign a value to its `color` property, as shown here:

```ruby
myCar.color = "Blue"
```

Once the property is set, you can access it whenever you need to. You can also execute the object's `drive` method, as shown here:

```ruby
puts "I love to drive my little " + myCar.color + " car."
myCar.drive
```

When executed, these two statements display the following results:

```
I love to drive my little Blue car.
Vroom!!!
```

Encapsulation

Encapsulation involves the restriction of access to one or more of the properties and methods defined within a class, thereby allowing the internal representation of objects to be hidden from view outside the object definition. It makes program code more reliable by limiting access to just the areas within the program where access is required, which helps prevent accidental modification or execution.

By default, any properties and methods that you define in a class are public, which means they can be accessed from outside the class. To control access to the properties and methods within a class, insert any of the following keywords into the class:

- **public**—Makes any specified properties or methods available throughout the program

- **private**—Restricts the access of any specified properties or methods defined within the object itself

- **protected**—Restricts the access of any specified properties or methods to objects of the same class or objects of subclasses of the class

To use these keywords, place them on a line by themselves immediately before the property or method definitions for which you wish to specify access. Access to any properties or methods that are defined after the occurrence of one of these keywords is governed by that keyword, which remains in effect until either the end of the class is reached or a different level of encapsulation is specified.

For an example of how to restrict access to a method located in a custom class, look at the following Ruby program, which prompts the user to enter the name of a superhero. In response, the program displays the superhero's secret identity (if it is known).

```ruby
class Superhero

  def initialize(name)
    secret_identity(name)
  end

  def display_identity
    puts "\n\nThis superhero's secret identity is " +
      @identity + "\n\n"
    print "Press Enter to continue."
  end

  private

  def secret_identity(name)
```

```
      if name =~ /Superman/i then
        @identity = "Clark Kent"
      elsif name =~ /Batman/i then
        @identity = "Bruce Wayne"
      elsif name =~ /Spiderman/i then
        @identity = "Peter Parker"
      else
        @identity = "Unknown"
      end

  end

end

loop do

  puts ("\n" * 25)
  puts "\n\nWelcome to the Superhero Identity Tracker!\n\n"
  print "Enter a superhero's name or type Q to quit: "

  input = STDIN.gets
  input.chop!

  break if input =~ /q/i

  puts ("\n" * 25)

  myHero = Superhero.new(input)
  myHero.display_identity

  STDIN.gets

end
```

Here, a class named Superhero is defined. Within the class, three methods are set up. The first method, initialize, executes as soon as an object is instantiated using this class, and it accepts as an argument a string representing a superhero's name. When the initialize method executes, it calls upon the Superhero class's third method, secret_identity, and passes the superhero's name to it.

When called, the Superhero class's second method, display_identity, displays a text string that contains a variable named @identity, which is populated with data supplied by the third method.

The third method, secret_identity, is preceded by the keyword private, which doesn't allow it to be accessed from outside the class. Within the secret_identity method, an if code block, when executed, analyzes the value of the superhero's name to see if it matches one of the known superhero names. If a match occurs, the value of @identity is assigned a text string containing the superhero's secret identity. If no match is found, a value of Unknown is assigned instead.

The rest of the program is made up of a loop that has been set up to run forever. Each time the loop repeats, it prompts the player to either enter a superhero's name or Q, for quit, terminating the program's execution.

Figure 8-8 shows the initial screen that is displayed when this program is run. As you can see, the user has been prompted to enter a superhero's name.

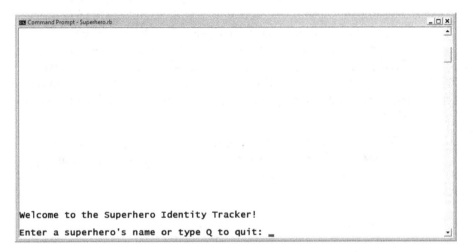

Figure 8-8 The user is prompted to enter a superhero's name or type Q to quit

After the user enters a name, the output shown in Figure 8-9 displays. Depending on whether the program was able to determine the hero's secret identity, either the superhero's real name is displayed, or the user is told that the superhero's identity is currently unknown.

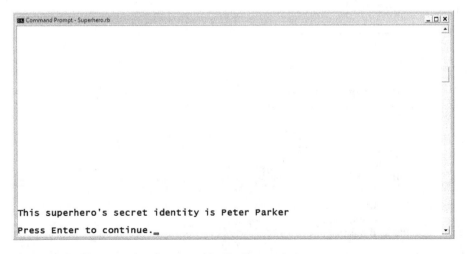

Figure 8-9 The superhero's secret identity is revealed

Inheritance

Inheritance is the process by which one class is derived from another class. The derived class, sometimes referred to as the child class, inherits all of the properties and methods of the parent class. In addition, you can modify the inherited properties and methods or add new ones to customize the child class.

With inheritance, it is possible to build an entire family of classes consisting of parents, children, grandchildren, siblings, and so on. When defining classes using inheritance, you should place the properties and methods common to all the classes in the top-most class, and place the properties and methods specific to individual classes within those individual classes. This allows you to customize the classes and also helps simplify the development and maintenance of your Ruby programs.

To see how inheritance works, look at the following program, which defines a class named Hero and then uses that class as the basis for defining three child classes:

```ruby
class Hero

  attr_accessor :power, :weakness

  def catch_phrase
   print "Halt in the name of the law! "
  end

end

class UnderDog < Hero

  def bark
    puts "Woof!"
  end

end

class Superman < Hero
  attr_accessor :cape
end

class Batman < Hero
  attr_accessor :mask
end

UD = UnderDog.new
SM = Superman.new
BM = Batman.new
```

```
SM.power = "Flight"
SM.weakness = "Kryptonite"
SM.cape = "red"

SM.catch_phrase
puts "Or I will fly over there in my " + SM.cape +
    "cape and capture you!"
```

Here, a class named Hero is created that defines two properties and a
method. Next, a new class named UnderDog is defined as a child class
of the Hero class. The UnderDog class is then assigned an additional
method. Two additional classes are then created that, like the
UnderDog class, inherit all of the properties and methods of the Hero
class. Unique properties have been included in each of the definitions
for these two classes.

Finally, three objects are instantiated, one from each class, and
the object based on the Superman class is then assigned various
properties, after which its catch_phrase method is executed,
resulting in the following output:

```
Halt in the name of the law! Or I will fly over there in my
red cape and capture you!
```

Polymorphism

Polymorphism is the ability to define objects and methods in
different forms. One way to implement polymorphism within Ruby
is to assign the same name to different methods, allowing Ruby to
execute the appropriate method based on the context in which the
method is executed. A good example of polymorphism is provided
by Ruby's + method. When used with two strings, the + method
concatenates the two strings, as shown here:

```
puts "Once upon " + "a time in a faraway land..."
```

After being executed, this statement displays the following output:

```
Once upon a time in a faraway land...
```

When used on two numbers, the + method adds them together, as
shown here:

```
puts 5 + 4
```

After being executed, this statement displays a value of 9.

When used with two arrays, the + method merges them into a new
array, as shown here:

```
x = [1, 2, 3] + [4, 5, 6]
puts x.inspect
```

After being executed, these statements display the following output:

```
[1, 2, 3, 4, 5, 6]
```

You can easily use polymorphic programming with your own custom methods, as shown here:

```ruby
class Hero
  attr_accessor :power, :weakness
  def catch_phrase
    puts "Here I come to save the day!"
  end
end

class UnderDog < Hero
end

class Superman < Hero
  def catch_phrase
    puts "Up, up and away!"
  end
end

class Batman < Hero
  def catch_phrase
    puts "Quick, to the batcave!"
  end
end
```

Here, a class named Hero is defined and assigned two properties and one method named catch_phrase. Next, three child classes are created based on the Hero class. The first, named UnderDog, inherits the properties and methods of its parent class. The other two classes inherit the same properties and methods that UnderDog does but overwrite the catch_phrase method with their own custom versions. Therefore, if you instantiate objects based on each of the three child classes, then execute their catch_phrase methods, you will see different results, as shown in the following example:

```ruby
UD = UnderDog.new
SM = Superman.new
BM = Batman.new

UD.catch_phrase
SM.catch_phrase
BM.catch_phrase
```

When executed, these statements display the following output:

```
Here I come to save the day!
Up, up and away!
Quick, to the batcave!
```

Short Quiz

1. (True/False) A class provides a template that specifies properties, methods, and data that are available for interacting with and controlling an object.

2. Which of the following is not a feature of object-oriented programming?

   a. Abstraction

   b. Encapsulation

   c. Visualization

   d. Polymorphism

3. Which if the following is a programming technique that restricts access to one or more of the properties and methods defined within a class?

   a. Encapsulation

   b. Abstraction

   c. Polymorphism

   d. Inheritance

4. Which of the following occurs when one class is derived from another class?

   a. Encapsulation

   b. Abstraction

   c. Polymorphism

   d. Inheritance

5. (True/False) Polymorphism is a term that refers to the process of organizing program code into classes.

Initializing Objects Upon Instantiation

You may want to instantiate an object and initialize it with one or more properties in a single step. To allow you to do so, Ruby provides a method named initialize. When included in a class definition, the initialize method is automatically executed any time an object is instantiated. By including the initialize method in a class definition, you can pass arguments to the class when you instantiate it, and these arguments will automatically be passed to the initialize method, after which they will be mapped to variables, as shown in the following example:

```
class Noise

  def initialize(number_beeps)
    @occurrences = number_beeps
  end

  def make_sound
    @occurrences.times {print "\a"}
  end

end
```

@occurrences is an example of an instance variable. Variable access is restricted to the object in which the variable resides.

Here, a class named Noise is set up that contains two methods. The first method, named initialize, is set up to process a single argument, which it then assigns to a variable named @occurrences. When called, the second method, named make_sound, plays a beep sound a specified number of times, as determined by the value assigned to @occurrences.

As with any class, you may instantiate as many object instances of the Noise class as you want. The following statements instantiate two objects based on the Noise class while initializing the @occurrences variable:

```
shortSound = Noise.new(1)
longSound = Noise.new(10)
```

The first statement instantiates an object named shortSound, based on the Noise object. Notice that a value of 1 has been passed as an argument. Therefore, when the new object is created, @occurrences is assigned a value of 1, and when the make_sound method is called, the method plays the beep sound one time.

The second statement creates an object named longSound. The only difference between this object and the shortSound object is that the longSound object will play the beep sound 10 times when the make_sound method is called. Once both objects have been instantiated, you can call the class's make_sound method for each of the objects using the method's initialized value for the @occurrences variable, as shown here:

```
shortSound.make_sound
STDIN.gets
longSound.make_sound
```

Here, the shortSound object's make_sound method is executed, playing a single beep sound, after which the program pauses until Enter is pressed. At this time, the longSound object's make_sound method is executed, playing 10 consecutive beep sounds.

Understanding Variable Scope

As you learned in Chapter 3, Ruby supports four different types of variables: local, global, instance, and class variables. Each of these variables is capable of storing a single instance of any type of object supported by Ruby. The difference among them is the scope—the area in the Ruby program—within which they can be accessed.

Working with Local Variables

A variable with a local scope can be accessed only within the scope that it was created in. As an example, consider the following statements, in which a class named Greeting that contains a method named display_msg is defined:

```
class Greeting

  def display_msg
    puts "Hello " + myName
  end

end
```

As a local variable, myName can only be accessed from within the method it was created in. If you specify a variable named myName outside that method, Ruby will regard it as a reference to a different variable, with its own scope, as shown here:

```
Msg = Greeting.new
myName = "Jerry Ford"
Msg.display_msg
```

When executed, these statements result in the following message: Undefined local variable or method error. Although the value of myName was set in the previous example, it remains unassigned in the Greeting class.

Working with Global Variables

One way around the problem shown in the previous example is to use a global variable. Global variables are accessible throughout a Ruby program and have an unlimited scope. Every class in the program is allowed to access them.

You should assign variables the lowest level of scope needed to provide the required access. Although it is easier to work with global variables, it can be a bad programming practice, because it renders variables susceptible to being accessed from other parts of the program.

To create a global variable, precede its name with the $ character, as shown in the following example:

```
class Greeting

  def display_msg
    puts "Hello " + $myName
  end

end

Msg = Greeting.new
$myName = "Jerry Ford"

Msg.display_msg
```

Since the myName variable has been changed from a local to a global variable, the previous error will not occur when the following statements are executed, because the $myName variable is accessible from the Greeting class's display_msg method.

```
Msg = Greeting.new
$myName = "Jerry Ford"
Msg.display_msg
```

Instead, the following output is displayed:

```
Hello Jerry Ford
```

The problem with using global variables is that they work against object-oriented programming principles. Specifically, they expose data located in other parts of a program file, opening up the possibility that the data might be accidentally changed. It is much better to isolate the various parts of a program file from one another, limiting the access to variables to those parts of the program that need to access them. Following this practice results in more modular code that is less prone to error and easier to maintain.

Encapsulation should be used to restrict access to variables. Whenever possible, you should use local variables and, as shown here, pass any values needed in different parts of a program rather than using global variables:

```
class Greeting

  def display_msg(userName)
    puts "Hello " + userName
  end

end

Msg = Greeting.new
name = "Jerry Ford"

Msg.display_msg(name)
```

Here, a value is assigned to a local variable called name. Next, the display_msg method is executed, and name is passed as an argument. The method then uses the userName parameter, which is local to the method, to display the following output:

```
Hello Jerry Ford
```

Working with Instance Variables

When working with variables that are defined within different methods belonging to the same class definition, it is sometimes helpful to increase the scope of the variables to allow them to be referenced by all the methods in that class definition. This allows you to keep pretty tight control over variable scope while making it easier to work with variables within objects instantiated from those classes. For example, earlier in this chapter you looked at a class named Noise, which contains two methods, initialize and make_sound. These two methods needed to share access to an argument passed during object instantiation. To accommodate this requirement, an instance variable was used, as shown here:

```
class Noise

  def initialize(occurrences)
    @occurrences = occurrences
  end

  def make_sound
    @occurrences.times {print "\a"}
  end

end
```

Instance variables begin with the @ character, global variables begin with the $ character, and local variables begin with a letter or underscore character. Although it's permitted, beginning a local variable name with an underscore character is not a good programming practice.

Working with Class Variables

Class variables are similar to instance variables, except they are accessible to all the instances of the same class, which makes it easier to make repeated references to variables. They begin with the @@ characters, as shown in the following example:

```
class Superman

  def initialize
```

```
    if defined?(@@myHero) then
        puts "Error: Only one instance of Superman is +
            #permitted at a time."
    else
        @@myHero = "Is alive"
        puts "Up, up and away!"
    end

  end

end
```

Here, a class named Superman is defined. It contains a single method named initialize, which automatically executes when an object is created using this class. The following statement creates an object based on the Superman class:

```
clarkKent = Superman.new
```

When executed, the clarkKent object creates a class variable named @@myHero and assigns it a value. If an attempt was made to create a second object based on the Superman class, as shown here, an error message will be displayed:

```
louisLane = Superman.new
```

The error message is displayed because of the @@myHero variable, which is accessible to any objects created from the Superman class and is found using the defined? method.

Notice that, in the previous example, the defined? method was used to verify the existence of the @@myHero variable. This method returns a value of true if the specified variable is found and false if it is not found.

Taking Advantage of Ruby's Built-in Classes

Ruby provides access to many built-in classes. By creating objects based on these classes, you instantly get access to all the predefined methods that Ruby defines for those objects. In addition, your objects have access to the properties belonging to these classes. As a result, programming is significantly simpler, because you do not have to reinvent the wheel every time you write a new program.

As an example, consider the Array class. Since every array automatically has access to all the methods defined by the Array class, you can sort the contents of an array by calling on the Array class's sort method. This gives you instant access to reliable source code. And you didn't have to spend the time required to write your own custom sort method.

You can even chain together different objects' methods to pass one method's output to another method as input, as shown in the following example:

```
myArray = [2, 8, 3, 5, 1]
puts myArray.sort.reverse.inspect
```

Here, the first statement creates an array object named myArray and assigns it a collection of numbers in no particular order. The second statement chains together a series of array methods that sorts the contents of the array, reverses their order, and then displays them as a string. This results in:

```
[8, 5, 3, 2, 1]
```

The advantage of chaining methods together is that you can perform complex tasks with a minimal amount of programming code. If you write less code, there will be less chance that you'll make an error, and the programs will be easier to maintain.

Modifying Ruby Classes

Ruby is an exceptionally flexible programming language, so much so that you can even modify the language itself by removing, redefining, or adding to parts of it. Ruby allows you to customize the language to suit your own preferences and needs.

For example, you can add more operator methods to Ruby's Numeric class. In Ruby, mathematical calculations are typically performed by defining an expression, as shown in the following statement:

```
x = 1 + 3
```

Here, a variable named x is assigned the value returned by the expression of 1 + 3. The following statement demonstrates another way of formulating the previous example:

```
x = 1.+ 3
```

Here, a value of 4 is assigned to x using an expression that uses dot notation to execute the Numeric class's + method, adding 1 and 3 together. If you want, you can add new methods to the Numeric class that you can use in place of Ruby's +, -, *, \ and other related methods, as shown here:

```
class Numeric
  def add(x)
    self.+(x)
  end
end
```

Here, a custom class named Numeric is defined. It contains a single method, named add. The add method contains a single statement.

Notice the use of the word "self." This is a shorthand way of referring to the current object. By adding this class to a Ruby program, you can use the newly defined add method in place of the + method to perform addition, as shown here:

```
x = 1.add 3
```

When executed, this statement will set x equal to 4.

If you want, you can expand the custom Numeric class to include a range of additional common mathematical operators that use English names, as shown here:

```
class Numeric

  def add(x)
    self.+(x)
  end

  def subtract(x)
    self.-(x)
  end

  def multiply(x)
    self.*(x)
  end

  def divide(x)
    self./(x)
  end
end
```

Short Quiz

1. (True/False) An instance variable restricts variable access to the object within which the variable resides.

2. When defined inside a class definition, the _____ method is automatically executed any time an object based on the class is instantiated.

3. Which of the following is not a valid Ruby variable scope?

   a. Local

   b. Global

   c. Abstract

   d. Class

4. (True/False) A variable with global scope is accessible from any location within a Ruby program.

5. Instance variable names begin with which of the following characters?

   a. @@

   b. $

   c. #

   d. @

Back to the Rock, Paper, Scissors Game

It is time to develop this chapter's game project, the Rock, Paper, Scissors game. As you work through the steps involved in developing this game, focus on the object-oriented aspects, especially the object and method definitions, but also object instantiation and execution.

Designing the Game

The development of the Rock, Paper, Scissors game is completed in 15 steps, as outlined here:

1. Open your text or program editor, and create a new file.

2. Add comment statements to the beginning of the script file to document the script and its purpose.

3. Define a Screen class representing the terminal window.

4. Define a Game class representing the Rock, Paper, Scissors game.

5. Add a display_greeting method to the Game class.

6. Add a display_instructions method to the Game class.

7. Add a play_game method to the Game class.

8. Add a get_player_move method to the Game class.

9. Add a get_computer_move method to the Game class.

10. Add an analyze_results method to the Game class.

11. Add a display_results method to the Game class.

12. Add a display_credits method to the Game class.

13. Instantiate script objects.

14. Prompt the player for permission to begin the game.

15. Set up the game's controlling logic.

Follow along carefully, do not skip any steps, and look out for typos.

Step 1: Create a New Ruby File

Open your text or script editor, and create a new Ruby script file. Save the file with the name RPS.rb, and store it in the folder with your other Ruby scripts.

Step 2: Document the Script and Its Purpose

Add the following comment statements to the new script file. These comments provide a description of the script and its purpose.

```
#------------------------------------------------------------
#
# Script Name: RPS.rb
# Version:     1.0
# Author:      Jerry Lee Ford, Jr.
# Date:        April 2010
#
# Description: This Ruby game is a computerized version of
#              the classic Rock, Paper, Scissors game, in
#              which the player goes head-to-head against
#              the computer.
#
#------------------------------------------------------------
```

Step 3: Define the *Screen* Class

The Rock, Paper, Scissors game uses two custom classes, screen and Game, each of which contains numerous methods for controlling the interaction with the user and executing the game. What follows are the program statements for the first of these two classes:

```
# Define custom classes -----------------------------------

#Define a class representing the console window
class Screen

  def cls  #Define a method that clears the display area
    puts ("\n" * 25)  #Scroll the screen 25 times
    puts "\a"       #Make a little noise to get the player's attention
  end

  def pause      #Define a method that pauses the display area
    STDIN.gets   #Execute the STDIN class's gets method to
                 #pause script execution until the player
                 #presses the Enter key
  end

end
```

The first method defined in the class is the cls method. It contains two statements. The first statement writes 25 blank lines to the terminal window to clear the screen. The second statement processes a string containing the \a escape character, which makes a beep sound, thus notifying the player each time the terminal screen is cleared.

Step 4: Define the *Game* Class

The Game class contains eight methods that control the execution of the game. To begin developing the Game class, add the following statements to the end of the script file:

```
#Define a class representing the Rock, Paper, Scissors game
class Game

end
```

Step 5: Define the *display_greeting* Method

The Game class's display_greeting method displays the game's welcome message. Define the display_greeting method by inserting the following statements between the class's opening and closing statements:

```
#This method displays the game's opening message
def display_greeting

    Console_Screen.cls  #Clear the display area

    #Display welcome message
    print "\t\t\tLet's Play Rock, Paper, Scissors!" +
    "\n\n\n\n\n\n\n\n\n\n\n\n\nPress Enter to " +
            "continue. "

    Console_Screen.pause      #Pause the game

end
```

Step 6: Define the *display_instructions* Method

The display_instructions method displays the instructions for playing the game. Define the second of eight methods belonging to the Game class by adding the following statements at the end of the class definition, immediately after the display_greeting method:

```
#Define a method to be used to present game instructions
def display_instructions

    Console_Screen.cls       #Clear the display area
    puts "INSTRUCTIONS:\n\n"  #Display a heading

    #Display the game's instructions
    puts "This game pits the player against the computer." +
        "To play, you must"
```

```
puts "enter one of the following moves when" +
   "prompted: Rock, Paper, or"
puts "Scissors.\n\n"
puts "The game will randomly select a move for the computer, and "
puts "the two moves will then be analyzed according" +
   "to the following"
puts "rules: \n\n"
puts "* Rock crushes Scissors, Rock equals Rock," +
   "and Rock is covered by"
puts " Paper.\n\n"
puts "* Paper covers Rock, Paper equals Paper, and" +
   "Paper is cut by"
puts " Scissors.\n\n"
puts "* Scissors cut Paper, Scissors equals" +
   "Scissors, and Scissors are"
puts " crushed by Rock.\n\n\n"
puts "Good luck!\n\n\n"
print "Press Enter to continue. "
Console_Screen.pause        #Pause the game

end
```

Step 7: Define the *play_game* Method

The third of the Game class's eight methods is the play_game method. It manages the execution of a round of play through the execution of other methods. To define this method, add the following statements at the end of the class definition, immediately after the display_instructions method:

```
#Define a method to control game play
def play_game

  Console_Screen.cls        #Clear the display area

  #Call on the method responsible for collecting the
  #player's move
  playerMove = get_player_move

  #Call on the method responsible for generating the
  #computer's move
  computerMove = get_computer_move

  #Call on the method responsible for determining the
  #results of the game
  result = analyze_results(playerMove, computerMove)

  #Call on the method responsible for displaying the
  #results of the game
  display_results(playerMove, computerMove, result)

end
```

The calls to the `playerMove` and `computerMove` methods retrieve the player's and the computer's moves, which are passed to the `analyze_results` method. The `analyze_results` method then determines the winner of the round and passes back its result. The result is passed to the `display_results` method, which informs the player.

Step 8: Define the get_player_move Method

The fourth of the `Game` class's eight methods is the `get_player_move` method. This method collects the player's move using a loop that runs forever. Each time the loop repeats, it displays a prompt that instructs the player to respond by entering a move (Rock, Paper, or Scissors). To define this method, add the following statements at the end of the class definition, immediately after the `play_game` method:

```
#Define the method responsible for collecting the player's move
def get_player_move

  Console_Screen.cls       #Clear the display area

  loop do #Loop forever

    Console_Screen.cls       #Clear the display area

    #Prompt the player to select a move
    puts "To make a move, type one of the following:\n\n"
    print "[Rock] [Paper] [Scissors]: "

    @choice = STDIN.gets   #Collect the player's answer
    @choice.chop!          #Remove any extra characters
                           #appended to the string

    #Terminate the loop if valid input was provided
    break if @choice  =~ /Rock|Paper|Scissors/i

  end

  #Convert the player move to uppercase and return it to the calling
  #statement
  return @choice.upcase

end
```

Within the loop, the player's input is analyzed using a regular expression. If the player's input matches one of the three words listed in the regular expression, the **break** command is executed, terminating the loop and allowing the game to continue. If the player fails to provide valid input, the **break** command is not executed, and the loop repeats, prompting the player to try again.

Step 9: Define the `get_computer_move` Method

Define the fifth of the Game class's eight methods by adding the following statements at the end of the class definition, immediately after the `get_player_move` method:

```
#Define the method responsible for making the computer's move
def get_computer_move

  #Define an array containing a list of three possible moves
  moves = ["ROCK", "PAPER", "SCISSORS"]

  #Generate and return a random number between 0 and 2
  randomNo = rand(3)

  #Return a randomly selected move to the calling statement
  return moves[randomNo]

end
```

This method generates a move on behalf of the computer by using the rand method to select a random number from 0 to 2. This number is then used to retrieve one of three moves stored in an array named moves. Once a move has been selected, it is returned to the statement that called upon the `get_computer_move` method.

Step 10: Define the `analyze_results` Method

The `analyze_results` method compares the player's and the computer's moves, which are passed to it as arguments, to determine the result of the current round of play. Define the sixth of the Game class's eight methods by adding the following statements at the end of the class definition, immediately after the `get_computer_move` method:

```
#Define the method responsible for analyzing and returning
#the result of the game (arguments are passed as upper
#case characters)
def analyze_results(player, computer)

  #Analyze the results of the game when the player selects ROCK
  if player == "ROCK" then
    return "Player wins!" if computer == "SCISSORS"
    return "Tie!" if computer == "ROCK"
    return "Computer wins!" if computer == "PAPER"
  end

  #Analyze the results of the game when the player selects PAPER
  if player == "PAPER" then
    return "Player wins!" if computer == "ROCK"
    return "Tie!" if computer == "PAPER"
    return "Computer wins!" if computer == "SCISSORS"
  end
```

```
#Analyze the results of the game when the player selects SCISSORS
if player == "SCISSORS" then
   return "Player wins!" if computer == "PAPER"
   return "Tie!" if computer == "SCISSORS"
   return "Computer wins!" if computer == "ROCK"
end
```

```
end
```

This method consists of three conditional tests that evaluate the player's and computer's moves to determine which side wins or if there is a tie. Based on the result, a text string is returned to the statement that called upon the method to execute.

Step 11: Define the `display_results` Method

The `display_results` method displays the result of the game, which is passed to it as an argument, along with the player's and the computer's moves. Define the seventh of the Game class's eight methods by adding the following statements at the end of the class definition, immediately after the `analyze_results` method:

```
#Define the method responsible for displaying the result of the game
def display_results(player, computer, result)

   #Display arguments passed to the method using the
   #following template
   Console_Screen.cls        #Clear the display area
   puts "\n\n\t\t\tRESULTS:"
   puts "\n\n\t\t\t================================="
   puts "\n\n\t\t\tPlayer's move:    " + player
   puts "\n\n\t\t\tComputer's move:  " + computer
   puts "\n\n\t\t\tResult:           " + result
   puts "\n\n\t\t\t================================="
   puts "\n\n\n\n"
   print "Press Enter to continue. "
   Console_Screen.pause       #Pause the game

end
```

Step 12: Define the `display_credits` Method

The `display_credits` method displays information about the game, including the developer's URL. Define the last of the Game class's eight methods by adding the following statements at the end of the class definition, just before its closing end statement:

```
#This method displays information about the Rock, Paper,
#Scissors game
def display_credits

   Console_Screen.cls #Clear the display area
```

```
#Thank the player and display game information
puts "\t    Thank you for playing the Rock, Paper," +
   "Scissors game."
puts "\n\n\n\n"
puts "\n\t\t\t Developed by Jerry Lee Ford, Jr.\n\n"
puts "\t\t\t\t Copyright 2010\n\n"
puts "\t\t\tURL: http://www.tech-publishing.com" +
   "\n\n\n\n\n\n\n\n\n\n"

end
```

Step 13: Instantiate Script Objects

Instantiate two objects named `Console_Screen` and RPS, based on the `Console_Screen` and Game classes, by adding the following statements to the end of the script file:

```
# Main Script Logic -------------------------------------

Console_Screen = Screen.new #Instantiate a new Screen object
RPS = Game.new              #Instantiate a new Game object

#Execute the Game class's display_greeting method
RPS.display_greeting

answer = ""  #Initialize variable and assign it an empty string
```

In addition to instantiating the `Console_Screen` and RPS objects, these statements define a variable named answer and assign it an empty string as an initial value. This variable will be used to control the execution of the loop defined in the next section.

Step 14: Get Permission to Start the Game

Set up the prompt for getting the player's permission to play the game by adding the following statements to the end of the script file:

```
#Loop until the player enters y or n and do not accept any
#other input
loop do

  Console_Screen.cls  #Clear the display area

  #Prompt the player for permission to start the game
  print "Are you ready to play Rock, Paper, Scissors? (y/n): "

  answer = STDIN.gets  #Collect the player's answer
  answer.chop!  #Remove any extra characters appended to the string

  #Terminate the loop if valid input was provided
  break if answer =~ /y|n/i

end
```

A loop is set up to control the execution of statements that prompt the player for permission to start a round of play. At the end of each iteration of the loop, a regular expression is used to evaluate the player's input, executing the break command if that input is valid.

Step 15: Control Game Play

Supply the programming logic that manages the overall execution of the game by adding the following statements to the end of the script file:

```
#Analyze the player's answer
.if answer =~ /n/i  #See if the player wants to quit

  Console_Screen.cls  #Clear the display area

  #Invite the player to return and play the game some other time
  puts "Okay, perhaps another time.\n\n"

else  #The player wants to play the game

  #Execute the Game class's display_instructions method
  RPS.display_instructions

  playAgain = ""

  loop do #Loop forever

    #Execute the Game class's play_game method
    RPS.play_game

    loop do #Loop forever

      Console_Screen.cls  #Clear the display area

      #Find out if the player wants to play another round
      print "Would you like to play again? (y/n): "

      playAgain = STDIN.gets  #Collect the player's response
      playAgain.chop!          #Remove any extra characters
                               #appended to the string

      #Terminate the loop if valid input was provided
      break if playAgain =~ /n|y/i

    end

    #Terminate the loop if valid input was provided
    break if playAgain =~ /n/i

  end

  #Call upon the Game class's determine_credits method
  RPS.display_credits
end
```

These statements are controlled by an `if` code block. If the player elects not to play the game, a message is displayed that invites the player to return and play another time. If the player decides to play, the Game class's `display_instructions` method is called on to execute. Next, a loop is set up to control the overall execution of the game. Within the loop, the Game class's `play_game` method is called, starting a new round of play. Once the `play_game` method has finished, the loop resumes execution and prompts the player to play again. Once the player decides to stop playing, the `break` command is executed, terminating the loop. This allows the `display_credits` method to execute, after which the game ends.

Running Your New Ruby Program Game

Save your Ruby script. If you typed the code statements correctly, the program should work as expected. If you run into any errors, read the error messages carefully to ascertain what went wrong. If necessary, review the script, and look for mistyped or missing statements.

Summing Up

- In object-oriented programming, data and code are stored together as objects.

- A class provides a template that specifies properties and methods that are available for interacting with and controlling an object.

- Object-oriented programming provides a number of key features, including abstraction, encapsulation, inheritance, and polymorphism.

- Abstraction is a term that refers to the process of organizing program code into classes.

- Encapsulation involves the restriction of access to one or more of the properties and methods defined within a class.

- You can insert the keyword `public` into a class, thereby making any properties or methods that follow the keyword available throughout the program.

- You can insert the keyword `private` into a class, thereby restricting the access of any properties or methods that follow the keyword to within the object itself.

- You can insert the keyword `protected` into a class, thereby restricting the access of any properties or methods that follow the keyword to objects of the same class or objects of subclasses of the class.

- Inheritance occurs when one class is derived from another class.

- Polymorphism is the ability to define something in different forms.

- Ruby provides access to a method named initialize that, when included in a class definition, automatically executes any time a new object based on that class is instantiated.

- Ruby supports four different scopes for variables: local, global, instance, and class.

- A local variable is one that can be accessed only within the scope in which it is created.

- Global variables are accessible throughout a Ruby program and have an unlimited scope.

- To create a global variable, precede its name with the $ character.

- The scope of an instance variable is limited to the object it is defined in.

- The scope of class variables is accessible to all instances of the same class.

- Local variable names begin with a letter or the underscore character.

- Global variable names being with the $ character.

- Class variable names begin with the @@ characters.

- Instance variable names begin with the @ character.

- The defined? operator looks for a variable and returns a value of true if the variable is found and a value of false if it is not found.

- self is a keyword used as a shorthand way of referring to the current object.

Comprehension Check

1. (True/False) In object-oriented programming, data and code are stored together as objects.

2. Which of the following is a term that refers to the process of organizing program code into classes?

    a. Abstraction

    b. Encapsulation

    c. Inheritance

    d. Polymorphism

3. Which of the following makes program code more reliable by restricting the parts of a program that can access class properties and methods?

    a. Abstraction

    b. Encapsulation

    c. Inheritance

    d. Polymorphism

4. (True/False) By default, any properties and methods that you add to a class are private, meaning that they cannot be accessed from outside the class.

5. A _____ class, sometimes referred to as a child class, inherits all the properties and methods of the parent class.

6. (True/False) You can modify any inherited properties and methods, or even add new ones, to customize a child class.

7. (True/False) When defining classes, programmers place properties and methods that are common to all the classes in the lower-most class, which allows the derived classes to inherit them.

8. _____ is the ability to define something in different forms.

9. (True/False) Ruby's * method is used to concatenate two strings to create a new string.

10. (True/False) In Ruby, objects must be instantiated and then initialized in two separate steps.

11. Ruby permits programmers to instantiate how many objects within a single program?

    a. 10

    b. 100

    c. 1,000,000

    d. Unlimited

12. Which one of the following variables can be accessed only within the scope it was created in?

    a. Local

    b. Global

    c. Instance

    d. Class

13. _____ variables have an unlimited scope.

    a. Local

    b. Global

    c. Instance

    d. Class

14. Global variable names begin with which of the following characters?

    a. @

    b. @@

    c. $

    d. %

15. Class variable names begin with which of the following characters?

    a. @

    b. @@

    c. $

    d. %

16. A(n) _____ variable's scope is limited to the object in which it is defined.

    a. Local

    b. Global

    c. Instance

    d. Class

17. A(n) _____ variable's scope is accessible to all instances of the same class.

    a. Local

    b. Global

    c. Instance

    d. Class

18. The _____ method determines whether a variable exists, returning a value of `true` if the variable is found.

19. Using the _____ method, you can reverse the order in which arrays are retrieved.

20. _____ is a keyword that can be used as a shorthand way of referring to the current object.

Reinforcement Exercises

The following exercises are designed to further your understanding of Ruby programming by challenging you to make improvements to the chapter's game project, the Rock, Paper, Scissors game.

1. Currently, the `Game` class's `get_player_move` method uses a regular expression to validate the player's moves of `Rock`, `Paper`, or `Scissors`, rejecting any input other than one of these words. Making the player enter entire words takes time and can lead to typos, however. Simplify game play by modifying the `get_player_move` method to also allow single-character input in the form of `R`, `P`, and `S`. Make sure you accommodate both uppercase and lowercase input.

2. The game allows players to play an unlimited number of times. To help them keep track of how many times they have played, modify the game by adding a global variable named `$gameCount` at the beginning of the program's Main Script Logic area, assigning it an initial value of 0. Next, add a method named `game_count` and set it to increment the value of `$gameCount` each time it is executed. Lastly, add a statement to the `play_game` method that executes the

game_count method, then modify the puts statements in the display_results method to accommodate the display of the $gameCount variable's value, with text describing its meaning.

3. The game lets players know whether they have won, lost, or tied a particular game. Modify the game so that players are told the number of games they have won, lost, or tied since the start of game play. Implement this change by adding three variables named $wins, $lost, and $ties to the program's Main Script Logic section, assigning each an initial value of 0. Next, modify the analyze_results method by adding programming logic that increments the values of $wins, $lost, and $ties, depending on the result of game play. Lastly, modify the display_results method so that it displays the values of $wins, $lost, and $ties each time it executes.

4. At the end of each round of play, the game analyzes the player's and the computer's input and determines the result. A message is then displayed, informing the player whether the game was won, lost, or tied. It is up to the player, however, to determine how that result was computed, which is done by comparing the player's and the computer's moves, both of which are displayed on the screen, to the game's rules.

Modify the game so that the game itself performs this task. To implement this change, start by modifying the analyze_results method so that instead of returning a simple string like Player wins! it returns a more detailed explanation like Rock crushes scissors. Player wins!. You'll need to do this for each of the nine possible game results.

5. The computer you're running the game on may automatically play a sound (beep) every time its screens are updated. However, you can ensure that the computer plays a sound, both when the game prompts the player to make a move and when the game displays the player's win-loss record, by embedding the \a escape character within a string. To implement this change, add the \a escape character to either a puts statement or a print statement within both the get_player_move method and the display_results method.

Discovery Projects

Discovery Project 8-1

Object-oriented programming (OOP) is a huge topic about which many books have been written. To learn more about it, visit Wikipedia's object-oriented programming page located at *http://en.wikipedia.org/wiki/Object-oriented_programming*. Using the information provided by this web page, write a two-page paper describing the fundamental concepts and features of OOP.

Discovery Project 8-2

Abstraction is a key feature of object-oriented programming, allowing you to organize program code into classes. This involves the specification of both properties and methods. To demonstrate your understanding of abstraction, complete the following exercises:

1. Create a Ruby program named AnimalFarm.rb, then begin developing a new script by adding a class definition to it. Name the class Animal and give it two properties, name and type. These two properties will be used in objects based on this class to store information about an object's (animal) name and type.

2. Modify the Animal class by adding two methods to it. Assign the name talk to the first method and configure it to display a string that identifies the sound Grrrrr!!!. Assign the name identify to the second method and configure it to display the animal class's type and the name of the object.

3. To verify that your Animal class has been correctly defined, modify the script by adding statements that instantiate two animal objects. Name the first object largeAnimal and the second object smallAnimal. Once the objects are instantiated, assign the name Leo to the largeAnimal object and then assign a value of Lion to the type variable. Next, assign the name Marvin to the smallAnimal object and then assign it a type value of Mouse. Lastly, add statements to the end of the program file that execute both of the Animal class's methods twice, once for each object.

4. Execute the AnimalFarm.rb program and ensure that it executes without error. Capture a screen print showing the script's output, and submit it to your instructor along with a copy of the program file.

Discovery Project 8-3

In Ruby, polymorphism is implemented through the assignment of the same name to different methods, and inheritance allows one class to be derived from another class. To demonstrate your understanding of these concepts, complete the following exercises:

1. Make a copy of the program that you created in Discovery Project 8-2, naming it AnimalFarm2.rb.

2. Add a new class to the program file named Lion. Using inheritance, create the Lion class using the Animal class as a parent class. By default, the Lion class inherits the talk method from the animal class. Next, use polymorphism to replace the Lion class's version of the talk method with a new method of the same name that displays a string of Roar!!!, which is more appropriate for this object.

    Next, add another class to the program named Mouse, once again using the Animal class as a parent class. Use polymorphism to replace the Mouse class's version of the talk method with a new method of the same name that displays a string of Eeek!!!, which is more appropriate for this object. Lastly, modify the two statements in the program that instantiate two instances of the Animal class. Modify the first statement so that it instantiates an instance of the Lion class and the second statement so that it instantiates an instance of the Mouse class.

3. To verify that your new class definitions have been correctly defined and that your polymorphic implementations of the talk and identify methods work as expected, add statements to the end of your new program that instantiate a new object named humanAnimal. Next, assign the new object the name Jerry and the type homosapien. Lastly, add statements to the end of the program file that execute both of the object methods.

4. Execute the AnimalFarm2.rb program, and ensure that it executes without error. Capture a screen print showing the script's output, and submit it along with a copy of the program file.

## CHAPTER 9

File and Folder Administration

In this chapter, you learn how to:

- ◎ Redirect file input and output
- ◎ Administer text files and folders
- ◎ Work with files and folders on different operating systems
- ◎ Read from and write to text files
- ◎ Create the Ruby Blackjack game

In this chapter, you learn how to develop scripts that interact with your computer's file system. In doing so, you learn how to create all kinds of text files, including log and data files and reports. You also learn how to read text files, which enables you to develop Ruby programs that use text files for program input. Finally, you learn the basic steps involved in administering files and folders, enabling you to develop Ruby programs that can administer your computer's file system.

Project Preview: The Ruby Blackjack Game

In this chapter, you create a computer game called the Ruby Blackjack game. In this game, a virtual blackjack dealer is pitted against the player, each of them trying to build a card hand that comes as close as possible to 21 without going over. The game begins by displaying the welcome message shown in Figure 9-1.

Figure 9-1   The welcome screen for the Ruby Blackjack game

After pressing Enter, the player is prompted for permission to begin the game, as shown in Figure 9-2.

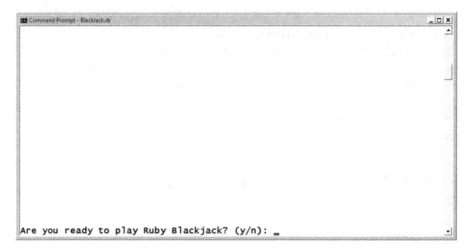

Figure 9-2   The player must respond with a y to begin the game

Once permission has been given, the instructions for playing the game are displayed, as shown in Figure 9-3.

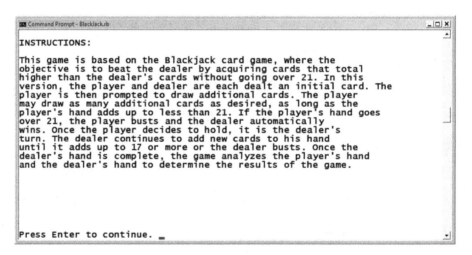

Figure 9-3   Instructions for how to play are provided

Both the player and the dealer are dealt an initial card, after which the player is prompted to play out the rest of her hand, as shown in Figure 9-4.

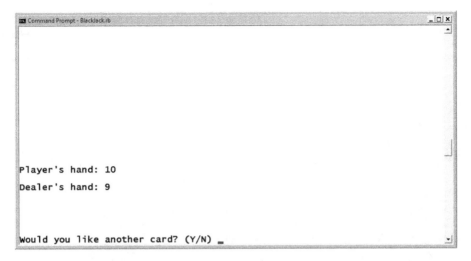

Figure 9-4   Once initial cards are dealt, the player goes first

The player may ask for as many additional cards as he wants, as long as the total value of his cards does not exceed 21. If this happens, the player busts and loses the hand, as shown in Figure 9-5.

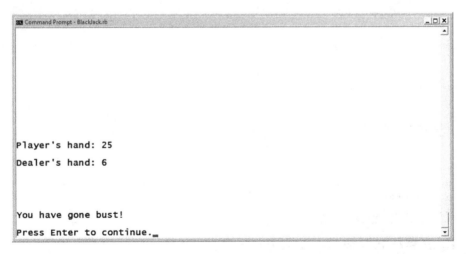

Figure 9-5   The player's hand has exceeded a total of 21, resulting in a loss

After each round of play, the player is prompted for permission to start a new hand, as shown in Figure 9-6.

298

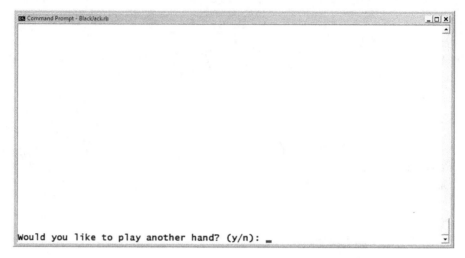

Figure 9-6 The player is invited to play again

Figure 9-7 shows an example of a game that the player has won. Here, the player's hand adds up to 21.

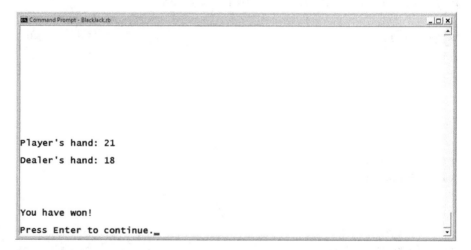

Figure 9-7 The player has won this hand

Once the player has decided to stop playing, the game ends after displaying the screen shown in Figure 9-8, which thanks the player and provides information about the game and its author.

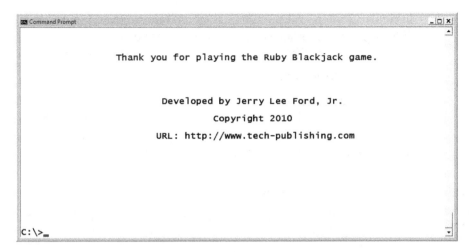

Figure 9-8 The game's closing screen

Redirecting File Input and Output

The movement of data from one place to another is referred to as data input and data output. By default, a computer receives standard input (STDIN) from the keyboard and sends standard output (STDOUT) to the computer's monitor.

If necessary, you can redirect STDIN and STDOUT. You can pull data from a different input source, say, or reroute data to a different output destination. Redirection is accomplished using the redirection output operator (>) and the redirection input operator (<).

The > redirection output operator allows you to pass the output from one source, such as a Ruby script, to another source, such as a text file. For example, suppose you created a Ruby script named Hello.rb that contained the following statement:

```
puts "Hello World!"
```

When executed from the command line, the words Hello World! are displayed on the computer screen. However, using the > redirection output operator, you can redirect the script's output to a text file, as shown here:

```
ruby Hello.rb > Hello.txt
```

When the Hello.rb script is executed this time, its output is redirected to a file named Hello.txt located in the current working directory (i.e., the directory where the script resides). If the Hello.txt file does not exist, it is created and then written to. If a file of the same name already exists, its contents are overwritten.

In similar fashion, you can use the < to redirect standard input from one resource to another. For example, suppose you created a Ruby script named DispMsg.rb that contained the following statement:

```
message = STDIN.gets
```

When executed from the command prompt, the script would wait for input to be provided by the user. Once the user types something and presses Enter, the script assigns the input to the message variable and then terminates. However, using the <, you can redirect STDIN from a file, as shown here:

```
ruby DispMsg.rb < Hello.txt
```

The Dispmsg.rb script reads the first line of text stored in a file named Hello.txt and then assigns it to the message variable.

> If an empty file were used as input in the previous example, a value of nil (Ruby's way of representing a value of nothing) would be assigned to the message variable.

The operating system provides both the > and the < redirection operators, and you can use them as an elementary way of writing to and reading from text files. However, Ruby provides a number of more elegant and sophisticated ways of administering files.

Administering Text Files and Folders

Ruby offers a number of ways to administer files and folders. You can create, rename, and delete files and folders through the Ruby File and Dir classes, which give you access to various file and folder administration methods.

Verifying Whether a File or Folder Exists

Before you administer a file or folder, you should check to see whether it already exists. Files and folders can disappear for a number of reasons. They may have been accidentally deleted or moved to different locations. If you discover that the file or folder you wanted to work with does not exist, you may want to terminate the script's execution or you may want to create a new folder.

To determine if a file or folder exists, use the File class's exist? method, which uses the following syntax:

```
File.exist?(Name)
```

Here, *Name* represents the name and path of the file or directory being looked for. To get a better feel for how to use the exist? method, look at the following example:

```
puts "Found it!" if File.exist?("Hello.txt")
```

Here, a statement is set up to look for a file named Hello.txt that's located in the current working directory. If the file is found, the string Found it! is displayed.

In the following example, a check is made to determine whether a folder exists:

```
if File.exist?("TestDirectory") then
  puts "TestDirectory folder found."
else
  puts "TestDirectory folder created."
  Dir.mkdir("TestDirectory")
end
```

Here, if the folder is not found, a message is displayed informing the user that the folder has been created, then the mkdir method is used to create the folder.

Retrieving Information About a File or Folder

The File and Dir classes provide you with access to a number of methods that you can use to get information about files and folders. Using these methods, you can determine whether a specified resource is a file, a folder, or something else. You can also determine whether a file is empty or how large it is, and you can retrieve a list of all the files and folders stored in a folder.

Determining if a Resource Is a File or a Folder

Using the File class's directory? method, you can determine if a resource is a folder or something else (socket, pipe, etc.). This method uses the following syntax:

```
File.directory?(Name)
```

Here, Name represents the name and path of the resource to be checked. To get a better feel for how to work with the directory? method, look at the following example:

```
if File.directory?("TestDir") then
  puts "It's a folder."
else
  puts "It is something else."
end
```

Here, the directory? method is used to determine if TestDir is a folder. The directory? method returns a value of true if the specified resource is a folder and a value of false if it is not. As a result of the analysis, one of two text messages is displayed: It's a folder. or It is something else.

The File class also contains a method named file?, which can be used to determine whether a resource is a file or something else. As you can see from the following syntax, the file? method is very similar to the directory? method:

```
File.file?(Name)
```

Here, *Name* represents the name and path of the resource to be checked. To get a better feel for how to work with the file? method, look at the following example:

```
if File.file?("Hello.txt") then
  puts "It's a file."
else
  puts "It is something else."
end
```

Here, the file? method is used to determine if Hello.txt is a file.

Checking a File's Size

Before reading from a file or overwriting an existing file with a new file, you may want to check to see if the file has anything in it. Based on this analysis, you can avoid trying to read from an empty file, or you can decide to append data to the end of a file instead of overwriting the existing data.

To determine if a file has any data in it, use the File class's size method, which returns a count of the specified file's size in bytes. The method has the following syntax:

```
File.size(Name)
```

Here, *Name* represents the name and path of the resource to be checked. To get a better feel for how to work with the size method, look at the following example:

```
puts "File Hello.txt is " + File.size("Hello.txt").to_s +
  " bytes in size."
```

Here, a text string is displayed that shows the size of a file named Hello.txt located in the current directory.

Examining Folder Contents

Ruby lists the contents of a folder using the Dir class's entries method, which returns the contents of the folder as an array. You can then iterate through the array and work with each individual file or folder as necessary. The entries method has the following syntax:

```
Dir.entries(Name)
```

Here, *Name* represents the name and path of the directory to be processed. To get a better feel for how to work with the `entries` method, look at the following example:

```
puts Dir.entries(".")
```

Here, the `puts` method is used to display the contents of the current directory, as provided by the `entries` method. When executed, this statement will display output similar to that shown here:

```
.
..
BlackJack.rb
Crazy8Ball.rb
NumberGuess.rb
RPS.rb
RubyJoke.rb
SupermanQuiz.rb
TallTale.rb
Test.rb
TypingChallenge.rb
WordGuess.rb
```

You can also produce a list of all the files stored in a folder using the `Dir` class's `foreach` method, as shown here:

In Ruby, the . character can be used as a shortcut for representing the current working directory.

```
Dir.foreach(".") do |resource|
  puts resource
end
```

Here, a loop is set up that iterates through every file and folder stored in the current directory. The advantage of using the `foreach` method is that it allows you to perform multiple actions on the contents of a folder by placing as many statements as you want inside the loop.

Creating New Folders

Ruby allows you to create new folders using the `Dir` class's `mkdir` method, which has the following syntax:

```
Dir.mkdir(Name)
```

Here, *Name* represents the name and path of the folder you want to create. To get a better feel for how to work with the `mkdir` method, look at the following example:

```
Dir.mkdir("TestDir")
```

When executed, this statement creates a new folder named TestDir. However, if a folder of the same name already exists, an error will occur, so you may want to first check whether a folder named TestDir already exists, as shown here:

```
if File.exist?("TestDir") then
  Dir.mkdir("TestDir")
end
```

Deleting Files and Folders

Ruby allows you to delete both files and folders using the `File` and `Dir` classes' `delete` method. The `File` class's `delete` method has the following syntax:

```
File.delete(Name,... Name)
```

Except for the class name, the syntax for the `Dir` class's `delete` method is the same, as shown here:

```
Dir.delete(Name,... Name)
```

In both cases, *Name, ...Name* represents any number of files or folders you want to delete. To get a better feel for how to work with the `delete` method, look at the following example:

```
Dir.delete("TestDir")
```

Here, a folder named `TestDir` is deleted if it exists.

> If you attempt to delete a file or folder that does not exist, or if you try to delete a folder that is not empty, an error will occur.

Renaming Files

Ruby allows you to rename a file using the `File` class's `rename` method, which has the following syntax:

```
File.rename(OldName, NewName)
```

Here, *OldName* represents the current name of the file to be renamed, and *NewName* represents the new file name that is to be assigned to the file. To get a better feel for how to work with the `rename` method, look at the following example:

```
File.rename("Hello.txt", "Greeting.txt")
```

A file named Hello.txt is renamed Greeting.txt. If the specified file or folder does not exist, an error will occur.

Short Quiz

1. (True/False) Using the redirection input operator (<), you can redirect a script's output to a text file.

2. Which of the following operators can be used to redirect STDIN from a file source?

   a. >

   b. <

   c. =

   d. ==

3. (True/False) Both the > and the < operators are provided by the operating system.

4. In Ruby, which of the following characters can be used as a shortcut for representing the current working directory?

   a. /

   b. +

   c. _

   d. .

5. (True/False) If you attempt to delete a file or folder that does not exist, or if you try to delete a folder that is not empty, an error will occur.

Working with Files and Folders on Different Operating Systems

So far, the examples in this chapter have been based on the assumption that the scripts were being executed from the same folder that the files and folders to be worked with resided in. This will not always be the case. Therefore, you need to be able to specify the path to the files and directories you want to work with.

To do so in Microsoft Windows, include the path in your script statements, as shown here:

```
puts File.exists?('C:\Test_Files\Hello.txt')
```

 Single quotes are used in this example because they keep character interpolation from occurring. As a result, the \ characters are taken literally, and everything works just fine. To get the expected result using double quotes, you would need to escape each instance of the \ character, as shown here:

```
puts File.exists?("C:\\Test_Files\\Hello.txt")
```

The File class's exists? method has been instructed to look in the C:\Test_Files folder for a file named Hello.txt.

If, instead of Microsoft Windows, you were working on a computer running UNIX or Linux, you could type the following:

```
puts File.exists?('/Test_Files/Hello.txt')
```

Here, the File class's exists? method has been instructed to look in a folder named Test_Files for a file named Hello.txt.

 Notice that Microsoft Windows uses backslashes when specifying path information, whereas UNIX and Linux use forward slashes.

If you develop a script that will run on different operating systems, you will need a way to determine which type of operating system your script is currently executing on. One way to do this is by taking advantage of Ruby's RUBY_PLATFORM special variable, as shown here:

```
if RUBY_PLATFORM =~ /win32/ then
  puts File.exists?('C:\Test_Files\Hello.txt')
else
  puts File.exists?('/Test_Files/Hello.txt')
end
```

Here, the value assigned to RUBY_PLATFORM is checked using a regular expression to see if it contains the characters win32. If it does, the script is executing on a Windows computer. Otherwise, it is assumed that the script is executing on a computer running some version of UNIX or Linux. In like fashion, you can use the regular expression /darwin/ to determine if a computer is running Mac OS X, or /linux/ to see if the computer is running Linux.

 A **special variable** is one that is automatically created and maintained by Ruby and can be referenced by any Ruby scripts. RUBY_PLATFORM contains a string that identifies the type of operating system on which a script is executing.

Reading From and Writing to Text Files

In addition to the < and > pipe operators, Ruby offers a number of different ways to write data to and read it from files by using methods belonging to the File class.

One way is to use the File class's new method to set up a reference to the file. Once the reference is established, you can refer to the file when you need to perform read and write operations. You can set up a file reference using the following syntax:

Reference = File.new("*Name*", "*Mode*")

Here, *Reference* is a placeholder for a variable that will be used to refer back to the file that will be read from or written to, *Name* represents the file that you want to interact with, and *Mode* represents one of the options listed in Table 9-1, which specify the mode you want the file opened in.

Mode	Description
r	Opens the file for reading only, placing the location pointer at the beginning of the file.
r+	Opens the file for both reading and writing, placing the location pointer at the beginning of the file.
w	Opens the file for writing only, overwriting any existing text by placing the pointer at the beginning of the file. If the specified file does not exist, it is created.
w+	Opens the file for both reading and writing, overwriting any existing text by placing the pointer at the beginning of the file. If the specified file does not exist, it is created.
a	Opens the file in append mode, placing the pointer at the end of the file to preserve any preexisting text while allowing new text to be added to the end of the file.
a+	Opens the file in append mode, allowing for both reading and writing, placing the pointer at the end of the file to preserve any preexisting text.

Table 9-1　File Class Mode Specifications

Notice the reference to the location pointer in Table 9-1. The location pointer identifies the place in the file where the next read or write operation will begin.

Writing Data to Text Files

One way to write data to a text file is to use the File class's new method to specify a write mode operation, as shown here:

```
outFile =
  File.new("Demo.txt We are already good here. ", "w")
  outFile.puts "Ho Ho Ho"
  outFile.puts "Merry Christmas!"
outFile.close
```

Here, a file reference is set up to open a file named Demo.txt using write mode. Once established, the file reference (outFile) can be used to write data to the file using the puts method. In this example, two lines of text are written to the file. If the file does not exist, it is created and then written to. If the file does exist, it is opened and then overwritten.

So far in this book, you have used the puts method only to display text on the computer screen. In this example, however, you have redirected the puts method's output to the specified file by appending the file reference to the puts method using dot notation.

Take special notice of the last statement: outFile.close. A statement like this is required for any file that is opened with a file reference. Failure to explicitly close an open file reference may result in the corruption of the file.

Figure 9-9 shows the contents of the text file that is created when this example is executed.

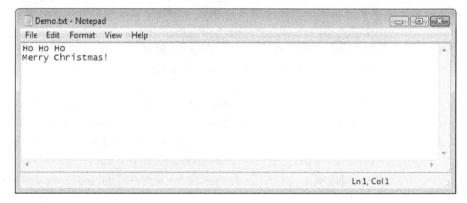

Figure 9-9 The contents of a text file written to by a Ruby script

Appending Data to the End of Text Files

Appending data to the end of a file is very similar to writing data to a file except that, in append mode, any data already written to the file is preserved. This makes append mode the appropriate option to use when adding data to the end of text files, as shown here:

```
outFile = File.new("Demo.txt", "a")
  outFile.puts "And a happy new year!"
outFile.close
```

Here, the Demo.txt file from the previous example is opened, and an additional line of text is written to it before it is again closed. Figure 9-10 shows how the contents of the text file have been modified after the script has executed.

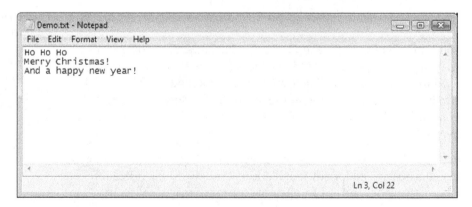

Figure 9-10 The contents of the Demo.txt file after additional data has been appended to it

Reading Data from Text Files

Reading data stored in text files is no more difficult than writing data to text files. First, the file must be opened in read mode. Then you can read the data from the text file, as shown here:

```ruby
File.new("Demo.txt", "r").each do |line|
  puts line
end
```

Here, the Demo.txt file is opened for reading using the File class's new method. Next, the each method is used to iterate through and display each line of text that is in the file. When executed, the following output is displayed:

```
Ho Ho Ho
Merry Christmas!
And a happy new year!
```

You can also use the gets method to read data from the file one line at a time, as shown here:

```ruby
inputFile = File.new("Demo.txt", "r")
puts inputFile.gets
inputFile.close
```

Here, the Demo.txt file is opened in read mode. Next, the gets method is used to read the first line of the file, which is then displayed by the puts method. The last statement closes the open file. When executed, these statements generate the following output:

```
Ho Ho Ho
```

To make things even easier, Ruby provides two shortcut methods for reading file contents without having to close the files when you are done: the read and readlines methods. These methods automatically handle the process of closing file access for you.

To use the read method, simply pass the method the name of the file that you want read, as shown here:

```ruby
inputFile = File.read("Demo.txt")
```

Here, the Demo.txt file is opened and read, and all of its contents are stored in a variable named inputFile. You can then process the data stored in inputFile as you see fit. For example, you might want to manipulate it using regular expressions, or simply display it, as shown here:

```ruby
puts inputFile
```

When executed, this statement displays the data stored in the inputFile variable, as shown here:

```
Ho Ho Ho
Merry Christmas!
And a happy new year!
```

The readlines method is similar to the read method except that, instead of the file's contents being read into a single variable, they are read line by line into an array, which allows you to reference and manipulate them using any of the Array class's methods. For example, the following statement uses the readlines method to read the Demo.txt file and store its contents in an array named inputArray:

```
inputArray = File.readlines("Demo.txt")
```

Once loaded into the array, the array's contents can be processed as you see fit. For example, the following statements could be used to loop through the array and print out its contents:

```
inputArray.each do |line|
  puts line
end
```

Though they are very easy to work with, using the read and readlines methods for a large file consumes a lot of computer memory, since they each require that the entire file be stored. A more efficient use of computer memory, in that case, is the File class's new method. When working with small- to medium-sized files, however, the read and readlines methods are a good option.

Short Quiz

1. (True/False) Both Microsoft Windows and UNIX/Linux-based operating systems use backslashes when specifying path information.

2. Which of the following is a special variable containing a string that identifies the type of operating system on which a script is executed?

    a. RUBY_SYSTEM

    b. RUBY_OS

    c. RUBY_PLATFORM

    d. RUBY_TYPE

3. (True/False) The readlines method is used to read a file's contents line by line into an array.

4. Which of the following methods can be used to open a file for reading?

    a. access

    b. new

c. get

d. b

5. The _____ method can be used to open a file
    without requiring you to explicitly close the file when done
    reading it.

Back to the Ruby Blackjack Game

It is time to develop this chapter's game project, the Ruby Blackjack game. As you create this script, focus on the way script variables are kept localized and programming logic is organized into distinct methods.

Designing the Game

The development of the Ruby Blackjack game is completed in 15 steps, as outlined here:

1. Open your text or script editor, and create a new file.

2. Add comment statements to the beginning of the script file to document the script and its purpose.

3. Define a Screen class representing the console window.

4. Define a Game class representing the Blackjack game.

5. Define the display_greeting method.

6. Define the display_instructions method.

7. Define the play_game method.

8. Define the get_new_card method.

9. Define the complete_player_hand method.

10. Define the play_dealer_hand method.

11. Define the determine_winner method.

12. Define the display_credits method.

13. Instantiate script objects.

14. Prompt the player for permission to begin the game.

15. Set up the game's controlling logic.

Step 1: Create a New Ruby File

Open your text or script editor, and create a new Ruby script file. Save the file with the name Blackjack.rb, and store it in the folder with your other Ruby scripts.

Step 2: Document the Script and Its Purpose

Add the following comment statements to the new script file. These comments provide a description of the script and its purpose.

```
#------------------------------------------------------------
#
# Script Name: BlackJack.rb
# Version:     1.0
# Author:      Jerry Lee Ford, Jr.
# Date:        April 2010
#
# Description: This Ruby game is a computerized version of
#              the casino card game in which the player
#              competes against the dealer (i.e., computer)
#              in an effort to build a hand that comes as
#              close as possible to 21 without going over.
#
#------------------------------------------------------------
```

Step 3: Define the *Screen* Class

The Ruby Blackjack game uses two custom classes, screen and Game, each of which contains numerous methods for controlling the interaction with the user and executing the game. What follows are the program statements for the first of these two classes:

```
#Define a class representing the console window
class Screen

  def cls  #Define a method that clears the display area
    puts ("\n" * 25)  #Scroll the screen 25 times
    puts "\a"    #Make a little noise to get the player's
                 #attention
  end

  def pause  #Define a method that pauses the display area
    STDIN.gets  #Execute the STDIN class's gets method to
                #pause script execution until the player
                #presses the Enter key
  end

end
```

The Screen class defines two methods. The cls method writes 25 blank lines to the console window and then plays a beep sound. The pause method pauses script execution whenever it is called and waits for the player to press Enter.

Step 4: Define the *Game* Class

The Game class contains eight methods that provide you with control over the game's execution. To begin the creation of the Game class, append the following statements to the script file:

```
#Define a class representing the Ruby Blackjack game
class Game

end
```

Step 5: Define the *display_greeting* Method

The display_greeting method is responsible for displaying the game's welcome message. Insert the following statements between the Game class's opening and closing statements:

```
#This method displays the game's opening message
def display_greeting

  Console_Screen.cls  #Clear the display area

  #Display a welcome message
  print "\t\t\tWelcome to the Ruby Blackjack Game!" +
    "\n\n\n\n\n\n\n\n\n\n\n\n\nPress Enter to " +
    "continue. "

  Console_Screen.pause       #Pause the game

end
```

Step 6: Define the *display_instructions* Method

The display_instructions method uses a series of text strings to display the game's instructions. Add the following statements to the Game class's definition, immediately after the display_greeting method:

```
#Define a method to be used to display game instructions
def display_instructions

  Console_Screen.cls       #Clear the display area
  puts "INSTRUCTIONS:\n\n"  #Display a heading

  #Display the game's instructions
  puts "This game is based on the Blackjack card game, " +
    "where the"
  puts "objective is to beat the dealer by acquiring " +
    "cards that total"
  puts "higher than the dealer's cards without going " +
    "over 21. In this"
  puts "version, the player and dealer are each dealt " +
    "an initial card. The"
```

```
puts "player is then prompted to draw additional " +
  "cards. The player"
puts "may draw as many additional cards as desired, " +
  "as long as the"
puts "player's hand adds up to less than 21. If the " +
  "player's hand goes"
puts "over 21, the player busts and the dealer " +
  "automatically"
puts "wins. Once the player decides to hold, it is " +
  "the dealer's"
puts "turn. The dealer continues to add new cards to " +
  "his hand"
puts "until it adds up to 17 or more or the dealer " +
  "busts. Once the"
puts "dealer's hand is complete, the game analyzes " +
  "the player's hand"
puts "and the dealer's hand to determine the results " +
  "of the game."
puts "\n\n\n\n\n\n\n"
print "Press Enter to continue. "

Console_Screen.pause        #Pause the game

end
```

Step 7: Define the *play_game* Method

The play_game method is responsible for managing an individual round of play. Add the following statements to the end of the Game class's definition, immediately after the display_instructions method:

```
#Define a method to control game play
def play_game

  Console_Screen.cls       #Clear the display area

  #Give the player and dealer an initial starting card
  playerHand = get_new_card
  dealerHand = get_new_card

  #Call the method responsible for dealing new cards to
  #the player
  playerHand = complete_player_hand(playerHand, dealerHand)

  #If the player has not busted, call the method
  #responsible for managing dealer's hand
  if playerHand <= 21 then
    dealerHand = play_dealer_hand(dealerHand)
  end

  #call the method responsible for determining the results
  #of the game
  determine_winner(playerHand, dealerHand)

end
```

The play_game method begins by calling on the get_new_card method two times to assign an initial card to both the player and the dealer. Since the player always goes before the dealer, the complete_player_hand method is called next and is passed the value of the player's and dealer's hands as arguments. The complete_player_hand method is responsible for adding new cards to the player's hand until the player busts or decides to stick with the cards currently in her hand, after which it returns a value representing the current value of the player's hand. This value is then examined to see if it exceeds 21, in which case the player has gone bust. If the player has not gone bust, the play_dealer_hand method is called and passed the current value of the dealer's hand as an argument. The play_dealer_hand method is responsible for playing out the dealer's hand and then returning the result of that hand. The last statement in the player_game method calls on the determine_winner method, passing it the current values of the player's and dealer's hands. The determine_winner method analyzes these two arguments to determine the result of the game.

Step 8: Define the get_new_card Method

The next method to be added to the Game class is the get_new_card method. This method is responsible for dealing a new card. The method's statements are shown here:

```
#Define a method responsible for dealing a new card
def get_new_card

  #Assign a random number from 1 to 13 as the value of the
  #card being created
  card = 1 + rand(13)

  #A value of 1 is an ace, so reassign the card a value of
  #11
  return 11 if card == 1

  #A value of 10 or more equals a face card so reassign
  #the card a value of 10
  return 10 if card >= 10

  return card  #Return the value assigned to the new card

end
```

When called, this method generates a random number from 1 to 13, which it assigns to a variable named card. If the value of card is set at 1, the card is considered to be an ace and therefore reassigned a value of 11. On the other hand, if the value of card is greater than or equal to 10, the card is considered either a 10 or a face card (Jack, Queen, or King) and assigned a value of 10. Once the value assigned to card is established, it is returned to the statement that called upon the method to execute.

Step 9: Define the *complete_player_hand* Method

The complete_player_hand method is responsible for helping the player play his hand. Add the following statements to the end of the Game class's definition, immediately after the get_new_card method:

```
#Define a method responsible for dealing the rest of the
#player's hand
def complete_player_hand(playerHand, dealerHand)

  loop do  #Loop forever

    Console_Screen.cls  #Clear the display area

    #Show the current state of the player's and dealer's
    #hands
    puts "Player's hand: " + playerHand.to_s + "\n\n"
    puts "Dealer's hand: " + dealerHand.to_s +
      "\n\n\n\n\n\n"
    print "Would you like another card? (Y/N) "

    reply = STDIN.gets  #Collect the player's answer
    reply.chop!  #Remove any extra characters appended
                 #to the string

    #See if the player decided to ask for another card
    if reply =~ /y/i then
      #Call method responsible for getting a new card
      #and add it to the player's hand
      playerHand = playerHand + get_new_card
    end

    #See if the player has decided to stick with the
    #current hand
    if reply =~ /n/i then
      break  #Terminate the execution of the loop
    end

    if playerHand > 21 then
      break  #Terminate the execution of the loop
    end

  end

  #Return the value of the player's hand
  return playerHand

end
```

This method is passed two arguments, playerHand and dealerHand, which represent the current values of the player's and the dealer's hands. These values are displayed, and the player is then asked if she would like another card. If the player decides to take another card, the value assigned to playerHand is incremented by adding the result returned by the get_new_card method to the value of playerHand. The player may add as many cards as desired, provided that the total value of the hand does not exceed 21. Once the player busts or decides not to draw any more cards, the method ends by returning the current value of the player's hand to the statement that called upon the method to execute.

Step 10: Define the *play_dealer_hand* Method

The play_dealer_hand method is responsible for completing the dealer's hand. Add the following statements to the end of the class definition, immediately after the complete_player_hand method:

```
#Define a method responsible for managing the dealer's hand
def play_dealer_hand(dealerHand)

  loop do  #Loop forever

    #If the value of the dealer's hand is less than 17
    #then give the dealer another card
    if dealerHand < 17 then
      #Call method responsible for getting a new card and
      #add it to the dealer's hand
      dealerHand = dealerHand + get_new_card
    else
      break  #Terminate the execution of the loop
    end

  end

  #Return the value of the dealer's hand
  return dealerHand

end
```

The play_dealer_hand method takes as an argument the current value of the dealer's hand. The method then repeatedly calls upon the get_new_card method, adding new cards to the dealer's hand until the total value of the dealer's hand exceeds 16, at which time the method returns the current value of the dealer's hand to the calling statement and then ends.

Step 11: Define the `determine_winner` Method

The `determine_winner` method is responsible for determining the
results of the game. Add the following statements to the end of the
class definition, immediately after the `play_dealer_hand` method:

```
#Define a method responsible for analyzing the player's
#and dealer's hands and determining who won
def determine_winner(playerHand, dealerHand)

  Console_Screen.cls  #Clear the display area

  #Show the value of the player's and dealer's hands
  puts "Player's hand: " + playerHand.to_s + "\n\n"
  puts "Dealer's hand: " + dealerHand.to_s +
    "\n\n\n\n\n\n"

  if playerHand > 21 then  #See if the player has busted
    puts "You have gone bust!\n\n"
    print "Press Enter to continue."
  else  #See if the player and dealer have tied
    if playerHand == dealerHand then
      puts "Tie!\n\n"
      print "Press Enter to continue."
    end
    #See if the dealer has busted
    if dealerHand > 21 then
        puts "The Dealer has gone bust!\n\n"
        print "Press Enter to continue."
    else
      #See if the player's hand beats the dealer's hand
      if playerHand > dealerHand then
        puts "You have won!\n\n"
        print "Press Enter to continue."
      end
      #See if the dealer's hand beats the player's hand
      if playerHand < dealerHand then
        puts "The Dealer has won!\n\n"
        print "Press Enter to continue."
      end
    end
  end

  Console_Screen.pause        #Pause the game

end
```

The `determine_winner` method is passed two arguments representing the current values of the player's and the dealer's hands. It then
displays these values and, using a series of nested `if` statements,
determines the winner of the game. The method then displays the
appropriate message.

Step 12: Define the `display_credits` Method

The `display_credits` method is responsible for displaying the game's credits, including the author's URL. Add the following to the end of the Game class's definition, immediately after the `determine_winner` method:

```
#This method displays information about the Ruby Blackjack
#game
def display_credits

   Console_Screen.cls  #Clear the display area

   #Thank the player and display game information
   puts "\t\t     Thank you for playing the Ruby " +
     "Blackjack game.\n\n\n\n"
   puts "\n\t\t\t Developed by Jerry Lee Ford, Jr.\n\n"
   puts "\t\t\t\t  Copyright 2010\n\n"
   puts "\t\t\tURL: http://www.tech-publishing.com" +
     "\n\n\n\n\n\n\n\n\n\n"

end
```

Step 13: Instantiate Script Objects

Instantiate the script's custom classes by appending the following statements to the end of the script file:

```
# Main Script Logic -------------------------------------

Console_Screen = Screen.new  #Instantiate a new Screen
                             #object
BJ = Game.new  #Instantiate a new Game object

#Execute the Game class's display_greeting method
BJ.display_greeting

answer = ""  #Initialize variable and assign it an empty
             # string
```

In addition to instantiating the `Console_Screen` and `BJ` objects, these statements both call the Game class's `display_greeting` method, which prompts the player for permission to begin the game, and define a variable named `answer`, which manages the execution of a loop.

Step 14: Get Permission to Start the Game

Set up the prompt for getting the player's permission to play the game by adding the following statements to the end of the script file:

```
#Loop until the player enters y or n and do not accept any
#other input
loop do
```

```
Console_Screen.cls  #Clear the display area

#Prompt the player for permission to start the game
print "Are you ready to play Ruby Blackjack? (y/n): "

answer = STDIN.gets  #Collect the player's answer
answer.chop!  #Remove any extra characters appended to
              #the string

#Terminate the loop if valid input was provided
break if answer =~ /y|n/i   #Accept uppercase and
                            #lowercase input
```

end

Here, a loop has been set up to run forever. Upon each iteration of
the loop, the player is prompted to enter a value of y or n to indicate
whether a new round of play should be initiated or the game should
be terminated. Any input other than a y or n is ignored. Once a valid
response has been entered, the **break** command is executed, terminating the loop and allowing the rest of the script to run.

Step 15: Control Game Play

The rest of the statements that make up the Ruby Blackjack game are
shown next. Add these to the end of the script file. These statements
are responsible for controlling the overall execution of the game.

```
#Analyze the player's answer
if answer =~ /n/i #See if the player wants to quit

  Console_Screen.cls  #Clear the display area

  #Invite the player to return and play the game some
  #other time
  puts "Okay, perhaps another time.\n\n"

else  #The player wants to play the game

  #Execute the Game class's display_instructions method
  BJ.display_instructions

  playAgain = ""  #Initialize variable and assign it an
                  #empty string

  loop do  #Loop forever

    #Execute the Game class's play_game method
    BJ.play_game

    loop do  #Loop forever
```

```
      Console_Screen.cls  #Clear the display area
      #Find out if the player wants to play another round
      print "Would you like to play another hand? (y/n): "

      playAgain = STDIN.gets  #Collect the player's
                              #response
      playAgain.chop!  #Remove any extra characters
                       #appended to the string

      #Terminate the loop if valid input was provided
      break if playAgain =~ /n|y/i  #Accept uppercase and
                                    #lowercase input

   end

   #Terminate the loop if valid input was provided
   break if playAgain =~ /n/i

end

#Call upon the Game class's display_credits method
BJ.display_credits

end
```

As you can see, these statements are controlled by a large if code block. The script statements that it executes depend on whether the player decides to terminate the game or play another round. If the player elects not to play, a message is displayed that encourages her to return and play another time. If the player elects to play, the Game class's display_instructions method is executed. Next, a loop executes the Game class's play_game method, beginning a new round of play. Once the current round of play has finished, control returns to the loop, which prompts the player to play again. If the player decides to play again, the loop iterates. Otherwise the break command is executed, terminating the loop and allowing the display_credits method to execute.

Running Your New Ruby Script Game

Save your Ruby script. If you typed the code statements correctly, the program should work as expected. If you run into any errors, read the error messages carefully to ascertain what went wrong. If necessary, review the script, and look for mistyped or missing statements.

Summing Up

- The movement of data from one source to another is commonly referred to as data input and output.

- By default, a computer receives standard input (STDIN) from the keyboard and sends standard output (STDOUT) to the computer's monitor.

- With the redirection output operator (>), you can redirect a script's output to a text file.

- With the redirection input operator (<), you can redirect standard input from one resource to another.

- Ruby offers a number of ways to perform file and folder administration through the File and Dir classes.

- To determine if a file or folder exists, you use the File class's exist? method.

- You can determine if a resource is a file or something else (socket, pipe, etc.) using the File class's directory? method.

- You can also use the File class's file? method to determine whether a resource is a file or something else.

- To determine if a file has any data in it, use the File class's size method.

- You can also use the size? method to determine the size of a file (in bytes).

- You can list a folder's contents using the Dir class's entries method, which returns the contents of the folder as an array.

- You can use the . character as a shortcut for representing the current working directory.

- You can produce a list of all the files stored in a folder using the Dir class's foreach method.

- You can create new folders using the Dir class's mkdir method.

- You can delete both files and folders using the File and Dir classes' delete methods.

- You can rename a file or folder using the File class's rename method.

- Microsoft Windows uses backslashes to specify path information. UNIX and Linux use forward slashes to specify path information.

- A special variable is a variable that is automatically created and maintained by Ruby and can be referenced by any Ruby scripts.

- RUBY_PLATFORM contains a string that identifies the type of operating system that a script is executing on.

- One way to interact with a file is to use the File class's new method to set up a reference to the file.

- You can use the gets method to retrieve data from a file one line at a time.

- Every time a file is opened for reading, you must remember to close it to keep the file from becoming corrupt.

- The readlines method reads a file's contents into an array, allowing you to reference and manipulate them using any of the Array class's methods.

- The read method reads the contents of a file into a single variable.

Comprehension Check

1. (True/False) The movement of data from one source to another is commonly referred to as data input and output.

2. (True/False) By default, a computer sends output (STDOUT) to the printer.

3. Which of the following operators facilitates the passage of output from one source to another source?

   a. >

   b. <

   c. =

   d. ==

4. (True/False) In Ruby, you redirect input and output using the < and > operators.

5. (True/False) If an empty file is read and stored in a variable, that variable is assigned a value of nil.

6. (True/False) If the > operator is used to redirect output to a file named Hello.txt, what happens if the Hello.txt file does not exist?

   a. The file is created and then written to.

   b. The file is created but not written to.

   c. An error occurs, and the script stops executing.

   d. An error occurs, but the script continues executing.

7. (True/False) If the < operator is used to redirect input from a file that is empty, what happens?

   a. An empty string is returned.

   b. An error occurs and the script stops executing.

   c. A value of nil is returned.

   d. An error occurs, but the script continues executing.

8. (True/False) The > and < operators are methods supplied by Ruby's Kernel class.

9. (True/False) Ruby facilitates file and folder administration through the File and Dir classes.

10. You can use the File class's _____ method to determine if a file or folder exists.

11. Which of the following methods is used to determine if a file has any data in it?

    a. size

    b. count

    c. length

    d. length?

12. The File class's _____ method returns the size of a file in bytes.

    a. size

    b. size?

    c. length

    d. length?

13. You can create a new folder using the `Dir` class's
    _____ method.

    a. make

    b. create

    c. mkdir

    d. rmdir

14. A(n) _____ is a variable automatically created
    and maintained by Ruby.

    a. local

    b. global

    c. special

    d. instance

15. Which of the following `File` class mode specifications opens
    a file for both reading and writing, placing the location
    pointer at the beginning of the file?

    a. r

    b. r+

    c. w

    d. a+

16. Which of the following `File` class mode specifications opens
    a file for both reading and writing, overwriting any existing
    text by placing the pointer at the beginning of the file?

    a. r+

    b. w+

    c. a+

    d. a

17. Which of the following `File` class mode specifications opens
    a file in append mode, placing the pointer at the end of the file
    to preserve any preexisting text?

    a. r+

    b. w+

    c. a

    d. a+

18. You can use the _____ method to read all the contents of a file and store them in a variable.

    a. readlines

    b. open

    c. get

    d. read

19. You can use the _____ method to read all the contents of a file and store them in an array.

    a. readlines

    b. open

    c. get

    d. read

20. (True/False) A special variable is a variable that is automatically created and maintained by Ruby and can be referenced by any Ruby program.

Reinforcement Exercises

The following exercises are designed to further your understanding of Ruby programming by challenging you to make improvements to the chapter's game project, the Ruby Blackjack game.

1. As currently designed, the game's instructions consist of a series of embedded strings that are displayed using the puts and print methods. This means that in order to make a change to the instructions you must change the program code. Anytime you have to modify program code, you run the risk of making a typo or other mistake. To reduce the possibility of an error occurring, move the game's instructions into a text file, where edits can be made without any chance of impacting the program's source code.

    To implement this change, create a text file named BJHelp.txt and copy the game's instructions text into it, then remove the display_instructions method from the program file. Next, add a method to the program file named get_help_file and add program logic to it that retrieves and displays the contents of the BJHelp.txt file. Finally, modify the Main Script Logic section by replacing the statement that calls on the display_instructions method with a statement that calls on the get_help_file method.

2. The game's welcome screen and credits screen are also stored as text strings within the program file. Externalize the content of these two screens in separate text files named BJWelcome.txt and BJCredits.txt. Once these files have been created, remove the display_greeting and display_credits methods from the program file. Next, change the name of the get_help_file to get_file and modify the method so that it accepts an argument named filename, representing the name of an external text file. Modify the method so that it retrieves and displays the contents of the text file passed to it as an argument. Next, modify the Main Script Logic section by replacing the statement that called on the get_help_file with a statement that calls on the get_file method.

Make sure this new statement passes the full name and path of the text file to be displayed. Finally, replace the two statements that call on the display_greeting and display_credits methods with statements that call on the get_file method and pass it the name of the appropriate external text file.

3. One possible maintenance issue with the current design of the Ruby Blackjack game is that the specification of external files is spread throughout the program file. Centralizing the specification would make the program file easier to maintain. To do so, add a new method to the program file named retrieve_files and add programming logic to it to load the contents of each external text file into a global variable. Name these variables $help_file, $welcome_file, and $credits_file.

To implement this change, modify the get_file method so that it displays the appropriate global variables based on a string argument of "Help", "Welcome", or "Credits". Modify the Main Script Logic section by adding a new statement to it that executes the retrieve_files method immediately after it instantiates the BJ object. Finally, replace the three statements in the Main Script Logic section with three statements that call upon the retrieve_files method, passing it a string identifying which of the three variables' contents the game should display.

4. As currently designed, the Ruby Blackjack game displays both the player's and the dealer's moves and declares a winner at the end of a round of play. What it doesn't do is keep a running record of which side won and what the final hands were. Rectify

this by adding a log file feature that shows the player's and the dealer's final hands and identifies the winner. To make the log file easy to view, use the hyphen character to add a dashed line of 50 hyphens at the end of each round of play, as shown below:

```
Player's hand: 6
Dealer's hand: 19
The Dealer has won!
--------------------------------------------------
Player's hand: 18
Dealer's hand: 18
The Player has won!
--------------------------------------------------
```

To implement this change, add a method to the program file named write_log_file and set the method up to process a single string argument, representing a message to be written to an external log file. Within the write_log_file method, add the program logic needed to append text data to the end of a text file named BJLog.txt, located in the temp (Windows) or tmp (Mac OS X, UNIX, or Linux) folder. Next, modify the determine_winner method so that when it displays a string representing the player's hand, dealer's hand, or the results of the current round of play, a corresponding string is passed to the write_log_file method.

So that the game's log file doesn't grow too large, make one last set of changes to the program file to ensure that the log file is overwritten each time the game is started. Do this by adding a method to the program file named remove_log_file and by adding program logic to the remove_log_file method so that it checks whether the BJLog.txt file exists and, if the file does exist, deletes it. To execute this method, add a new statement to the Main Program Logic section that calls on the method if the player selects y when prompted to begin game play.

5. As written, the Ruby Blackjack game only executes on an operating system that supports the file and path syntax that has been specified for it. One way around this limitation is to create a second copy of the game using a file and path specification supported by a different operating system. Rather than adopting this approach, modify the Ruby Blackjack game so that it can be played on various operating systems. To implement this change, use the RUBY_PLATFORM special variable to control the file and path specification based on operating system type in the retrieve_files, write_log_file, and remove_log_file methods.

Discovery Projects

 Project 9-1

This chapter presented different ways of reading data from files. Create a text file named Story.txt, type the following statements into the file, and save it:

```
Once upon a time, there was a little boy who went on a
great adventure.

Unfortunately, nothing happened.

The End
```

Next, create a Ruby program named StoryCheck.rb and add the program logic needed to perform the following tasks:

- Verify that the file exists.

- If the file exists, read it, and display the contents of the text file.

- If the file does not exist, display an error message.

 Project 9-2

This chapter showed how to work with directories. Create a Ruby program file named DirChecker.rb, and add the program logic needed to perform the following tasks:

- Prompt the user to type the path and name of a folder whose contents will be displayed.

- Capture and analyze user input to determine whether the specified folder exists.

- Tell the user whether or not the folder exists.

- If the folder exists, prompt the user to press Enter to view the folder's contents.

- If the folder does not exist, display an error message.

Project 9-3

This chapter showed how to write out to files, which enables you to create reports and log files. Create a Ruby program that prompts users to type in their Christmas lists. Do this by creating a program file named ChristmasList.rb and adding the program logic needed to perform the following tasks:

- Assign the complete path and file name of the output file to a variable named outFile.

- Programmatically write the following statement to the beginning of the file:

  Dear Santa, here is my wish list!

- Create a loop that repeatedly prompts the user to add an item to the list.

- Continue collecting list items until the user types q and presses Enter.

- Close the output file.

## CHAPTER 10

Debugging

In this chapter, you learn:

◎ About syntax, runtime, and logical errors

◎ How to create error handlers that react to and handle
errors

◎ How to track the logical execution flow of statements within
your program files

◎ How to use Ruby's debugger to run and monitor the
execution of Ruby programs

Until now, your main way to deal with program errors has been to carefully review error messages and the statements that make up your program files. And since this book has explained how to create and execute all of its examples and game programs, this is all you have needed to do. As you venture out on your own, however, and as your programs become more complex, errors will become more difficult to track down. This chapter teaches you how to track down and deal with program errors. You learn how to add error-handling logic to your Ruby programs and how to work with Ruby's built-in debugger to correct errors and test the execution of your program files.

Project Preview: The Ruby Tic-Tac-Toe Game

In this chapter, you learn how to create a computer program called the Ruby Tic-Tac-Toe game. This program is designed to bring together all the programming concepts presented throughout the book. The two-person game begins by displaying the welcome screen shown in Figure 10-1.

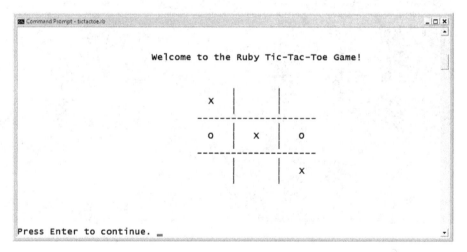

Figure 10-1   The Ruby Tic-Tac-Toe game's welcome screen

After pressing the Enter key, the players are prompted for permission to begin the game, as shown in Figure 10-2.

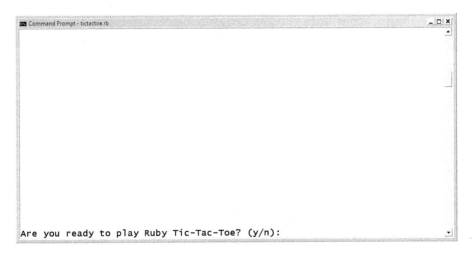

Figure 10-2   The game prompts the players for permission to begin

Once the players have decided to play, the instructions shown in
Figure 10-3 are displayed.

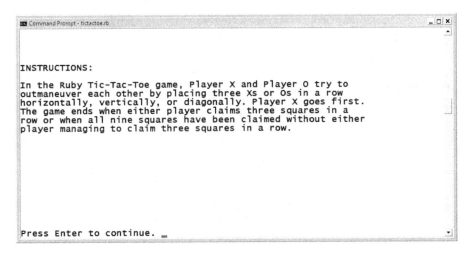

Figure 10-3   The game provides the players with instructions on how to play

Moves are made by entering the coordinates of a Tic-Tac-Toe square. As Figure 10-4 shows, Player X goes first.

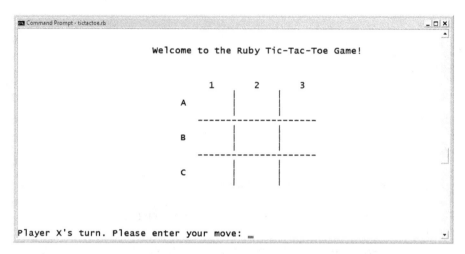

Figure 10-4   Player X is prompted to make the game's first move

As game play progresses, the letters identifying each player's moves are displayed on the Tic-Tac-Toe game board, as demonstrated in Figure 10-5.

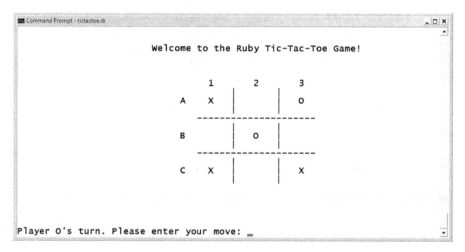

Figure 10-5   It is Player O's turn to make a move

After each move, the game examines the game board, looking for a winner. To win, a player must line up three squares in a row horizontally, vertically, or diagonally. Figure 10-6 shows a game that Player X won.

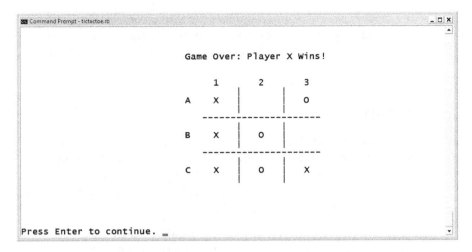

Figure 10-6   Player X has won the game

At the end of each game, the players are prompted for permission to start another game. When the players decide to quit playing, the screen shown in Figure 10-7 displays.

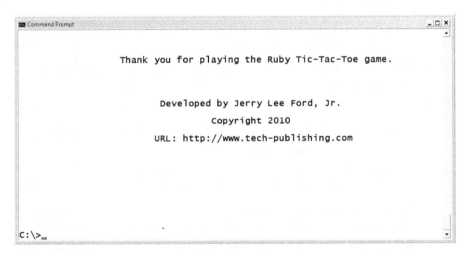

Figure 10-7   The final screen for the Tic-Tac-Toe game

Types of Script Errors

Undoubtedly, you have encountered some errors as you worked your way through this book. Maybe you made a few typos when testing the examples that were provided, or maybe you accidentally skipped a step or two when creating the Ruby game programs. That's okay. Even the most experienced programmers run into errors. Dealing with programming errors, which are sometimes referred to as bugs, is a part of every programmer's life. The trick is learning how to identify and fix bugs when they occur, which is the focus of this chapter.

Syntax Errors

Errors fall into different categories. One category is syntax errors. **Syntax errors** are ones that occur if you do not correctly follow Ruby's syntactical rules when writing your program statements—for example, if you mistype a keyword or fail to add closing quotation marks or parentheses, as required.

Ruby checks programs for syntax errors before executing them. Any program that contains one will not compile and execute until the error has been corrected. Generally, all you need to track down and fix a syntax error is the information provided by Ruby's error messages.

Runtime Errors

Another category of errors is **runtime errors**. These occur when a program attempts to perform an illegal action. For example, a runtime error will occur if you attempt to divide a number by zero, as shown here:

```
puts 10 / 0
```

When executed, this statement produces the following error, then terminates the execution of the program.

```
C:/Ruby_scripts/Test.rb:2:in, '/': divided by 0
        (ZeroDivisionError) from C:/Ruby_scripts/Test.rb:2
```

Runtime errors can sometimes be buried deep inside seldom-used methods and may not make their presence known until a particular set of circumstances occurs. As a result, it is extremely important that you thoroughly test your Ruby programs, ensuring that every part of every method works as expected.

Unfortunately, runtime errors can also occur for a variety of reasons that are outside your control. For example, if your program tries to access a network drive and the drive or network crashes, your program will experience a runtime error. In these situations, the best you can do is gracefully handle the situation, perhaps by displaying a more user-friendly error message. (Error-handling techniques are discussed later in this chapter.)

Logical Errors

A final category of errors is logical errors. A **logical error** occurs because of a mistake made in the formulation of the logic used to accomplish a particular task. For example, if you wrote a statement that was supposed to multiply two numbers but you accidentally divided one number by the other, a logical error would occur—i.e., your program's output would be different from what you wanted.

The best way to avoid logical errors is to carefully plan out the design of your programs before writing them. However, even the most experienced programmers sometimes make logical errors. Using the debugging techniques discussed in this chapter, you will be able to monitor the execution of your Ruby programs to track down and correct logical errors.

Handling Exceptions

When an error occurs in a Ruby program, an exception object is generated, and information about the error is assigned to it. When an exception occurs, the interpreter displays an error message and forces the immediate termination of the program. Rather than accept this behavior, Ruby allows you to programmatically deal with the error by handling exceptions.

Dealing with errors may mean displaying more useful error messages. Or it may mean finding ways of allowing programs to continue executing without the users even knowing that something has gone wrong. For example, you might include additional logic in a program so that a given operation is retried a number of times. Alternatively, let's say you have a program that needs to access a file on a network drive and the network drive becomes unavailable while the program is executing. You could add an error handler to the program that allows the program to use default data instead.

 One way to handle errors is to provide users with additional information. To do so you can execute the Kernel class's `system` method, which runs an external command or application as a separate process, as shown here:

```
system('start http://www.google.com')
```

When executed, this statement loads Google's home page in the user's default browser.

Creating Exception Handlers

When an exception is generated, it is said to be raised. Whenever an exception is raised, Ruby looks for an exception handler capable of handling it. If it finds one, control is transferred to the handler.

Otherwise, an error message is displayed, and the program termi-nates. As an example, suppose you created a program made up of the following statement:

```
puts x
```

When executed, the following error would be reported:

```
Test.rb:2: undefined local variable or method 'x' for
main:Object (NameError)
```

As you can see, the error occurred because the program attempted to reference an undefined variable.

To define an error handler, you need to first identify a statement within your Ruby program where you think an error may be able to occur, then precede it with the **begin** keyword. Next, place the **rescue** keyword after the location, then add any statements intended to deal with the exception immediately after that. Finally, add the **end** keyword.

To prevent the previous error from terminating the program, you could develop an exception handler, as shown here:

```
begin
  puts x
rescue
  #No actions defined
end
```

Here, the statement with the error in it has been placed between the **begin** and **rescue** keywords. As a result, when the error occurs, handling does not perform any further processing of the error. Since there are no statements between the **rescue** and **end** keywords, the error is simply disregarded. If there were any statements following the **end** statement associated with the **rescue** statements, the program would continue and allow those statements to execute.

Accessing Error Information

Exceptions that occur within Ruby programs are treated as objects from the Exception class and its family of subclasses. Using the => operator, you can access information about an exception, as shown here:

```
begin
  puts x
rescue => e
  puts "\n\nSorry. An error has occurred. Please report " +
    "the following"
  puts "error information to the help desk.\n\n"
  puts "ERROR CLASS: " + e.class.to_s
  puts "ERROR MESSAGE: " + e
end
```

Here, a user-friendly error message is displayed instead of the default error message. The user-friendly message identifies both the class and text of the error and requests that the user inform the help desk of the error. What follows is the output from the previous statements:

```
Sorry. An error has occurred. Please report the following
error information to the help desk.

ERROR CLASS: NameError
ERROR MESSAGE: undefined local variable or method 'x' for
main:Object
```

Handling Different Types of Errors

The error handler discussed previously is a generic error handler that will catch any type of error. You can also define error handlers to handle specific types of errors, as shown here:

```
begin
  puts x
rescue NameError
  puts "An name error has occurred!"
rescue ArgumentError
  puts "Incorrect use of arguments!"
rescue RangeError
  puts "A range error has occurred!"
rescue
  puts "Unexpected error!"
end
```

Here, separate `rescue` statements have been defined, each designed to handle a different type of error. The first three `rescue` statements trap specific types of errors. The last `rescue` statement traps any error that does not match up against the three previously defined error types.

Retrying Failed Statements

If your program recovers from an exception, you can use the `retry` statement to repeat the execution of an entire `begin/end` code block. To do this, you must place the `retry` statement on a line by itself, at the end of the `rescue` section of the code block, as shown here:

```
print "\nEnter a numerator: "
numerator = STDIN.gets    #Collect the numerator
numerator.chop!           #Remove the end-of-line marker

print "\nEnter a denominator: "
denominator = STDIN.gets #Collect the denominator
denominator.chop!         #Remove the end-of-line marker

numerator = numerator.to_i
denominator = denominator.to_i
```

```
begin
  calculation = numerator / denominator
  print "\nResult = " + calculation.to_s
  puts "\n"
rescue
  denominator = 10
  retry
end
```

Here, the user is prompted to enter two numbers, representing a numerator and a denominator. The user input is then converted to integer values. The value of the numerator is then divided by the denominator, and the result is displayed. Everything works fine as long as the user does not enter a value of 0 for the denominator. If this occurs, a division-by-zero runtime error occurs, terminating the program's execution. To prevent this error from terminating the program, the rescue statement located in the exception handler assigns a default value of 10 to the denominator, and the retry statement executes the division operation again, this time with a result that does not generate an error, as shown by the following output:

```
C:\Users\Jerry\Desktop\>test.rb

Enter a numerator: 50

Enter a denominator: 0

Result = 5

C:\>
```

Adding the retry statement to an exception handler can generate an endless loop, creating an entirely new problem. Therefore, exercise caution when including this statement in an exception handler.

As you can see, the user specified 50 as the numerator and 0 as the denominator. The denominator value results in an error that is handled by the program's exception handler, where a value of 10 is substituted as the denominator, resulting in a calculated value of 5.

Short Quiz

1. Programming errors, sometimes referred to as _____, are a part of every programmer's life.

2. _____ occur if you do not follow Ruby's syntactical rules when formulating code statements.

    a. Runtime errors

    b. Syntax errors

    c. Logical errors

    d. None of the above

3. Which of the following statements about runtime errors is true?

   a. They can be buried inside seldom-used methods and only surface in very specific circumstances.

   b. They are the result of faulty programming logic.

   c. They occur if you fail to follow Ruby's syntactical rules.

   d. They result in the display of error messages but do not halt program execution.

4. (True/False) Whenever a runtime error occurs within a Ruby program, an exception is generated.

5. (True/False) If an exception occurs and an exception handler has been defined, Ruby will transfer control to the handler.

Tracking a Script's Logical Flow

Sometimes, the contents of a Ruby error message make it difficult to track the error down. You can determine what is happening in a Ruby program, however, by strategically embedding print or puts statements throughout the program. These statements identify when specified methods are being executed, and they display the contents of variables whose values you suspect may not be getting set correctly. To see how to use the print and puts statements in this way, take a look at the following method, which is a modified version of a method used in Chapter 9's Ruby Blackjack game. The added code appears in bold.

```ruby
def play_game

  puts "Method play_game starting execution."

  Console_Screen.cls

  playerHand = get_new_card
  dealerHand = get_new_card

  puts "Initial value of playerHand = " + playerHand
  puts "Initial value of dealerHand = " + dealerHand

  playerHand = complete_player_hand(playerHand,
     dealerHand)

  puts "Updated value of playerHand = " + playerHand

  if playerHand <= 21 then
    dealerHand = play_dealer_hand(dealerHand)
    puts "Updated value of dealerHand = " + dealerHand
  end
```

```
determine_winner(playerHand, dealerHand)
puts "Calling determine_winner"

puts "Method play_game has completed execution."
```

end

Once you are confident that your program is working as expected, you can either remove the extra puts statements or comment them out by preceding them with the # character, but you should keep them available, in case you later need to conduct further testing.

Finding Bugs Using the Ruby Debugger

The use of print and puts statements as a debugging tool is fine for small programs. As your Ruby programs grow larger and more complex, however, this approach becomes too difficult and time consuming to implement. To monitor and debug larger Ruby programs, you need to work with Ruby's built-in debugger. It allows you to monitor and control the execution of your programs on a statement-by-statement basis, pausing to check on the value of variables when necessary.

Starting the Debugger

Ruby's debugger provides you with a test environment for running and monitoring your programs. (Before you can use it, however, the program must be free of syntax errors.) To start the debugger, execute the following command:

```
ruby -r debug
```

Here, the debugger is loaded by starting the Ruby interpreter with the -r debug option. For the rest of this section, the following Ruby program, which is in a file called test.rb, will be used to demonstrate how to work with the debugger:

```
x = 1
loop do
  puts x
  x += 1
  puts "We are half way there!" if x == 3
  break if x == 5
end
```

If you run this program without the debugger, it would generate the following output:

```
1
2
We are half way there!
3
4
```

To load the program and execute it using the Ruby debugger, use the following command at the operating-system command prompt:

```
ruby -r debug test.rb
```

Ruby loads your program in the debugger and generates the following output:

```
Debug.rb
Emacs support available.

test.rb:1:x = 1
(rdb:1)
```

The first two lines indicate that the debugger is active. The third line provides the line number of the program statement that will run next. Since the program has just been loaded into the debugger, this program statement has not yet executed. The last line displays the debugger's command prompt.

To get a feel for how to work with the debugger, let's run the test.rb program. If you have not already done so, create and save your own version of the test.rb program, and then start executing it in the debugger. The debugger loads and prepares to execute the program, as shown here:

```
Debug.rb
Emacs support available.

test.rb:1:x = 1
(rdb:1)
```

Let's allow the first program statement to be executed. You do this by executing the step command, as shown here:

```
(rdb:1) step
test.rb:2:loop do
(rdb:1)
```

Here, the debugger shows that the second program statement is ready for execution. Before executing it, however, check on the value assigned to the x variable now that the first statement has been run. One way of doing this is to simply type the name of the variable at the debugger prompt, as shown here:

```
(rdb:1) x
1
(rdb:1)
```

Here, x has been assigned a value of 1.

Another way of examining the value assigned to x is to type var local and press Enter, as shown here:

```
(rdb:1) var local
  x => 1
(rdb:1)
```

The var local command tells the debugger to list all the local variables within the current scope. (Type var global to view global variables and var instance to view instance variables.)

As you work your way through your program, you may lose track of where you are. To get your bearings, enter the list command. In response, the debugger identifies the next statement to be executed, as well as a number of statements that surround it, with the => marker, as shown here:

```
(rdb:1) list
[-3, 6] in test.rb
   1  x = 1
=> 2  loop do
   3    puts x
   4    x += 1
   5    puts "We are half way there!" if x == 3
   6    break if x == 5
(rdb:1)
```

Rather than stepping through a program line by line, you may want to set a breakpoint. A **breakpoint** is a marker placed in a program that pauses program execution when it is reached. Once the program's execution is paused, you can execute debugger commands.

To set up a breakpoint, use the break command, passing as an argument the line number at which you want to set the break. Here's how to set up a breakpoint on the fourth line of our sample program:

```
(rdb:1) break 4
Set breakpoint 1 at test.rb:4
(rdb:1)
```

Once the breakpoint has been set, type the cont command at the debugger prompt, as shown here:

```
(rdb:1) cont
1
Breakpoint 1, toplevel at test.rb:4
test.rb:4:  x += 1
(rdb:1)
```

The cont command executes the program without any stepping, stopping execution when a breakpoint is reached or the program ends. Here, after the cont command is executed, the program executes the second and third statements and then pauses execution before executing the fourth statement, where the breakpoint is set.

Next, use the step command to execute the fourth statement and check on the value assigned to x, as shown here:

```
(rdb:1) step
test.rb:5:  puts "We are half way there!" if x == 3
(rdb:1) x
2
(rdb:1)
```

The value of x is now equal to 2. Now, remove the breakpoint that was set. You can do that by typing **del** and the number that was previously assigned to the breakpoint, or you can do it by telling **del** to delete all breakpoints, as shown here:

```
(rdb:1) del
Clear all breakpoints? (y/n) y
(rdb:1)
```

Now that the breakpoint has been removed, set a conditional breakpoint, also known as a watchpoint, and allow the program to execute without stepping through it. The **watch** command is used to set conditional breakpoints, which are only triggered if a value within a statement meets a predefined value, as shown here:

```
(rdb:1) watch x = 3
Set watchpoint 4
(rdb:1) cont
Watchpoint 4, toplevel at test.rb:5
test.rb:5:  puts "We are half way there!" if x == 3
(rdb:1)
```

Here, the conditional breakpoint has been set up to pause program execution when the value assigned to x is equal to 3. Then the **cont** command is used to continue the program's execution, pausing again when the value of x is 3.

Next, display the conditional breakpoint, as shown here:

```
(rdb:1) break
Breakpoints:

Watchpoints:
   4 x = 3
```

Now, remove the breakpoint, as shown here:

```
(rdb:1) del
Clear all breakpoints? (y/n) y
```

Finally, verify that the breakpoint has been removed, as shown here:

```
(rdb:1) break
Breakpoints:

Watchpoints:

(rdb:1)
```

Wrap up the current debugging session by telling the debugger to terminate, as shown here:

```
(rdb:1) quit
Really quit? (y/n) y
```

Here, the **quit** command instructs the Ruby debugger to terminate, returning you to the operating system's command prompt. By executing debugger commands, you can exercise detailed control

You can type the word **break** to generate a list of all currently set breakpoints and to see the line number associated with each breakpoint.

over the execution of a Ruby program. You can control when statements execute and keep track of the order in which things are occurring. In addition, you can inspect the values assigned to variables to ensure that they are being appropriately set. Once you have identified the source of your program errors, you can make changes to your programs and test them again.

Short Quiz

1. You can use Ruby's built-in _____ to monitor and debug Ruby programs.

    a. exception handler

    b. analyzer

    c. debugger

    d. All of the above

2. To load Ruby's debugger, you start the Ruby interpreter by using which of the following commands?

    a. `ruby -debugger`

    b. `ruby -r analyze`

    c. `ruby -i debug`

    d. `ruby -r debug`

3. A _____ is a marker placed in a program that, when reached, pauses the program's execution.

4. Which of the following commands is used to terminate Ruby's debugger?

    a. `break`

    b. `pause`

    c. `quit`

    d. `exit`

5. Breakpoints are set using which of the following commands?

    a. `pause`

    b. `break`

    c. `halt`

    d. `break -i`

Back to the Ruby Tic-Tac-Toe Game

It is time to develop this chapter's game project, the Ruby
Tic-Tac-Toe game. As you work on this program, notice the way
variables are used. In particular, keep track of the global variables
that are used to represent each of the game board's nine squares.
Whereas the rest of the variables used in this program are local
variables and are passed, when needed, as arguments to methods,
the variables representing the game-board squares have been made
global because there are so many variables and because they are used
throughout the program.

Designing the Game

The development of the Ruby Tic-Tac-Toe game is completed in 16
steps, as outlined here:

1. Open your text or script editor, and create a new file.

2. Add comment statements to the beginning of the script file to
   document the script and its purpose.

3. Define a Screen class representing the terminal window.

4. Define a Game class representing the Ruby Tic-Tac-Toe game.

5. Define the display_greeting method.

6. Define the display_instructions method.

7. Define the display_game_board method.

8. Define the validate_player_move method.

9. Define the play_game method.

10. Define the clear_game_board method.

11. Define the check_results method.

12. Define the display_game_results method.

13. Define the display_credits method.

14. Instantiate script objects.

15. Prompt the player for permission to begin the game.

16. Administer game play.

Step 1: Create a New Ruby File

Open your favorite text or script editor, and create a new Ruby script file named TicTacToe.rb. Store it in the same folder as your other Ruby game programs.

Step 2: Document the Script and Its Purpose

Add the following comments to the new script file. These comments provide a description of the script and its purpose.

```
#------------------------------------------------------------
#
# Script Name: TicTacToe.rb
# Version:     1.0
# Author:      Jerry Lee Ford, Jr.
# Date:        March 2010
#
# Description: This Ruby script is a version of the popular
#              Tic-Tac-Toe game in which two players try to
#              outmaneuver each other by placing three Xs
#              or Os in a row horizontally, vertically, or
#              diagonally.
#
#------------------------------------------------------------
```

Step 3: Define a *Screen* Class

The Ruby Tic-Tac-Toe game uses two custom classes, Screen and Game, each of which contains numerous methods for controlling the interaction with the user and executing the game. Define a class named Screen by adding the following statements to the end of the script file:

```
# Define custom classes -------------------------------------

#Define a class representing the console window
class Screen

  def cls  #Define a method that clears the display area
    puts ("\n" * 25)  #Output 25 blank lines to the screen
    puts "\a"    #Make a little noise to get the player's
                 #attention
  end

  def pause    #Define a method that pauses the display
               #area
    STDIN.gets  #Execute the STDIN class's gets method to
                #pause script execution until the player
                #presses the Enter key
  end

end
```

Step 4: Define the *Game* Class

The Game class contains nine methods used to control the execution of the game. To define the Game class, add the following statements to the end of the script file:

```
#Define a class representing the Ruby Tic-Tac-Toe game
class Game

end
```

Step 5: Define the *display_greeting* Method

Define the first of nine methods belonging to the Game class by inserting the following statements between the class's opening and closing statements. These statements define the display_greeting method, which is responsible for displaying the game's welcome message.

```
#This method displays the game's opening message
def display_greeting

   Console_Screen.cls   #Clear the display area

   #Display the game's welcome screen
   puts "\t\t\tWelcome to the Ruby Tic-Tac-Toe Game!" +
      "\n\n\n\n"
   puts "\t\t\t                |         |"
   puts "\t\t\t         X      |         |"
   puts "\t\t\t                |         |"
   puts "\t\t\t         ----------------------"
   puts "\t\t\t                |         |"
   puts "\t\t\t         0      |    X    |    0"
   puts "\t\t\t                |         |"
   puts "\t\t\t         ----------------------"
   puts "\t\t\t                |         |"
   puts "\t\t\t                |         |    X"
   puts "\t\t\t                |         |"
   print "\n\n\n\n\nPress Enter to continue. "

   Console_Screen.pause      #Pause the game

end
```

Step 6: Define the *display_instructions* Method

Define the second of nine methods belonging to the Game class by adding the following statements at the end of the class definition, immediately after the display_greeting method. These statements define the `display_instructions` method, which is responsible for displaying the game's instructions.

```
#Define a method to be used to display game instructions
def display_instructions

  Console_Screen.cls        #Clear the display area

  puts "INSTRUCTIONS:\n\n"  #Display a heading

  #Display the game's instructions
  puts "In the Ruby Tic-Tac-Toe game, Player X and " +
    "Player O try to "
  puts "outmaneuver each other by placing three Xs or " +
    "Os in a row "
  puts "horizontally, vertically, or diagonally. " +
    "Player X goes first. "
  puts "The game ends when either player claims three " +
    "squares in a "
  puts "row or when all nine squares have been claimed " +
    "without either "
  puts "player managing to claim three squares in a row."
  puts "\n\n\n\n\n\n\n\n\n\n\n"
  print "Press Enter to continue. "

  Console_Screen.pause        #Pause the game

end
```

Step 7: Define the `display_game_board` Method

Define the third of nine methods belonging to the Game class by adding the following statements at the end of the class definition, immediately after the `display_instructions` method:

```
#Define a method to display the game board and collect
#player moves
def display_game_board(player)

  move = ""   #Assign a default value

  loop do   #Loop forever

    Console_Screen.cls  #Clear the display area

    #Display the game board
    puts "\t\t\tWelcome to the Ruby Tic-Tac-Toe Game! " +
      "\n\n\n\n"
    puts "\t\t\t           1         2          3\n"
    puts "\t\t\t                |         |"
    puts "\t\t\t    A    #{$A1}   |   #{$A2}    |    #{$A3}"
    puts "\t\t\t                |         |"
    puts "\t\t\t          ---------------------"
    puts "\t\t\t                |         |"
    puts "\t\t\t    B    #{$B1}   |   #{$B2}    |    #{$B3}"
    puts "\t\t\t                |         |"
```

```
      puts "\t\t\t            --------------------"
      puts "\t\t\t           |        |"
      puts "\t\t\t      C    #{$C1}  |  #{$C2}  |   #{$C3}"
      puts "\t\t\t           |        |"

      #Prompt the player to enter a move
      print "\n\n\n\n\nPlayer " + player + "'s turn. " +
        "Please enter your move: "

      move = STDIN.gets  #Collect the player's move
      move.chop!  #Remove the end-of-line marker
      move = move.upcase  #Convert to uppercase

      #Terminate the loop if a valid move was entered
      if move.length == 2 then   #Must be at 2 character long
        if move =~ /[A-C][1-3]/i  #Must be A1, A2, A3, B1,
                               #B2, B3, C1, C2, C3
          #Call method responsible for determining if the
          #board square was available
          validMove = validate_player_move(move)
          if validMove == true  #The move was valid
            break  #Terminate the execution of the loop
          end
        end
      end

    end

    return move  #Return the player's move back to the
                 #calling statement

end
```

This method is controlled by a loop that has been set up to run forever. Each time the loop repeats, it displays the Tic-Tac-Toe game board. Embedded within the game board is a series of variable references. These variable references are filled in using variable interpolation during game play. After displaying the game board, the method displays a message prompting the current player, as specified by the value assigned to the player variable, to enter a move.

The player's input is converted to all uppercase and checked to see if it is two characters long. If it is, a regular expression is used to further validate the player's input, ensuring that the first character is an A, B, or C and that the second character is a 1, 2, or 3. If the player's input passes these validation checks, it is passed as an argument to the validate_player_move method, which checks to see if the game-board square selected by the player is available for selection (i.e., that it has not already been assigned). If the value returned by the validate_player_move method is equal to true, a break command is executed, and the player's move is returned to the statement that called upon the method to execute. Otherwise, the player is again prompted to enter a move.

Step 8: Define the `validate_player_move` Method

Define the fourth of nine methods belonging to the Game class by adding the following statements at the end of the class definition, immediately after the `display_game_board` method. The `validate_player_move` method is responsible for ensuring that the game-board square specified by the player is available for selection.

```
#Define a method that determines if the square selected by
#the player is still available
def validate_player_move(move)

    #Return a value of false if the square has already been
    #selected
    return false if move == "A1" && $A1 != " "
    return false if move == "B1" && $B1 != " "
    return false if move == "C1" && $C1 != " "
    return false if move == "A2" && $A2 != " "
    return false if move == "B2" && $B2 != " "
    return false if move == "C2" && $C2 != " "
    return false if move == "A3" && $A3 != " "
    return false if move == "B3" && $B3 != " "
    return false if move == "C3" && $C3 != " "

    #Return a value of true if the square is available
    return true

end
```

When called, this method checks to see if the player's move, passed to the method as an argument, is available. This is accomplished by checking to see if the value assigned to the game-board square is a blank space, which means the square is available.

A value of `false` is returned if the specified game-board square is not available. Otherwise, a value of `true` is returned.

Step 9: Define the `play_game` Method

Define the fifth of nine methods belonging to the Game class by adding the following statements at the end of the class definition, immediately after the `validate_player_move` method. The `play_game` method is responsible for managing the play of a complete game.

```
#Define a method to control game play
def play_game

    player = "X"   #Make Player X the default player for each
                   #new game

    noOfMoves = 0  #Reset the value of the variable used to
                   #keep track of the total number of moves
                   #made in a game
```

```ruby
#Clear out the game board to get it ready for a new game
clear_game_board

loop do  #Loop forever

  Console_Screen.cls        #Clear the display area

  #Call on the method that displays the game board and
  #collects player moves
  square = display_game_board(player)

  #Assign the selected game-board square to the player
  #that selected it
  $A1 = player if square == "A1"
  $A2 = player if square == "A2"
  $A3 = player if square == "A3"
  $B1 = player if square == "B1"
  $B2 = player if square == "B2"
  $B3 = player if square == "B3"
  $C1 = player if square == "C1"
  $C2 = player if square == "C2"
  $C3 = player if square == "C3"

  #Keep count of the total number of moves that have
  #been made
  noOfMoves += 1

  #Call on the method that is responsible for
  #determining if the game has been won
  winner = check_results(player)

  #See if player X has won
  if winner == "X" then
    #Call on the method that displays the game's final
    #results
    display_game_results("Player X Wins!")
    break  #Terminate the execution of the loop
  end

  #See if player O has won
  if winner == "O" then
    #Call on the method that displays the game final
    #results
    display_game_results("Player O Wins!")
    break  #Terminate the execution of the loop
  end

  #See if the game has ended in a tie
  if noOfMoves == 9 then
    #Call on the method that displays the game's final
    #results
    display_game_results("Tie")
    break  #Terminate the execution of the loop
  end
```

```
#If the game has not ended, switch player turns and
#keep playing
if player == "X" then
  player = "O"
else
  player = "X"
end

  end

end
```

This method begins by assigning a value of X to a variable named player and a value of 0 to a variable named noOfMoves. The value assigned to player specifies the game's starting player. noOfMoves will be used to keep track of the total number of moves made by both players during game play.

Next, the clear_game_board method is called, resetting all the game board's embedded variables to blank spaces, thus readying the game for a new round of play. The rest of the method is controlled by a loop. Each time the loop repeats, the display_game_board method is called and passed the value assigned to the player variable. The display_game_board method returns a value representing the game-board square selected by the player. A game-board square is then assigned to the player based on the square that was selected, and the value of noOfMoves is incremented to keep track of the number of moves that have been made by both players.

Next, the check_results method is called. This method checks to see if the current player has won the game, returning a value of X or 0 if one of the players has won. If this is the case, the display_game_results method is called, and a break command is executed, terminating the loop and ending the play_game method. If neither player has won the game, the value of noOfMoves is checked to see if it is equal to 9, in which case every game-board square has been selected without either player winning the game.

If neither player has won the game and all of the squares have not been played, the last thing the loop does before it repeats is switch whose turn it is, from Player X to Player O or vice versa, as appropriate.

Step 10: Define the clear_game_board Method

Define the sixth of nine methods belonging to the Game class by adding the following statements at the end of the class definition, immediately after the play_game method. The clear_game_board method is responsible for resetting the value of each variable embedded in the game board.

```
#Define a method that is responsible for clearing out the
#game board
def clear_game_board

  #Assign a blank space to each game-board square
  $A1 =  " "
  $A2 =  " "
  $A3 =  " "
  $B1 =  " "
  $B2 =  " "
  $B3 =  " "
  $C1 =  " "
  $C2 =  " "
  $C3 =  " "

end
```

When called, this method assigns each of the game board's nine
embedded variables a blank space, visually clearing each square and
making it available for selection in the next round of play.

Step 11: Define the check_results Method

Define the seventh of nine methods belonging to the Game
class by adding the following statements at the end of the class
definition, immediately after the clear_game_board method. The
check_results method is responsible for determining whether the
current player, passed to the method as an argument, has lined up
three squares in a row.

```
#Define a method to examine the game board and determine
#if the current player has won the game
def check_results(player)

  winner = ""   #Assign a default value

  #Check diagonally
  winner = player if $A1 == player && $A2 == player &&
    $A3 == player
  winner = player if $B1 == player && $B2 == player &&
    $B3 == player
  winner = player if $C1 == player && $C2 == player &&
    $C3 == player

  #Check vertically
  winner = player if $A1 == player && $B1 == player &&
    $C1 == player
  winner = player if $A2 == player && $B2 == player &&
    $C2 == player
  winner = player if $A3 == player && $B3 == player &&
    $C3 == player
```

```
#check diagonally
winner = player if $A1 == player && $B2 == player &&
   $C3 == player
winner = player if $A3 == player && $B2 == player &&
   $C1 == player

return winner   #Return the result back to the calling
                #statement
```

```
end
```

The method checks horizontally, vertically, and diagonally for a winner. If a winner is identified, the method returns a letter representing the winning player (X or O). Otherwise, an empty string is returned to the calling statement.

Step 12: Define the `display_game_results` Method

Define the eighth of nine methods belonging to the Game class by adding the following statements at the end of the class definition, immediately after the check_results method. The display_game_results method is responsible for displaying the results of the current round of play.

```
#Define a method that will be used to displays the game's
#final result
def display_game_results(message)

    Console_Screen.cls  #Clear the display area

    #Display the results of the game
    puts "\n\n\n"
    puts "\t\t\t    Game Over: " + message + "\n\n\n"
    puts "\t\t\t        1      2      3\n"
    puts "\t\t\t            |      |"
    puts "\t\t\t    A    #{$A1}    |  #{$A2}    |   #{$A3}"
    puts "\t\t\t            |      |"
    puts "\t\t\t      ---------------------"
    puts "\t\t\t            |      |"
    puts "\t\t\t    B    #{$B1}    |  #{$B2}    |   #{$B3}"
    puts "\t\t\t            |      |"
    puts "\t\t\t      ---------------------"
    puts "\t\t\t            |      |"
    puts "\t\t\t    C    #{$C1}    |  #{$C2}    |   #{$C3}"
    puts "\t\t\t            |      |"
    print "\n\n\n\n\nPress Enter to continue. "

    Console_Screen.pause        #Pause the game

end
```

This method displays a message, passed to it as an argument, at the top of the game's Tic-Tac-Toe board.

Step 13: Define the `display_credits` Method

The `display_credits` method displays information about the game and its developer, including the developer's URL. Define this ninth of nine methods belonging to the Game class by adding the following statements to the end of the class definition, immediately after the `display_game_results` method:

```
#This method displays information about the Ruby
#Tic-Tac-Toe game
def display_credits

  Console_Screen.cls  #Clear the display area

  #Thank the player and display game information
  puts "\t\t  Thank you for playing the Ruby " +
    "Tic-Tac-Toe game.\n\n\n\n"
  puts "\n\t\t\t Developed by Jerry Lee Ford, Jr.\n\n"
  puts "\t\t\t  Copyright 2010\n\n"
  puts "\t\t\tURL: http://www.tech-publishing.com\n\n" +
    "\n\n\n\n\n\n\n\n"

end
```

Step 14: Initialize Script Objects

Initialize an instance of the Screen and Game classes by adding the following statements to the end of the script file:

```
# Main Script Logic --------------------------------------

Console_Screen = Screen.new  #Instantiate a new Screen
                             #object
TTT = Game.new  #Instantiate a new Game object

#Execute the Game class's display_greeting method
TTT.display_greeting

#Execute the Game class's clear_game_board method
TTT.clear_game_board

answer = ""  #Initialize variable and assign it an empty
             #string
```

In addition to instantiating the Console_Screen and TTT objects, these statements also execute the Game class's `display_greeting` method and define a variable named answer, which will be used to manage the execution of a loop that prompts the player for permission to begin a new round of play.

Step 15: Get Permission to Start the Game

Set up the prompt for getting the player's permission to play the game by adding the following statements to the end of the script file:

```
#Loop until the player enters y or n and do not accept any
#other input
loop do

   Console_Screen.cls  #Clear the display area

   #Prompt the player for permission to start the game
   print "Are you ready to play Ruby Tic-Tac-Toe? (y/n): "

   answer = STDIN.gets  #Collect the player's answer
   answer.chop!  #Remove the end-of-line marker

   #Terminate the loop if valid input was provided
   break if answer =~ /y|n/i

end
```

Here, a loop is set up to run forever. Upon each iteration of the loop, the player is prompted to enter a value of y or n to indicate whether a new round of play should be initiated or the game should be terminated. Any input other than a y or n is rejected. Once valid input is provided, a **break** command is executed, terminating the loop and allowing the program to continue running.

Step 16: Control Game Play

The remainder of the script file consists of statements responsible for controlling the overall execution of the game. The program's remaining statements are shown here:

```
#Analyze the player's answer
if answer =~ /n/i  #See if the player wants to quit

   Console_Screen.cls  #Clear the display area

   #Invite the player to return and play the game some other
   #time
   puts "Okay, perhaps another time.\n\n"

else  #The player wants to play the game

   #Execute the Game class's display_instructions method
   TTT.display_instructions

   playAgain = ""  #Initialize variable and assign it an
                   #empty string
```

```
loop do   #Loop forever

  #Execute the Game class's play_game method
  TTT.play_game

  loop do   #Loop forever

    Console_Screen.cls   #Clear the display area
    #Find out if the player wants to play another round
    print "Would you like to play another round? (y/n): "

    playAgain = STDIN.gets   #Collect the player's
                             #response
    playAgain.chop!   #Remove the end-of-line marker

    #Terminate the loop if valid input was provided
    break if playAgain =~ /n|y/i

  end

  #Terminate the loop if the player wants to quit
  break if playAgain =~ /n/i

end

#Call upon the Game class's display_credits method
TTT.display_credits

end
```

The execution of these statements is controlled by an if statement
code block. If the player decides not to play, a message is displayed
encouraging the player to return and play another time, and the
game terminates. If the player decides to play, the Game class's
display_instructions method is run. A loop then repeatedly
executes the Game class's play_game method, allowing the players
to play as many times as they want. The loop continues to iterate
until the players decide to quit, at which time a break command is
executed, terminating the loop and allowing the display_credits
method to execute.

Running Your New Ruby Script Game

Save your Ruby script. If you typed the code statements correctly,
the program should work as expected. If you run into any errors,
however, read the error messages carefully to ascertain what went
wrong. Then review the script, looking for mistyped or missing
statements. If necessary, crank up Ruby's debugger, and use it to
debug your program. In fact, even if your program runs fine, run it
in the debugger anyway, just to get some additional experience.

Summing Up

- Dealing with programming errors, which are sometimes referred to as bugs, is a part of every programmer's life.

- Syntax errors are ones that occur if you do not correctly follow Ruby's syntactical rules when writing your program statements.

- Runtime errors occur when a program attempts to perform an illegal action.

- Logical errors occur because of a mistake made in the formulation of the logic used to accomplish a particular task.

- The best way to avoid logical errors is to carefully plan the design of your programs before you start writing them.

- An exception is generated any time a runtime error occurs within a Ruby program.

- By default, when an exception occurs, the interpreter displays an error message and forces the immediate termination of the program.

- Whenever an exception is raised, Ruby looks for an exception handler capable of handling the exception, and if it finds one, control is transferred to the handler.

- Exceptions that occur within Ruby programs are managed as objects from the `Exception` class.

- To monitor and debug larger Ruby programs, you need to learn how to work with Ruby's built-in debugger.

- The debugger allows you to monitor and control the execution of your programs on a statement-by-statement basis, pausing whenever necessary to check on the value of variables.

- The debugger is loaded by starting the Ruby interpreter with the `-r debug` option.

- In debug mode, the `step` command causes the next program statement to be executed.

- The `var local` command tells the debugger to list all the local variables within the current scope.

- The `var global` command tells the debugger to list all the global variables, and the `var instance` command tells the debugger to list all the instance variables.

- In debug mode, the `list` command displays the next statement to be executed as well as a number of statements that surround it.

- A breakpoint is a marker placed in a program that pauses the program's execution when it is reached.

- To set up a breakpoint, you use the `break` command.

- The `cont` command runs the program without any stepping, stopping execution when a breakpoint is reached or the programs ends.

- Remove breakpoints using the `del` command.

- You can type the word `break` to generate a list of all the currently set breakpoints and to see the line number associated with each breakpoint.

- Use the `watch` command to set conditional breakpoints.

- The `quit` command instructs the Ruby debugger to terminate.

Comprehension Check

1. (True/False) Depending on the error, a Ruby program with a syntactical error may still compile.

2. _____ errors occur when Ruby programs perform illegal actions.

3. What type of error will occur when the following statement is executed?

        puts 100 / 0

   a. Syntax

   b. Runtime

   c. Logical

   d. Terminal

4. _____ errors occur because of mistakes in the formulation of the logic used to accomplish a given task.

5. (True/False) By default, when an exception occurs, the interpreter displays an error message and forces the immediate termination of the program.

6. (True/False) When an exception is raised, Ruby looks for an exception handler capable of handling the error.

7. To define an error handler, you must precede a statement where the error might occur with which of the following keywords?

   a. rescue

   b. begin

   c. capture

   d. exception

8. (True/False) Exceptions that occur within Ruby programs are managed as objects from the Error class.

9. To define an error handler, you must add which of the following keywords immediately after the statement where the error might occur?

   a. rescue

   b. begin

   c. capture

   d. exception

10. Which of the following statements is true about Ruby's built-in debugger?

   a. It allows you to control statement execution on a statement-by-statement basis.

   b. It pauses the program's execution, allowing you to monitor variable values.

   c. It supports the use of breakpoints, allowing you to predetermine the locations where the program's execution is paused.

   d. All of the above

11. Ruby's debugger is a _____ component.

   a. Third-party

   b. Add-on

   c. Built-in

   d. GUI

12. (True/False) In order to use Ruby's debugger, your Ruby program must be free of all syntax errors.

13. In debug mode, the _____ command is used to display a list of local variables within the current scope.

    a. `var local`

    b. `list local`

    c. `list var`

    d. `var`

14. In debug mode, the _____ command is used to display the next statement to be executed.

    a. `display`

    b. `line`

    c. `list -a`

    d. `list`

15. A(n) _____ is a marker placed in a program to pause the program's execution when it is reached.

    a. halt mark

    b. break

    c. breakpoint

    d. interrupt

16. The _____ command runs a program without any stepping.

    a. `cont`

    b. `exec`

    c. `jump`

    d. `skip`

17. The _____ command removes a breakpoint.

    a. `rem`

    b. `del`

    c. `remove`

    d. `delete`

18. When used by itself, the _____ command generates a list of all the currently set breakpoints.

    a. breakpoint

    b. break

    c. halt point

    d. rem

19. The _____ command is used to set conditional breakpoints.

    a. set

    b. break

    c. rem

    d. watch

20. The _____ command instructs the Ruby debugger to terminate.

    a. quit

    b. halt

    c. step

    d. pause

Reinforcement Exercises

The following exercises are designed to further your understanding of Ruby programming by challenging you to make improvements to the chapter's game project, the Ruby Tic-Tac-Toe game.

1. Currently, any time a player makes an invalid move, the game rejects it without an explanation. Player input may be invalid for several different reasons, however. A player may attempt to choose a game-board square that has already been assigned, or a player may submit invalid game-board coordinates or the wrong number of characters. Modify the game to display text messages that identify when an invalid move has been made and explain why that move was invalid.

   To implement this change, add a method to the Game class. Name the method display_error and configure it to accept a single argument, a text string containing the error message to be displayed. Modify the `display_game_board` method so that it calls upon the `display_error` method whenever invalid input is received from a player. Make sure that calls to the `display_error` method contain suitable error messages in the form of a text string.

2. The game allows players to play as many times as they wish. However, it is currently up to players themselves to keep track of the number of games they win. Relieve players of this burden by having the game keep track of the number of games each player wins. Rather than displaying this statistical information after each game, make it available to the players as a hidden cheat. And make the statistics accessible during game play, allowing players to access this data by typing the letter h or H in place of a move during game play.

To implement this change, add two variables named `$xWins` and `$oWins`. Add the definition statement for these two variables at the beginning of the program's Main Script Logic section, and assign both variables a starting value of 0. Add a new method named `display_statistics` to the Game class. Configure the method so that it converts the numeric value stored in the two variables to a string and then displays its values so that players can see it. Next, add two statements to the `display_game_board` method that increment the value of `$xWins` and `$oWins` each time Player X or Player O wins a game. Lastly, modify the `display_game_board` method so that it executes the `display_statistics` method whenever a player enters H and presses Enter.

3. Currently, the game requires Player X to go first, putting Player O at a disadvantage. To make things fairer, modify the Main Script Logic section so that Player X begins the first round of play, but after that the players take turns beginning a round of play. In addition, modify the call to the `play_game` method so that it includes the passage of the `player` variable. Provide that method with instruction (e.g., a text string of X or O) on whose turn it is. Then modify the `play_game` method to accept a text string as a parameter representing the player whose turn it is. Lastly, remove the hardcode statement at the beginning of the `play_game` method, which makes Player X begin every round of play.

4. Currently, the game's welcome screen instructs players to press Enter to continue. No option is provided for immediate termination of the game should the players decide not to play.

Instead, the players have to press Enter and then respond to a different prompt to terminate game play. Remove this unnecessary step.

To implement this change, modify the Game class's display_greeting method so that it prompts the players to either type q or Q and press Enter to terminate game play or press Enter to continue playing. Collect this input using the STDIN class's gets method, and then use the chop! method to remove the end-of-line marker from the input. Add a statement at the end of the method that returns the player's response to the statement that called on the method for execution. Next, modify the statement at the beginning of the Main Script Logic section that executes the display_greeting method so that it captures the result now returned by that method. Lastly, add programming logic that either terminates the game or allows game play to continue, based on the value returned from the display_greeting method.

5. Currently, the game assumes that both players already know how to play the game. However, this may not always be the case. To make the game more user friendly, add an option that allows players to view Wikipedia's Tic-Tac-Toe page.

To implement this change, modify the Game class's display_greeting method so that it presents players with the option of typing m or M and pressing Enter to load the Wikipedia page into their default Web browser. Further, modify the display_greeting method so that it executes the following statement whenever a player elects to view more information about Tic-Tac-Toe:

```
system('start http://en.wikipedia.org/wiki/↵
Tic_tac_toe')
```

Discovery Projects

Discovery Project 10-1

An important part of programming is identifying the areas in your programs where errors are likely to occur and adding the program logic to deal with those errors, should they occur. In Ruby, this means creating exception handlers. To demonstrate your understanding of how to create exception handlers, add one to the following example, which is susceptible to a runtime error if an external text file named input.txt is removed or renamed in the current directory.

```
fileName = "input.txt"

file = open(fileName)

if file

    puts "\n" + fileName + " found. Contents:\n\n"
    puts File.read(fileName)

end
```

When adding the exception handler to this program, also add program logic that, in the event the input.txt file is not found, continually prompts the user to enter the name of an alternative text file until a valid filename in the current working directory is provided.

Discovery Project 10-2

There is a lot more to debugging than can be covered in a single chapter. To further your understanding of debugging techniques and strategies, go to *http://www.wikipedia.org* and search on the keyword "debugging." Review the material presented, and prepare a one-page paper on the subject.

Discovery Project 10-3

Testing allows you to make sure that your program works as expected and that you have not made any logic errors in your program's design. Proper testing also helps weed out possible runtime errors that may be hiding in seldom-exercised methods within your programs.

To further your understanding of testing techniques and strategies, go to *http://www.wikipedia.org* and search on the keywords "software testing." Review the material presented, and prepare a one-page paper on the subject. Identify a number of additional benefits provided by program testing and then review the different testing methods that can be employed.

## CHAPTER 11

Ruby on Rails Web Development

In this chapter, you:

- ◎ Get an overview of Ruby on Rails
- ◎ Learn how to get Ruby on Rails up and running
- ◎ Learn how to verify that Ruby on Rails is set up correctly
- ◎ Create a Ruby on Rails blog application

As was discussed in Chapter 1, Ruby has become a popular programming language in part because of Ruby on Rails, which is an open-source, web-based application-development framework. Ruby on Rails simplifies web-application development by making assumptions about how those applications should be created, based on industry standards and conventions, and by using default configurations that support most web applications. Once the applications have been created, you can further customize them to suit your own needs.

Project Preview: The Blog Application

In this chapter, you create a Ruby on Rails blog application. This application, which you develop and test on your own computer, will allow you to create, view, and modify blog entries, as shown in Figure 11-1.

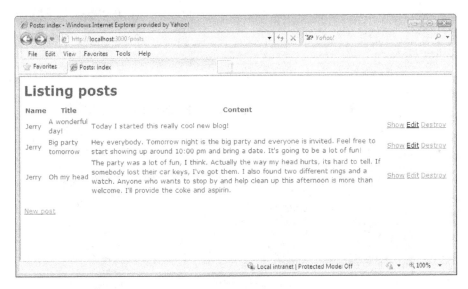

Figure 11-1 Sample entries in the blog application

As you can see, the blog application supports the collection of name, title, and content data. It allows any number of blog entries to be created, and the entries can be viewed, modified, or destroyed.

Overview of Ruby on Rails

Ruby on Rails, sometimes referred to as **RoR** or **Rails**, includes a collection of scripts used to automate the creation of web-based applications. Web developers have chosen to use Ruby on Rails in large part because it handles most of the work involved in developing new applications—tasks like database access, output display, and data validation. As a result, you spend less time and effort creating web applications than if you worked with other web-development frameworks and programming languages.

Ruby on Rails was developed by David Heinemeier Hansson, who wrote it in Ruby and released it as open-source software in July 2004. In October 2007, Apple began shipping Ruby and Ruby on Rails as part of its Mac OS X 10.5 distribution, thereby signaling the acceptance of Ruby as a mainstream web-development tool. Ruby on Rails 2.3 was released in March 2009. The next version, Ruby on Rails 3.0, was under development when this book was published. The information presented in this chapter is applicable to both versions of Ruby on Rails.

As shown in Figure 11-2, the official Ruby on Rails website is located at *http://www.rubyonrails.org*.

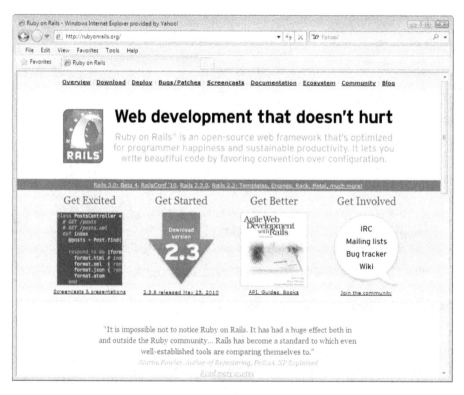

Figure 11-2   The official Ruby on Rails website

There are many ways to customize your Ruby on Rails applications. You can, for example, edit your application's HTML code or modify the CSS style sheets to alter the application's appearance. You can change the application's database management system or modify its URL associations by changing the application's routing information.

You can also add new application features and functionality by executing additional Ruby on Rails helper scripts and by making use of a feature known as scaffolding.

Skills Needed to Work with Ruby on Rails

To work with Ruby on Rails, you need a basic understanding of HTML, web-page construction, and how the Internet works. You also need to understand Cascading Style Sheets (CSS), which Ruby on Rails uses to configure the presentation of the content viewed by web browsers. Finally, you need to understand web-server and database management systems. This chapter assumes that you already understand these areas. Its focus is on providing you with a basic understanding of Ruby on Rails and demonstrating the steps involved in creating Ruby on Rails applications.

Required Software

To create applications using Ruby on Rails, you must have Ruby installed on your computer. In addition, Ruby on Rails applications usually require a database management system to facilitate the management of a database in which the application's data is stored. As for database management systems, Ruby on Rails can work with many types, but all you will usually need, to create and test the execution of your web applications, is the SQLite web server, which you can download for free using RubyGems, as discussed later in this chapter. In addition to a database management system, you must have access to a web server that can host your Ruby on Rails web applications as you develop them. When Ruby on Rails is installed on your computer, so is a small web server called WEBrick, which you use as your Ruby on Rails development environment.

Development Philosophy

Ruby on Rails follows a number of guiding principles, which allow it to deliver full-featured web applications quickly and with less effort than other web-development frameworks. These principles include:

Convention Over Configuration

Using a set of assumptions, Ruby on Rails configures a new application based on best practices and common standards, resulting in general-purpose applications that can be further customized as necessary. This allows you to avoid working through numerous configuration files.

Don't Repeat Yourself, or DRY

The DRY principle is the idea that you should avoid writing the same program code more than once within a web application. Doing so results in larger applications that are more difficult to maintain and, therefore, subject to more errors.

Architecture

The Ruby on Rails framework is a collection of programs that provides everything needed to develop database-driven web applications. It is designed to handle most of the basic development, leaving it up to you to customize your applications to your own needs.

Ruby on Rails is built on a Model-View-Controller (MVC) architecture, which organizes your applications into three primary components: models, views, and controllers. The relationship among these three components is depicted in Figure 11-3.

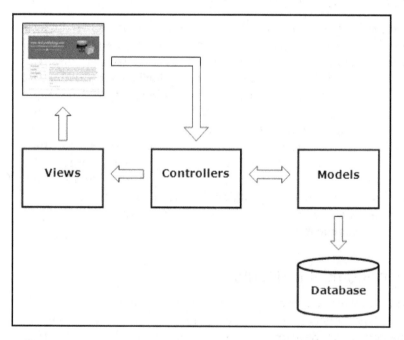

Figure 11-3   Relationships among the three main components of MVC architecture

As shown in Figure 11-3, models are Ruby on Rails programs that manage the relationship between controllers and the application's database. They are also responsible for performing data validation. Most application code is contained in its models. Models are implemented via Ruby on Rails' **Active Record** library. Active Record provides Ruby on Rails with database independence, allowing it to work with all major database management systems.

Every Ruby on Rails application displays its data using one or more views. These programs are responsible for an application's user interface, presenting data in a predefined format. Views help maintain a separation between an application's programming logic and the presentation of its data. The data displayed by a view is updated based on the actions of controllers. Views are implemented via Ruby on Rails' **Action View** library, which defines presentation templates that are used in displaying data. These views are usually in HTML and contain embedded Ruby code that performs tasks needed to properly present application data within the browser windows, as shown in Figure 11-3.

Ruby on Rails uses controllers to process data and manage the flow of data communication with web browsers. As shown in Figure 11-3, controllers tie together different models and views, processing application input and output. They are responsible for querying models for data and then organizing the received data into a format that can be displayed by a view. Controllers are implemented by Ruby on Rails' **Action Controller**, which serves as an interface between Active Record, which interfaces with the database, and Action View, which manages data presentation.

The MVC architecture facilitates DRY programming and keeps the programming logic that controls application execution separate from the programming logic that manages the presentation of data, resulting in an application that is much easier to support and maintain. Another result of the MVC architecture is a clear directory structure that maintains a separation between different pieces of code as well as a separation between application code and other application resources.

Other Ruby on Rails Libraries

In addition to Active Record, Action View, and Action Controller, Ruby on Rails contains a number of important libraries that are automatically installed by RubyGems. These include the following:

- **Action Mailer**—Provides a framework for adding e-mail services to Ruby on Rails applications, enabling applications to send e-mail and receive e-mail.

- **Active Resource**—Manages the connections between application objects and database tables, mapping local application objects to web resources.

- **Railties**—Provides the program code (help scripts) that actually creates Ruby on Rails applications and ties everything together.

- **Active Support**—A library of classes used by Ruby on Rails programs.

Working with Database Management Systems

Almost every Ruby on Rails application involves the storage and retrieval of information using a database. By default, every new Ruby on Rails project is configured to use the SQLite database management system, which is easily installed using RubyGems. However, you can configure Ruby on Rails to work with just about any distributed database management system, including MySQL, SQL Server, DB2, and Oracle.

All Ruby on Rails applications are built to support three environments: development, test, and production environments. The development environment is where you work when you are building your Ruby on Rails application. The test environment is where you make sure your application works as expected, fixing any errors you come across. The production environment is where your application goes once it's ready to be sent out into the world. The configuration settings for these are specified within a file named database.yml. By editing this file, you can configure a Ruby on Rails application to work with different database management systems.

SQLite is well suited to the development of small applications. However, by modifying the configuration setting for its production environment, you can configure your application to use a more powerful database management system, which is needed to support data storage in larger applications.

In this chapter, everything is done using the default development environment, which is designed to support local application development. In addition, this chapter uses SQLite as the database management system for its web-application project. This keeps things simple and allows you to focus on the overall development of your Ruby on Rails application without getting bogged down in database details.

Short Quiz

1. (True/False) Ruby on Rails does not make any assumptions about the application it creates, leaving it up to you to supply all of the application's configuration.

2. Which of the following is a way to configure a Ruby on Rails application?

   a. Edit the application's HTML

   b. Modify the application's cascading style sheet

   c. Modify the application's URL associations

   d. All of the above

3. Which of the following best describes Ruby on Rails' Convention Over Configuration philosophy?

    a. Applications should be created without making any assumptions about application configuration.

    b. Applications should be created using a set of assumptions based on best practices and common standards.

    c. Configuration information should be embedded within program code.

    d. None of the above

4. (True/False) Controllers are Ruby on Rails programs that manage the relationship between models and an application's database.

5. Under Ruby on Rails' Model-View-Controller (MVC) architecture, applications are organized into three primary components, including which of the following?

    a. Models

    b. Views

    c. Controllers

    d. All of the above

Getting Ruby on Rails Up and Running

Before you can begin developing Ruby on Rails applications, you must install various pieces of software, thereby establishing a web-application development environment on your computer. This software includes the Ruby on Rails framework, a web server, and a database management system.

Installing Ruby On Rails

The easiest way to install Ruby on Rails is through RubyGems. **RubyGems** is a package installer program that comes as part of Ruby. It automates the downloading and installation of Ruby on Rails programs and related development-software tools. Before installing Ruby on Rails, make sure you have a working Internet session.

 Once Ruby on Rails is installed on your computer, you can keep it up to date by connecting to the Internet, accessing the command prompt, and typing the following command:
`gem update rails.`
Then press Enter.

Installing Ruby on Rails on Windows

RubyGems should already be installed on any computer running Windows that has Ruby installed on it. From the Windows command prompt, issue the following command to install Ruby on Rails:

```
gem install rails --include-dependencies
```

This command installs Ruby on Rails on your computer and then downloads and installs various Ruby on Rails libraries, along with their documentation.

Installing Ruby on Rails on Mac OS X

The first step in installing Ruby on Rails on a computer running on Mac OS X is to make sure RubyGems is installed and to install it if it is not. To determine if RubyGems is installed, issue the following command:

```
$gem -v
```

If RubyGems is already installed, its version number will be displayed. Otherwise, a `command not found` message is displayed. If RubyGems is not installed, open your web browser and go to *http://rubygems.org/pages/download*, which is shown in Figure 11-4.

Figure 11-4   Web page for downloading RubyGems on Mac OS X

Click one of the links to download the latest version of RubyGems. Unpack the download into a folder, and, via the terminal window, use the `cd` command to navigate to that folder. Next, type `sudo ruby setup.rb`, and press Enter. When prompted, type your password, and press Enter. The RubyGems installation should take only a few minutes. Once it's completed, you can install Ruby on Rails by executing the following command and pressing Enter:

```
sudo gem install rails --include-dependencies
```

The Ruby on Rails installation should take only a few minutes.

Selecting a Web Server

Ruby on Rails applications require a web server. Luckily, Ruby on Rails can work with any web server. In addition, it comes with its own web server, named WEBrick.

The WEBrick web server is automatically installed as part of Ruby. For simplicity, this chapter's project will use WEBrick as the web server. To do so, execute the following command from the command prompt, and press Enter while you're within the folder where your Ruby on Rails application has been stored:

```
script/server
```

In response, the WEBrick server starts up and waits for incoming requests from a web browser on your computer. If you choose to work with a different web server, consult its documentation for instructions on its installation and startup.

Installing the SQLite Database Management System

SQLite is a small, compact database management system well suited to small- and moderate-sized applications. For Mac OS X 10.5 users and newer users, it should already be installed on your computer. On other operating systems, you can easily install it using RubyGems. To do so, establish an Internet connection, and then execute the following command from the command prompt and press Enter:

```
gem install sqlite3-ruby
```

 Before installing SQLite, you should download the most current version of RubyGems. To do so, establish an Internet connection and execute the following command from the command prompt, then press Enter:

```
gem update --system
```

Verifying Ruby on Rails Setup

Once you have installed Ruby on Rails, a web server, and a database management system, you should test your Ruby on Rails development environment by creating a demo project. This involves just two commands. The first command builds the demo application, validating that Ruby on Rails has been properly installed. The second command starts the WEBrick web server, validating the operation of your web server.

377

Creating a Demo Application

Access the command prompt, and navigate to a folder in which you will store the demo application. Since you are validating the installation of Ruby on Rails by creating this demo application, type rails demo, and press Enter. This command will create a folder named demo containing all of the files and folders that make up the application. As the following example shows, Ruby on Rails automatically does a lot of work for you.

Although the rails demo command is shown here executing on Windows, the same command is used to create the demo application on computers with different operating systems.

```
C:/RoR_Projects>rails demo
    create
    create    app/controllers
    create    app/helpers
    create    app/models
    create    app/views/layouts
    create    config/environments
    create    config/initializers
    create    config/locales
    create    db
    create    doc
    create    lib
    create    lib/tasks
    create    log
    create    public/images
    create    public/javascripts
    create    public/stylesheets
    create    script/performance
    create    test/fixtures
    create    test/functional
    create    test/integration
    create    test/performance
    create    test/unit
    create    vendor
    create    vendor/plugins
    create    tmp/sessions
    create    tmp/sockets
    create    tmp/cache
    create    tmp/pids
    create    Rakefile
    create    README
    create    app/controllers/application_controller.rb
    create    app/helpers/application_helper.rb
    create    config/database.yml
    create    config/routes.rb
    create    config/locales/en.yml
    create    db/seeds.rb
    create    config/initializers/backtrace_silencers.rb
    create    config/initializers/inflections.rb
    create    config/initializers/mime_types.rb
    create    config/initializers/new_rails_defaults.rb
    create    config/initializers/session_store.rb
    create    config/initializers/cookie_verification_secret.rb
    create    config/environment.rb
    create    config/boot.rb
    create    config/environments/production.rb
```

```
create   config/environments/development.rb
create   config/environments/test.rb
create   script/about
create   script/console
create   script/dbconsole
create   script/destroy
create   script/generate
create   script/runner
create   script/server
create   script/plugin
create   script/performance/benchmarker
create   script/performance/profiler
create   test/test_helper.rb
create   test/performance/browsing_test.rb
create   public/404.html
create   public/422.html
create   public/500.html
create   public/index.html
create   public/favicon.ico
create   public/robots.txt
create   public/images/rails.png
create   public/javascripts/prototype.js
create   public/javascripts/effects.js
create   public/javascripts/dragdrop.js
create   public/javascripts/controls.js
create   public/javascripts/application.js
create   doc/README_FOR_APP
create   log/server.log
create   log/production.log
create   log/development.log
create   log/test.log
```

```
C:\RoR_Projects>
```

rails is a Ruby script installed as part of Ruby on Rails. When executed, it creates a Ruby on Rails project, including its directory structure and its core application files. The rails script requires a single argument, the name of the application to be created, which in this case is demo.

Assuming that there were no issues with the installation of Ruby on Rails on your computer, a new folder named demo is created within the current directory. In the command's output, you will see a listing of all the files and folders that are created within the demo folder.

 The demo project uses the SQLite database management system by default, which you should have previously installed. Therefore, you do not have to concern yourself with making any configuration changes that would otherwise be required to instruct Ruby on Rails on how to work with your database management system.

Verifying the Execution of Your Web Server

To verify that you have a working copy of the WEBrick web server, you need to start it on your computer. To do so, navigate to the newly created demo folder using the following command:

```
cd demo
```

Once inside the folder, type ruby script/server at the command prompt, and press Enter. This command will generate output similar to that shown here:

```
C:\RoR_Projects\demo>ruby script/server
=> Booting WEBrick
=> Rails 2.3.8 application starting on http://0.0.0.0:3000
=> Call with -d to detach
=> Ctrl-C to shutdown server
[2010-06-27 14:30:42] INFO WEBrick 1.3.1
[2010-06-27 14:30:42] INFO ruby 1.8.6 (2007-03-13)
    [i386-mswin32]
[2010-06-27 14:30:42] INFO WEBrick::HTTPServer#start:
  pid=1328 port=3000
```

At this point, WEBrick pauses and begins monitoring port 3000, waiting for incoming requests from a web browser. As requests are received, they are processed, and you will see text displayed on the terminal window that reflects the actions that WEBrick takes when processing those requests.

You can also access your computer's locally installed web server by using http://127.0.0.1:3000/.

Now that you have created your new Ruby on Rails project and started up the WEBrick web server, you can review the results of your efforts by opening your web browser and loading the following URL:

http://localhost:3000

If everything works, you should see the Ruby on Rails web page displayed in your web browser, as shown in Figure 11-5.

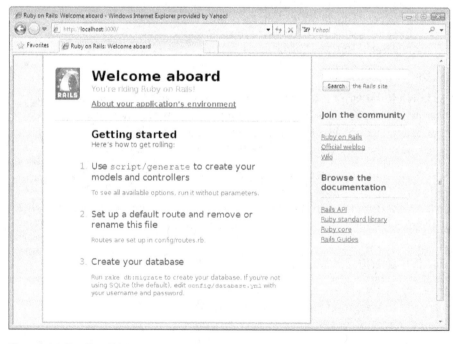

Figure 11-5 The "Welcome aboard" message verifies that your Ruby on Rails development environment is functional

Ruby on Rails' home page is actually an HTML page named index.html, which is stored in every Ruby on Rails application's public folder. By default, Ruby on Rails looks in this folder for the application's home page. However, as demonstrated later in this chapter, you can instruct it to use a different web page as the application's home page.

When you are done testing the execution of the demo application, halt the execution of the WEBrick web server, access the terminal window where it is running, and press Ctrl-C. This will shut down the web browser and return the command prompt.

Ruby on Rails Applications Files

As you have seen, Ruby on Rails applications are created using helper programs, like the `rails` program. When executed, these programs create the program files required for a basic web application. The files are stored using a specific directory structure. Ruby on Rails creates the same directory structure for each new web application. As a result, Ruby on Rails applications have a clearly defined structure, making them easier to maintain. The following list shows the directory structure that Ruby on Rails created for the demo application:

```
demo/
..../app
........./controller
........./helpers
........./modules
........./views
............./layouts
..../config
..../db
..../doc
..../lib
..../log
..../public
..../script
..../test
..../tmp
..../vendor
README
Rakefile
```

Once you become familiar with this structure, you will find its consistency across different applications a major advantage that simplifies and speeds up application development. The following list provides a brief overview of the resources you will find in these folders:

- **app**—Stores most of the source code and templates for Ruby on Rails applications. Organizes the application's controllers, helpers, models, and views in separate folders, keeping application components separate.

- **app/controller**—Organizes application controller classes, each of which manages a different type of user request supported by the application.

- **app/helpers**—Stores helper classes that the application needs when working with model, view, and controller classes.

- **app/models**—Stores classes designed to model and format data in a form required by the application's database.

- **app/views**—Stores templates used to format the display of data, which the application converts to HTML and returns to the browser for display.

- **app/views/layouts**—Stores template files used with views.

- **config**—Stores configuration files that specify application settings that affect database configuration, the processing of web requests, and other application environment settings. Included here is the database.yml file, which contains database configuration information, and the `routes.rb` script, which instructs Ruby on Rails on how to find the web pages that you add to your applications.

- **db**—Stores scripts that manage the application's database.

- **doc**—Stores documentation that is generated for the application.

- **lib**—Stores application libraries with program code that does not fit into the controller, model, or help classifications.

- **log**—Stores application-error log data. Separate log files are maintained for development, text, and production.

- **public**—Stores application files that do not change often, including JavaScript, graphics, CSS style sheets, and HTML files.

- **script**—Stores program files that manage various Ruby on Rails tools, including ones used to create and develop new Ruby on Rails applications.

- **test**—Stores various test scripts and files created by Ruby on Rails when your application is created.

- **tmp**—Stores temporary files generated by the application.

- **vendor**—Stores third-party libraries/plugins.

- **README**—Contains documentation about Ruby on Rails applications.

- **Rakefile**—Builds, packages, and deploys Ruby on Rails program code.

As you can see, each Ruby on Rails application contains a robust directory structure filled with various files. However, you will find that, thanks to Ruby on Rails' default settings, most of the time you will only have to work with a handful of these files when fine-tuning your applications.

Short Quiz

1. Before developing Ruby on Rails applications, you must install various pieces of software, including:

   a. The Ruby on Rails framework

   b. A web server

   c. A database management system

   d. All of the above

2. (True/False) The easiest way to install Ruby on Rails on a computer running Windows is through the fxri-interactive Ruby and Help Console.

3. To determine if RubyGems is installed, you must issue which of the following commands?

   a. gem -r

   b. gem -i

   c. gem -v

   d. gem -h

4. Ruby on Rails supports many web servers. In addition, it comes with its own web server, named _____ .

5. _____ is a small, compact database management system that Ruby on Rails is automatically configured to use, one that is well suited to meet the needs of applications with small- to moderate-sized storage requirements.

Back to the Blog Application

It is time to develop this book's final project, the blog application. By following the steps described here, you will create a web application that can capture, store, retrieve, and display blog data.

Although using Ruby on Rails effectively requires a basic understanding of HTML, web servers, and database management systems, this particular blog application is designed to eliminate the need for these prerequisites. Instead, the instructions provided will guide you through the creation of the blog application while focusing only on information that is essential to the development of the application. You will not have to write a single Ruby code statement to develop this blog application. And modification of the configuration files will be kept to an absolute minimum. All you have to do is execute a number of Ruby on Rails commands and statements and edit a couple of configuration files.

As you develop the blog application, don't try to understand every command or statement that is presented. Instead, focus on understanding the overall development process.

In previous chapters, you were guided through the creation of complete Ruby programs, which you then enhanced in the chapters' reinforcement exercises. In this chapter, you will have to complete both the main project and the reinforcement exercises to develop a complete Ruby on Rails application.

Design the Blog Application

The development of the core program files that make up the blog application is completed in five steps, as outlined here:

1. Create an application folder.

2. Create a new Ruby on Rails application.

3. Create a database for your application.

4. Create a controller and a view for the blog application.

5. Edit the application's index page.

Step 1: Create an Application Folder

Create a folder on your computer where you would like to store the application's files. You can do so from the command prompt by executing the following command:

```
mkdir RoR_Apps
```

Here, a new folder named RoR_Apps is created. Now, execute the following command to navigate into the new folder:

```
cd RoR_Apps
```

Step 2: Create a New Ruby on Rails Application

Create the blog application's base file and folder structure. Do this by using the `rails` command, as shown here:

```
rails blog
```

When executed, this command creates a Ruby on Rails application and configures it to work with a SQLite database, which will be used to store the application's data.

Step 3: Create a Database for Your Application

Create the application's database. Do this from within the blog folder that was created in the previous step. To navigate to this folder, execute the following command:

```
cd blog
```

Next, use the `rake` command to create the application's database, as shown here:

```
rake db:create
```

Rake is a Ruby on Rails program that is used to perform different administrative tasks. One of its most common uses is the creation of databases. In the previous statement, `rake` is used to create a new SQLite database within the current folder.

Step 4: Create a Controller and a View for the Blog Application

Every Ruby on Rails application needs at least one controller and a view. To set this up, you need to execute the `generate` program (script/generate), passing it the arguments shown here in bold:

```
C:\:RoR_Apps\blog>ruby script/generate controller home index
      exists  app/controllers/
      exists  app/helpers/
      create  app/views/home
      exists  test/functional/
      create  test/unit/helpers/
      create  app/controllers/home_controller.rb
      create  test/functional/home_controller_test.rb
      create  app/helpers/home_helper.rb
      create  test/unit/helpers/home_helper_test.rb
      create  app/views/home/index.html.erb

C:\RoR_Apps\blog>
```

Although the example in Step 4 shows the `generate` command running on Microsoft Windows, the same command is used when creating the application on Mac OS X or Linux/UNIX.

As is shown in the resulting command output, the `generate` script adds a number of additional files to the blog application. One of these files, named index.html.erb, provides a template that Ruby on Rails uses to display results when it needs to process a request to show the application's home page.

Step 5: Edit Your Application's Index Page

At this point, the home page created for the application does not have any content to display. You therefore need to customize it to provide some. To do so, use your favorite program or text editor to open the index.html.erb file. This file resides in the app/views/home folder.

By default, the index.html.erb file contains the following statements:

```
<h1>Home#index</h1>
<p>Find me in app/views/home/index.html.erb</p>
```

Modify this file so that it contains a single statement, as shown here:

```
<h1>Jerry Ford's Blog</h1>
```

This modification displays a Level 1 HTML heading, "Jerry Ford's Blog," on the application's home page.

Running Your New Ruby on Rails Project

You are ready to test the blog application's execution. If you have followed the instructions without making any typos, your copy of the blog application should display a customized web page with the heading "Jerry Ford's Blog."

You have created the overall file and folder structure for the blog application, and you have created a home page for it, but the programming logic needed to support the posting of blog entries still needs to be added. The steps for doing this and for adding other enhancements to the application are provided in the chapter's reinforcement exercises.

Starting Your Web Server

Before you can test the execution of the blog application, you must start the WEBrick web server. To do so, access the command prompt, navigate to the application blog folder, and execute the `ruby script/server` command, as shown here:

```
C:\RoR_Apps\blog>ruby script/server
=> Booting WEBrick
=> Rails 2.3.8 application starting on http://0.0.0.0:3000
=> Call with -d to detach
=> Ctrl-C to shutdown server
[2010-07-03 18:10:31] INFO WEBrick 1.3.1
```

```
[2010-07-03 18:10:31] INFO ruby 1.8.6 (2007-03-13)
   [i386-mswin32]
[2010-07-03 18:10:31] INFO WEBrick::HTTPServer#start:
   pid=2080 port=3000
```

Viewing the Blog Application

To review the results of your efforts so far, open your web browser, and load the following URL:

http://localhost:3000

In response, a copy of the Ruby on Rails "Welcome aboard" page is displayed. Next, you need to modify the URL to load the application's home page into the browser window, as shown in Figure 11-6. Load the following URL:

http://localhost:3000/home/index

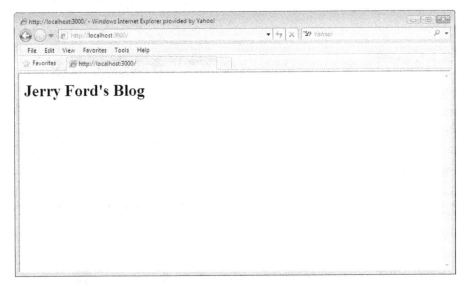

Figure 11-6 The blog application's index page

Learning More About Ruby on Rails

Ruby on Rails is not easily mastered. Entire books have been dedicated to it. This chapter has provided you with a basic overview of its features and capabilities. To learn more about Ruby on Rails, visit its official website at *http://rubyonrails.org/*.

Another valuable online resource is the Ruby on Rails documentation site at *http://api.rubyonrails.org/*, the home page for which is shown in Figure 11-7. Here you will find documentation of the classes that make up the Ruby on Rails framework.

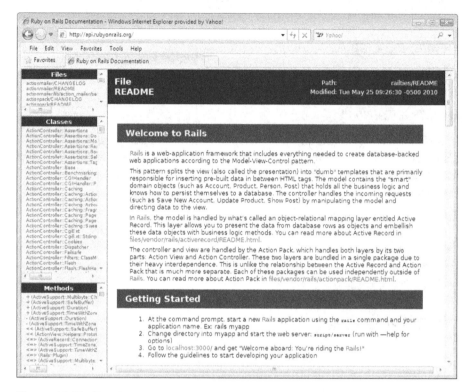

Figure 11-7 The documentation site for Ruby on Rails

Summing Up

- Ruby on Rails, sometimes referred to as RoR or Rails, is an open-source, web-based application-development framework.

- Ruby on Rails simplifies web-application development by making assumptions about the applications it creates.

- Once you have created Ruby on Rails applications, you can customize them to suit your purposes.

- You can also add new application features and functionality by executing additional Ruby on Rails helper scripts and by making use of scaffolding.

- Ruby on Rails applications usually require a database management system to facilitate the management of the database in which the application's data is stored.

- All you usually need to create and test the execution of new web applications is the SQLite web server, which Ruby on Rails is configured to use by default.

- When Ruby on Rails is installed on your computer, so is a small web server called WEBrick, which you can use as part of your Ruby on Rails development environment.

- The principle known as Convention Over Configuration refers to the emphasis on best practices and common standards in Ruby on Rails development.

- The principle known as Don't Repeat Yourself (DRY) is the idea that you should avoid writing the same program code more than one time within your web applications.

- Ruby on Rails is based on a Model-View-Controller (MVC) architecture.

- Within the MVC architecture, your Ruby on Rails applications are organized into three primary components: models, views, and controllers.

- Models manage the relationship between program data and the application's database. They are implemented via Ruby on Rails' Active Record library, which serves as an interface between program code and the application's database.

- Views are an application's user interface, presenting application data in a predefined format. They help to maintain a separation between Ruby on Rails' programming logic and the presentation of its data and are implemented via Ruby on Rails' Action View library.

- Ruby on Rails uses controllers to process data and direct data communication from web browsers. Controllers tie together different models and views, processing application input and output. They are implemented by Ruby on Rails' Action Controller system.

- All Ruby on Rails applications support three environments: development, test, and production environments.

- The easiest way to install Ruby on Rails on a computer running Windows is with RubyGems, which is a package installer program that's part of Ruby.

- To determine if RubyGems is installed, issue the `gem -v` command.

- Ruby on Rails supports many types of web servers. In addition, it comes with its own lightweight web server, named WEBrick.

- SQLite is a small, compact database management system well suited to the development of small- and moderate-sized applications.

- Ruby on Rails' "Welcome aboard" home page is actually an HTML page named index.html, which is stored in the application's public folder.

- Ruby on Rails applications are created using helper scripts, like the `rails` script.

Comprehension Check

1. Which of the following best describes Ruby on Rails?

   a. It is an open-source web-development database management system that supports the storage of application data.

   b. It is a closed-source web-application framework that supports the development of desktop and web applications.

   c. It is an open-source web-application framework that supports the development of database-driven web applications.

   d. All of the above

2. Ruby on Rails is capable of handling which of the following types of tasks?

   a. Database access

   b. Data validation

   c. Data display

   d. All of the above

3. Ruby on Rails is based on which of the following architectures?

   a. Build-Test-Execute

   b. Model-View-Controller

   c. Prototype-Test-Controller

   d. None of the above

4. _____ are responsible for managing the relationship between program data and the application's database.

   a. Views

   b. Models

   c. Controllers

   d. Builds

5. _____ represent an application's user interface, presenting application data using a predefined format.

   a. Views

   b. Models

   c. Controllers

   d. Builds

6. _____ tie together different models and views, processing application input and output.

   a. Views

   b. Models

   c. Controllers

   d. Builds

7. _____ provides e-mail services within Ruby on Rails applications.

   a. Action Mailer

   b. Active Resource

   c. Railties

   d. Active Support

8. _____ provides the program code (help scripts) that actually creates Ruby on Rails applications and ties everything together.

   a. Action Mailer

   b. Active Resource

   c. Railties

   d. Active Support

9. (True/False) Ruby on Rails can be configured to work with just about any distributed database management system.

10. (True/False) All Ruby on Rails applications are built to support four environments: development, test, debug, and production.

11. _____ is a package-installer program that is used to install Ruby on Rails.

12. _____ is a small, compact database management system well suited to small- and moderate-sized application development.

13. _____ is a Ruby script installed as part of Ruby on Rails that you use to create new projects, including a directory structure and key application files.

14. Which of the following commands starts the WEBrick web server?

 a. webrick -s

 b. start webrick

 c. webrick script/server

 d. ruby script/server

15. Which of the following commands terminates the execution of the WEBrick web server?

 a. ctrl-c

 b. ctrl-z

 c. ctrl-x

 d. ctrl-q

16. The _____ folder stores most of the source code and templates for a Ruby on Rails application.

 a. config

 b. lib

 c. app

 d. db

17. The _____ folder stores classes designed to model and format data in the way required by the application's database.

 a. app/controllers

 b. app/models

 c. app/helpers

 d. app/view/layouts

18. The principle known as _____ emphasizes that Ruby on Rails applications should be created based on a set of best practices and common standards.

19. The principle known as _____ is the idea that you should avoid writing the same program code more than one time within your web applications.

20. (True/False) The WEBrick web server monitors incoming requests on port 2000.

Reinforcement Exercises

The following exercises are designed to further your understanding of Ruby on Rails applications development by challenging you to complete the chapter's project, the blog application.

1. Replace the Ruby on Rails "Welcome Aboard" page with the new "Jerry Ford's Blog" page, making it the home page for the website. To do this, you must delete the application's default web page. This page, named index.html, is located in the blog application's public folder (demo/public/index.html).

   To perform this operation, execute one of the following commands from the command prompt while in the blog folder:

   Mac OS X   `rm public/index.html`

   or

   Windows   `del public\index.html`

   Next, specify the location of the application's new home page. To do this, edit the routes.rb file, which is located in the application's config folder (blog/config/routes.rb). This file contains entries written in domain-specific language (DSL), which instruct Ruby on Rails how to connect inbound requests to controllers. At the bottom of this file, you will see the following pair of statements, which represent the application's default routes:

   ```
   map.connect ':controller/:action/:id'
   map.connect ':controller/:action/:id.:format'
   ```

   Place the following statement immediately before the two preceding statements:

   ```
   map.root :controller => "home"
   ```

   This statement instructs Ruby on Rails to route requests for the application's default index action to the application's new index.html page. To verify that the application's home page has been replaced, the WEBrick web server must be running. If it is not running, open a new command prompt, navigate to the blog folder, and execute the following command to start the WEBrick web server:

```
ruby script/server
```

Open your preferred web browser, type the following command, and press Enter:

```
http://localhost:3000/
```

The new home page for the blog application should be displayed. Leave your WEBrick web server running as you complete the remaining reinforcement exercises.

You may, of course, choose to develop application source code from scratch rather than using scaffolding. However, doing so means a lot more work for you and negates a primary advantage of using Ruby on Rails.

2. For the blog application to be of any use, it must support the posting of blog entries. To accomplish this, you need to make changes to the application's database, adding table entries representing two strings and a text column. The two strings will be used to store name and title data for blog postings, and the text column will be used to store blog-content data entries.

Ruby on Rails provides programs that facilitate the speedy development of new web applications using a tool known as **scaffolding**. Scaffolding programs add specific functionality to Ruby on Rails applications, enabling you to get up and running quickly without having to develop things from scratch.

When creating scaffolding, Ruby on Rails examines the application's database tables and, based on what it finds, creates a controller, model, and view that match up with the table's structure. In the process, new application files, stylesheets, and other application resources are added to your Ruby on Rails applications.

To provide the blog application with the ability to post entries, type the following command, and press Enter:

```
ruby script/generate scaffold Post name:string ↵
    title:string content:text
```

This command generates scaffolding that enables users to post blog entries. When executed, the command generates output similar to that shown here:

```
C:/RoR_Apps/blog>ruby script/generate scaffold ↵
    Post name:string title:string content:text
        exists  app/models/
        exists  app/controllers/
        exists  app/helpers/
        create  app/views/posts
```

```
    exists   app/views/layouts/
    exists   test/functional/
    exists   test/unit/
    exists   test/unit/helpers/
    exists   public/stylesheets/
    create   app/views/posts/index.html.erb
    create   app/views/posts/show.html.erb
    create   app/views/posts/new.html.erb
    create   app/views/posts/edit.html.erb
    create   app/views/layouts/posts.html.erb
    create   public/stylesheets/scaffold.css
    create   app/controllers/posts_controller.rb
    create   test/functional/posts_controller_
       test.rb
    create   app/helpers/posts_helper.rb
    create   test/unit/helpers/posts_helper_
       test.rb
     route map.resources :posts
dependency   model
    exists   app/models/
    exists   test/unit/
    exists   test/fixtures/
    create   app/models/post.rb
    create   test/unit/post_test.rb
    create   test/fixtures/posts.yml
    create   db/migrate
    create   db/migrate/20100704153401_create_
       posts.rb
```

One of the resources added to the blog application by the scaffolding command is a database migration. A **migration** is a Ruby class that makes changes to the application's database tables. Ruby on Rails uses the `rake` command to process migrations. To make the required changes to the application's database that stores the name, title, and content data for the blog entries, you must use the `rake` command to process the application's migration, which is stored in `db/migrate`. To do so, execute the following command, and press Enter:

```
rake db:migrate
```

When executed, this command yields output similar to that shown here:

```
C:\RoR_Apps\blog>rake db:migrate
(in C:/RoR_Apps/blog)
== CreatePosts: migrating
===================================================
====
-- create_table(:posts)
   ->0.0030s
== CreatePosts: migrated (0.0110s)
=======================================
====
```

3. The blog application is almost complete. However, you still need to connect the application's index.html page to the blog. To do so, open the index.html.erb file (/app/views/home/index.html.erb) and change its content, as shown here:

```
<h1>Jerry Ford's Blog</h1>
<%= link_to "View/Create Blog Entries", posts_path %>
```

Here, the Ruby on Rails link_to method is used to create a hyperlink to posts_path, which is the path to the application's postings. Once you have made this change, reload the *http://localhost:3000/* URL in your web browser. Assuming the WEBrick web server is still running, the updated home page should be displayed, as shown in Figure 11-8.

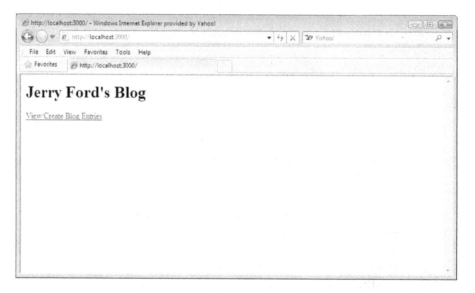

Figure 11-8   The "Jerry Ford's Blog" web page now contains a link to the blog application

Click the **View/Create Blog Entries** link. The web page shown in Figure 11-9 should be displayed.

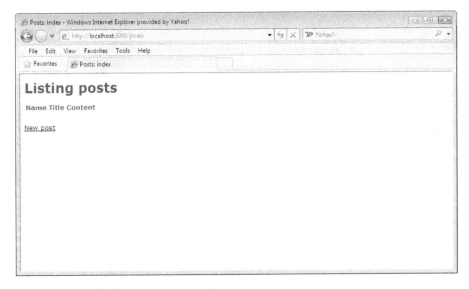

Figure 11-9   The blog with no current entries

4. Test the operation of the blog application by adding a blog
    posting. To do so, click the **New post** link. The page shown in
    Figure 11-10 is displayed.

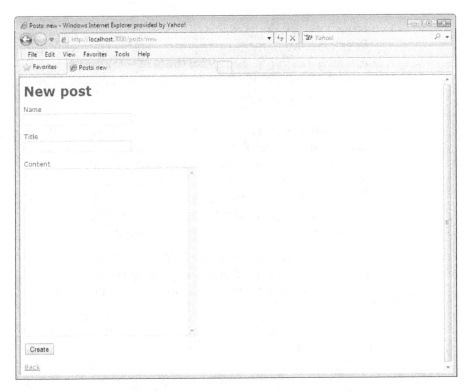

Figure 11-10   Ready to create a new blog entry

Type Jerry in the Name field, Author in the Title field, and This is my first blog entry! in the Content field, and then click the **Create** button. The blog entry should then be displayed as shown in Figure 11-11.

Figure 11-11 View your first blog entry

From here, you can click **Edit** to modify your blog entry or **Back** to return to the "Listing posts" page, where your blog will be listed. Just to the right of the blog entry are links labeled **Show**, **Edit**, and **Destroy**, which, when clicked, allow you to view, modify, or delete the blog entry.

5.   Click **New post** to add a new blog entry. Enter Jerry in the name field, and click **Create**. A new empty blog entry with no title or content is added. All blog entries should contain Name, Title, and Content entries. All three of these fields should be filled in before a blog entry is accepted. An informational message should be displayed explaining to the user that an incomplete entry has been submitted.

Remove this entry by clicking the **Back** link, then click the **Destroy** link to the right of the empty blog entry. Click **OK** when prompted for confirmation to delete the blog entry.

To change the blog application so that only complete blog entries are permitted, modify the contents of the post.rb script (app/models/post.rb). By default, this file contains a single statement, as shown here:

```
class Post < ActiveRecord::Baseend
```

Modify the contents of post.rb, as shown here:

```
class Post < ActiveRecord::Base
  validates_presence_of :name, :title, :content
  validates_length_of :name, :minimum => 2
  validates_length_of :title, :minimum => 5
  validates_length_of :content, :minimum => 10
end
```

What these statements do is validate that something has been typed into each of the blog entry text fields and verify that a minimum amount of text is entered into each text field. Figure 11-12 shows an example of the type of error message the user will see if an invalid blog entry is submitted.

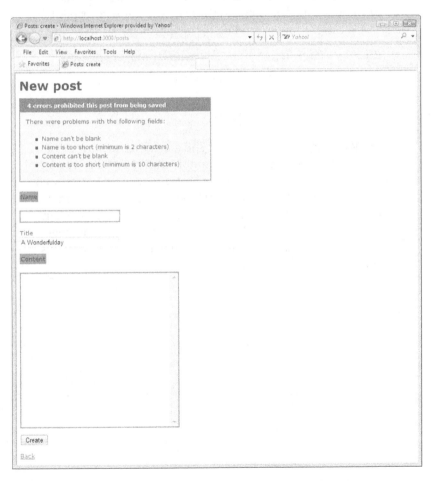

Figure 11-12   Error messages notify the user of an incomplete blog entry

Discovery Projects

Project 11-1

Ruby on Rails is based on a Model-View-Controller (MVC) architecture. This chapter provided a brief overview of MVC and its three primary components: models, views, and controllers. To learn more, visit *http://en.wikipedia.org/wiki/Model-view-controller*, and then write a one-page paper that demonstrates your understanding of MVC.

Project 11-2

Ruby on Rails follows a number of guiding principles for web-application development. These include Convention Over Configuration and Don't Repeat Yourself (DRY). To learn more, visit the following web pages at Wikipedia.com, and then write a one-page paper that demonstrates your understanding of these principles:

- *http://en.wikipedia.org/wiki/Convention_over_configuration*

- *http://en.wikipedia.org/wiki/Don%27t_repeat_yourself*

Project 11-3

Ruby on Rails requires a web server and a database management system. The WEBrick web server is automatically installed as part of Ruby on Rails, and Ruby on Rails applications are automatically configured to work with the SQLite database management system. Select either WEBrick or SQLite and, using your preferred search engine, search the Internet for more information. Then write a one-page paper that demonstrates your understanding of the Ruby on Rails development tool that you selected.

Glossary

.NET framework A Microsoft program-development infrastructure that supports the development of desktop, network, and Internet-based applications and programs.

A

Abstraction An OOP term that describes the ability to make important object features available while hiding nonessential details, thereby focusing on the outside view of an object.

Action Controller An MVC architecture component that serves as an interface between Active Record and Action View.

Action Mailer A Ruby on Rails framework that provides e-mail services within Ruby on Rails applications.

Action View A library that Ruby on Rails uses to define presentation templates, which are used in displaying data.

Active Record A library that Ruby on Rails uses to implement models and which serves as an interface between program code and the application's database.

Active Resource A Ruby on Rails feature that manages connections between application objects and database tables in Restful applications, mapping local application objects to Web resources.

Active Support A library of classes used by other Ruby on Rails components.

Argument Data that is passed to a program or method as input.

Array An indexed collection of items stored as a list.

Assembler A program used to translate assembly programs into executable programs.

Assembly language A programming language that replaces machine language and its 0s and 1s with sets of symbols or mnemonics.

Associative array A list of data stored in key-value pairings that is sometimes referred to as a hash or a dictionary.

B

Breakpoint A marker used to pause the execution of programs run using the Ruby debugger.

C

Call The process of calling upon a method within a Ruby program.

Case sensitivity The differentiation of uppercase and lowercase letters in the formulation of Ruby variables and strings.

Central processing unit (CPU) The computer component (sometimes referred to as a microprocessor chip) that is responsible for performing most of the data processing.

Chaining The process of passing one method's output to another method as input.

Class A template that can be used to create or instantiate individual objects based on definitions made within the class.

Class variable A variable with a scope that allows it to be referenced by all instances of the same class.

Code block A group of statements that is executed as a unit.

Command prompt A text-based interface used to accept commands and display the results of those commands.

Comment A statement embedded within a program for the purpose of documenting the program's internal design and logic.

Compiler A program that converts program statements into an executable file that can be executed by the computer.

Compiling The process that the Ruby interpreter goes through in order to convert a program into a format that can be executed by the operating system.

Computer programming Often referred to simply as programming, the process of developing, testing, debugging, and updating the code statements that make up computer programs.

Concatenation The process of combining two strings in order to create a new string.

Conditional logic The analysis of two or more conditions in order to determine the execution of statements within a program.

Constant A value that is defined within a program and cannot be changed.

Controller An MVC architecture component that ties together different models and views, processing application input and output in Ruby on Rails applications.

Convention Over Configuration A guiding principle in Ruby on Rails development that emphasizes creating applications based on a set of assumptions, which results in general-purpose applications that can be further tweaked as necessary.

Cross-platform program A software program that can be run on different computer operating systems without changing its program code.

D

Debug To track town and fix an error within a program file.

Decrement To decrease a numeric value during the execution of a loop, method, or program.

Delimiter A marker used to separate arguments passed to commands, methods, and programs.

Don't Repeat Yourself or DRY A guiding principle in Ruby on Rails development emphasizing that you should avoid writing the same program code more than once within a web application.

Dot notation The syntax used when referencing object properties and methods.

E

Element An individual item stored in an array.

Encapsulation The restriction of access to one or more of the properties and methods defined within a class, thereby allowing the internal representation of objects to be hidden from view outside the object definition.

Endless loop A loop that repeats forever without a means of terminating its execution.

Error A problem that occurs during the execution of a program.

Escape character A two-character sequence made up of the \ character followed by a letter, another \ character, or a double-quote, which is embedded within a string as a means of issuing instructions to Ruby.

Escaping A programming technique in which the \ character is pre-appended to a character within a string in order to instruct Ruby to interpret the character literally.

Expression A programming statement that, when evaluated, returns a value.

F

Floating point A real number containing a decimal point, thereby representing a fractional value.

Flowchart A tool used to graphically represent some or all of a program's logical flow or design.

G

Global variable A variable that can be accessed from any location within a program.

H

Hash Sometimes referred to as an associative array; a list of data stored in key-value pairings.

I

Increment To increase a numeric value during the execution of a loop, method, or program.

Index A numeric value used to specify the location of an element in an array.

403

Inheritance The process whereby one class is derived from another class and in which the child class inherits all the properties and methods of the parent class.

Input Data passed to a method or program for processing.

Instance variable A variable with a scope that allows it to be referenced by all methods residing inside the class definition.

Instantiation An OOP process in which objects are created based on classes.

Integer A whole number.

Integrated Development Environment (IDE) A graphic program tool used in the development of software programs.

Interpolation The process by which Ruby replaces a variable embedded within a string with the variable's assigned value.

Interpreted language A programming language used to develop programs that must be compiled each time they are executed.

Interpreter A program that is used to convert a program into executable code.

Irb (interactive Ruby) An interactive environment that can be used to submit Ruby statements for immediate execution and which is commonly used by Ruby programmers as a means of tinkering with Ruby and testing different language features to see how they work.

IronRuby A Ruby environment that facilitates the development and execution of Ruby programs that interact with the Microsoft .NET framework.

Iteration The process of repeating the execution of a loop.

Iterator A variable used as a counter when using a loop to process the contents of a list.

J

JRuby A virtual machine developed by Sun Microsystems that provides a Java-based Ruby environment.

K

Key-value pair An individual data item stored within a hash along with its associated label.

L

Language constructs Commands that are part of the core Ruby programming language.

Linux An open-source computer operating system derived from UNIX.

List A collection of data items that are stored and managed as a unit.

Local area network (LAN) A local computer network that enables communication among computers.

Local variable A variable that can be accessed only within the scope in which it is created.

Logical error Error that occurs because of a mistake made in the formulation of the logic used to accomplish a particular task.

Loop A collection of statements that execute repeatedly as a unit.

M

Mac OS X A proprietary operating system based on UNIX that is provided by Apple for use on Macintosh computers.

Machine code The programming language (sometimes referred to as machine language) used to develop the programs that ran on early computers.

Machine language The programming language (sometimes referred to as machine code) used to develop the programs that ran on early computers.

Metacharacter A character that alters the way a pattern match occurs in a regular expression.

Method A collection of statements defined within a class that can be called upon to interact with and control the operation of objects instantiated from that class.

Model An MVC architecture component that is responsible for managing the relationship between program data and the application's database in Ruby on Rails applications.

Model-View-Controller (MVC) A Ruby on Rails architecture in which applications are organized into three primary areas: models, views, and controllers.

Modifier An expression that alters the execution of a statement to which it is appended.

Module A structure used to store collections of classes, methods, and constants.

N

Nesting The process of embedding one conditional statement within another in order to facilitate the development of complex conditional logic.

Nil A Ruby value that indicates a value of nothing.

O

Object A self-contained entity that includes information about itself in the form of properties and contains program code stored in methods.

Object-oriented programming (OOP) A programming technique made popular in the late-1970s and early-1980s in which programmers create and interact with object-based classes that define object properties and methods.

Operator precedence The process a programming language uses to determine the order in which mathematic operations are evaluated.

Output Data generated by a procedure or program and returned as a result.

P

Parameter An argument passed to a command, method, or program for processing as input.

Pattern matching The process of identifying matching string values based on a search performed using a regular expression.

Polymorphism The ability to define objects and methods in different forms.

Porting The process of converting a program to allow it to execute on a different type of computer operating system.

Procedure A collection of program statements, sometimes called functions or subroutines, that is designed to accept and process predefined types of data (input) and return a result (output).

Procedure-oriented programming A programming technique in which program code is organized into collections of procedures, sometimes called functions or subroutines.

Program A collection of compiled code statements that make up an application.

Programming Also referred to as computer programming, the process of developing, testing, debugging, and updating the code statements that make up computer programs.

Property An attribute that describes or characterizes a specific feature of an object.

R

Railties A Ruby on Rails feature that provides the program code (helper programs) that creates applications and ties everything together.

Rapid Application Development (RAD) A programming methodology that facilitates the quick development of high-quality applications.

RDoc Provides access to documentation about Ruby classes and methods.

Regular expression A pattern used to identify matching character data.

ri A command-line Ruby documentation viewer.

Ruby A modern, interpreted, object-oriented programming language.

RubyGems A package installer program that comes as part of Ruby, which can be used to install Ruby on Rails and SQLite.

Ruby on Rails (Rails or RoR) A web-based application-development framework that facilitates the development of database-driven applications.

Runtime error An error that occurs when a program attempts to perform an illegal action.

S

Scaffolding Ruby on Rails programs that add specific functionality to Ruby on Rails applications.

Scope Refers to the accessibility of a variable within a program.

Script A plain text file that contains program code, which can then be interpreted and executed.

Script Editor A specialized text editor that is used to develop program files.

Scripting language An interpreted programming language (such as Python, Java, and Ruby) that is used in the development of programs that must be converted to executable code each time they are run.

Special variable A variable that is automatically created and maintained by Ruby and can be referenced by any Ruby program.

SQLite A serverless database system that is well suited to the development of new Ruby on Rails applications.

Statement An executable line of code within a program file.

STDIN (Standard Input) The default location where Ruby retrieves input (e.g., the keyboard).

STDOUT (Standard Output) The default location where Ruby sends output (e.g., the screen).

String A group of text characters enclosed within matching quotation marks.

String interpolation Variable substitution performed by embedded variables within text strings.

Syntax The rules that govern the formulation of commands and program statements.

Syntax error An error that occurs if Ruby's syntactical rules have not been correctly followed when writing program statements.

U

UNIX A computer operating system created by AT&T Bell Labs in the 1960s that has been ported to every major computing platform.

V

Validation The process of analyzing data input to ensure that it meets required specifications.

Value The data assigned to a variable.

Variable A pointer to a location in memory where a piece of data is stored.

View An MVC architecture component that represents an application's user interface in a Ruby on Rails application, presenting application data using a predefined format.

Virtual machine A program that looks and operates as if it were its own computer, running as a computer within a computer.

W

WEBrick web server A small database server that comes as part of Ruby on Rails and can be used in the development and testing of web applications.

Wide area network (WAN) A distributed network that connects computers in different geographic locations.

Windows A proprietary operating system created by Microsoft for use on personal computers.

Index

Aaron Yorek

...Got a Job in Computing

Aaron is an IT and Security Compliance Manager at BioScrip, Inc. He graduated from St. Cloud State University in 2006 with a major in Computer Information Systems. He provides testing and regulatory oversight to ensure compliance with audits. He also manages participation in developing and monitoring corrective action programs and plans to address identified deficiencies.

What are your hobbies when you're not at work?
I enjoy reading—almost always nonfiction. Another favorite pastime is attempting to complete the crossword puzzle.

What is the best career advice you could give to an IT student about to graduate?
Accept every interview you're offered. It gives great practice at refining your responses and making you more comfortable with the whole process.

What has surprised you most about the IT industry?
I am continually surprised by how quickly the IT business changes. It's a challenge trying to stay current but interesting to see how the industry grows and changes.

What is your favorite thing about your job?
I receive satisfaction knowing every day, in a small way, I am directly helping the company and its employees and I'm helping make their entire IT structure more secure.

Where do you see yourself professionally in 10 years?
Ten years from now I see myself working as a CIO for a medium sized business. I prefer small to medium sized businesses because it seems more like a team when you know everyone who works there.

As a child, what did you think you'd be doing at this age?
When I was young I knew I would either be doing something with computers or nuclear medicine. I'm not sure why I thought nuclear medicine, but it sounded intriguing. I'm glad I stuck with computers though!

Create. Contribute. Lead. www.cengage.com/coursetechnology